||| || ||||| | || ||||||| ||| |||||| || |||
W9-BHB-880

# Embrace the Angel

## Amber's Journey

by
Patti DiMiceli

*Deluxe Color Edition*

*This book contains images which some may find disturbing.
Please use your parental discretion wisely. There is a
TEXT-ONLY edition available, on our website and through
retailers, that does not contain photographs.*

Copyright © 2011 by Patti DiMiceli
All rights reserved
ISBN: 978-0-9831803-8-8
Deluxe Color Edition

Printed in the United States of America. No part of this book may be used
or reproduced, either electronically or in any manner whatsoever, without
written permission except in the case of brief quotations embodied in
critical articles and reviews. For more information, contact:

**Tobias & Co.**
P.O. Box 4475
Annapolis, Md. 21403
www.tobiasandcompany.com
www.embracetheangel.com

**Editions of *Embrace the Angel*:**
- *Print:* Deluxe text edition with color photographs
- *Print:* Text with black & white photographs
- *Print:* Text-only
- *eBook:* Text with color photographs between paragraphs
- *Adobe PDF:* Text with color photographs integrated throughout
- *Enhanced eBook:* Text with audio, video, documents, links, etc.

**1st Edition: September 1996**
Stiewing, Patricia
ISBN-10: 0-9654102-0-X
ISBN-13: 978-0-9654102-0-5
Library of Congress Card Number: 96-90574

A very special "Thank you!" to Sony Music Publishing for permission to
print the words to Amber's favorite song from *"The Muppet Movie:"* *"I'm
Going to Go Back There Someday"* by Paul Williams and Kenny Asher.
Copyright 1979 Jim Henson Productions, Inc., all rights administered by
Sony/ATV Tunes, LLC, 8 Music Square West, Nashville, TN 37203
All rights reserved. Used by permission.

*Cover photograph courtesy of Quality Images*

# Table of Contents

**Amber's "Spontaneous Drawing" for Bernie**

October 5, 1980

# Foreword

Amber has been a part of my life since the first day I met her thirty years ago. At each of my lectures I show a slide of the drawing she did of a purple balloon, draped in black, about to go off the top of the page. Purple is a spiritual color and it said to me she is ready to leave her body. At the bottom of the drawing is a child crying, in the healthy colors, yellow and green. That confused me so I asked Amber about it. Amber said, "That's the girl in the next room." I was also puzzled by the many dots of various colors and a basket with a four-pointed star rising out of it. It looked so joyful it was hard for me to understand how it fit with the images of dying. I said to Patti, "Take her home and love her. She is ready to go. I just don't understand the decorations and 'basket'."

Patti called me several weeks later to say, "It's my birthday today. Amber woke up and said, 'Mom, I'm dying today as a gift to you to free you from all your troubles'." Amber understood that life is about beginnings and she was freeing her mother to begin a new life; a graduation is called a commencement and this is what Amber gave Patti as a birthday present.

Many of you may not understand the importance of that statement. First, counting the colorful dots revealed them to be the number of days left in her life, the basket is her party basket, and the rising star at age four. Secondly—and most importantly—Patti and Amber were a team. Love was what united them. Amber knew she would be given permission to go. Patti would not say, "Don't die" or "Try a new treatment" or "Fight, Amber, fight." So, a tired Amber was free to go surrounded by love.

How does a four year old know how to die? She knows because it is an innate ability in all of us that is often taken away by the medical profession and our families. I have seen this kind of peaceful death, supported by loved ones in my family and many of my patients. I have shared my experiences in my books. You don't need Jack Kevorkian or a book on how to commit suicide. You just leave when you are ready to "fall up;" to share my father-in-law's words. He did just that when he was tired of his ninety-seven year old quadriplegic body. When you are tired of your body and turn off the "will to live switch," your body gets the message and does what you want. Your body knows that dying is not the worst outcome; it leaves you un-alive and perfect again.

I have also learned from children that what we come here for does not take many years to accomplish. We are here to love and be loved and Amber certainly did that. She lived a lifetime. She understood about love and forgiveness and did not need all the years most of us do to learn the lessons we are here to learn. As a child said, when his dog was about to be euthanized, animals have shorter lives because they don't need all the time we need to learn what Amber knew.

I have also learned that what is evil is not the disease nor is the disease God's way of punishing us. Disease is a loss of health and when one cannot find what one has lost then it is time to move on to a new existence. And what is evil is to not respond with love and compassion towards the afflicted person. When we do that, we become co-creators and angels. We are doing God's work.

I invite you to read this moving story. It will take courage on your part to feel and be aware of the suffering Amber endures, but be aware also of the love that heals and strengthens her to endure. As hard as it may seem to you, Amber was a fortunate child. She had love and with love one can handle any of the difficulties life presents us with. If you did not grow up with love, let Amber and Patti be your new parents and help you to love yourself, your life and your body and care for them because you are a divine child, too.

As I said, Amber was one of my teachers. Let Patti and Amber teach you how to survive. No one's life is free of difficulties, so learn how to deal with them and survive. To survive, is to feel all the feelings and go on. You must feel if you are going to heal your life. The feelings aren't only the loving ones, which so impressed me about Amber, but the pain, anger, questioning, resentment, and more towards life, death, disease, doctors, God, one's self and more.

So prepare yourself for the truth and meet a teacher who will help you to live—Amber and Patti tell your story. And remember my statement: Dying is easy; living is hard. To live your life full of love and empowerment, will show you that both life and death can be accomplished as intended by our creator. Not an easy thing to do.

Walking in the cemetery one day, I saw a headstone of a child's grave: "His life taught us how to live. His death taught us how to die." So it is with Amber. She is immortal because bodies perish but love is permanent.

**Forever Amber**

Bernie S. Siegel MD

**Bernie S. Siegel, MD**

Amber "playing doctor" while waiting for Bernie in his office.

# A Special Note

"Living well" is no easy task for any of us. In order to live well it helps to have a strong, loving, and curious spirit, much as Amber had during her time here. Her zeal for life and her courage in facing her illness and eventual death is inspiring to us all. If only, we often wonder, the good like Amber could stay with us longer. Our grief and tears in losing her represent the love that we will always hold for her.

As difficult as living well may be, "dying well" is even more challenging. As a natural part of the life cycle, the ability to accept and integrate the death of a loved one into our psyche is a daunting task. The death of a young child is even harder to take and can leave us feeling like we are being deprived of the chance to see the bloom of a flower when it is fully open.

Allowing our loved ones to "die well" may indeed be one of the most difficult challenges in living. Dying well means being able to "let go" or encouraging our loved ones to let go of our temporal world in order to transform into the next stage of life. To courageously face that transformation, we need to have confidence in the life process and understand that all energy, and thus life, is neither created nor destroyed, it is merely transformed.

Amber and Patti's story in *Embrace the Angel* is a powerful lesson in dying well. It raises the question: How we can survive the loss of a child and rebuild life after such a devastating blow? Their story provides insight into how we can achieve joy in life through release from it, rather than by clinging to it. Their experiences help us to discover openness about the subject of death and about our ability to truly love. For in order for us to love, we have to open our heart, open our arms and open our soul.

*Embrace the Angel* chronicles the journey of Amber and Patti's willingness to look at life, and thus death, differently. Dying well means being in touch with your body and with your soul in order to know when it is time to let go and release for transformation.

I never met Amber in person during her life here, but I feel that I know her through the love I see in her mother's eyes when she speaks of her. It is the energy of that love that helped Amber to let go and leave life so gracefully. Amber and Patti's journey serves as a beautiful and loving testimony to one of the most important and difficult tasks life can challenge us with: Letting go to live and letting go to die.

**Scott E. Smith, PhD**
Annapolis, Maryland

# With Open Heart

I was facilitating a public meeting about Emergency Management when amidst formal introductions I heard a soft yet firm voice say "Hi, my name is Patti, I am a mother of two. One is an angel, my daughter Amber who died from cancer, the other is my son Toby, who is in the United States Navy..." I don't recall any of the other introductions that day, but I remember vividly that moment, the moment Amber's spirit entered my life and an amazing friendship with her mother Patti began.

Every year on the anniversary of Amber's heaven day (passing) I feel 'prompted' to buy a particular birthday gift and card for her mother. I have jokingly told Patti, "I didn't pick it, Amber did!"

Patti's drive and determination to share the lessons learned from her daughter have helped strengthen my belief that there is indeed a heaven. Often on lazy summer days, a tiny purple butterfly has landed on my hand and stayed with me for some time. I have felt unexplainable warmth, as if Amber has stopped by to say hello.

It is my hope for you as you read this book, that you feel the same warmth and love. Open your heart as you turn the pages, be comforted by Amber's strength and believe that you can hold the key to the gates of heaven, just like she did.

**Alison Kelly**
Annapolis, Maryland

Author, *Through My Irish Eyes*

# Preface

In 1996, sixteen years after Amber died, the first edition of *Embrace the Angel* was published. It was the catalyst that propelled me to resume my "Cancer Crusade"… to speak for the millions who have been touched by cancer, wake up the world to its horrors, and shake the foundation of the "Cancer Industry." But it was my crusade, not Amber's, not God's. As time went on, I grew weary, tired of being in the "public eye," frustrated at the seeming indifference I encountered. My attempts were noble, but my methods were not. I was too angry, impatient, and unsettled. It took me a few more years to realize this and retreat into my life to find peace, happiness, anonymity, and contentment.

I focused on raising my son, Toby, varnishing boats for a living, and finally finding "The Man of My Dreams," John. Making the decision to pull out was easy. I needed to create space between me and the "Cancer World…" to enjoy a simple life filled with love and caring. Married for over ten years, we have enjoyed sharing our lives, creating a home (the "oasis" I always wanted) and spending time with family, friends, and Annie, our Jack Russell. I wallowed in the sweet, minute, simplicity of living my life day to day… of pulling weeds… of growing a garden… of tending to the birds and creatures in our yard. I also knew it could not last. Like instinct denied, I had to rewrite this book and return to the world to complete my "Life Task" of bringing Amber's message to the world, not carry on my "Cancer Crusade."

Another fifteen years passed before I would revisit the task of rewriting this book… before I would allow myself to dig down and resurrect my long-buried feelings and emotions. Gratefully, time and distance gave me much needed perspective, as well as the tools and skills to know myself… to understand the "how and why" of my time with Amber and the years that followed. I began to discover the deeper meaning of my actions, my decisions, and my emotions. Taking on a life of their own, they began to bubble up until I could no longer hold them in. I longed to tell you, the reader… to explain and define myself… to share the miracle of

Amber's life and her death... to give you the same gift she gave me: Her words of wisdom. "Live now and live life to the fullest, for 'now' is all we have. Do all you can to elevate others, for the power you possess must be shared. Leave this world knowing you have done your best to make it better—one smile, one embrace, one thoughtful gesture at a time. And when your time to crossover comes, use The Key to open the Gates of Heaven and enter the next world with open arms waiting."

I set up a studio in our spare bedroom, a place where I could finally assemble all of the materials I'd collected and stored. Knowing then that I would need them someday, I documented everything—from before Amber's birth to the moment she died. Everything. The letters, newspaper articles, movies, TV shows, drawings, photographs, audio tapes, and my journal were scanned and digitized. I secured the domain name, applied for the trademark, got a new computer with writing software, and suspended my professional organizing business, Organizing Made Simple. With preparations complete, I was ready to embark, once again, on Amber's journey. Unlike last time, *this* time, I went willingly. I knew that the only time I had was now, not later.

Reading the collection of letters I wrote to and received from well-known and accomplished people during my first crusade in 1984, my heart stopped at one. The words that Paula D'Arcy, author of *Song for Sarah*, wrote to me have finally come true: "You want to leave them (the reader) with knowing not just the details of your circumstances, but also feeling as if they know the ticking of your heart. The famous film director Elia Kazan said, 'To succeed as a writer, you have to be naked'." Finally, I was ready to disrobe. Baring my soul to the world and my heart to God, I took the plunge. I began to write... to give life to these words once more.

However, this book did not come easy. It is the product of thirty years of hard work, sacrifice, many revealing—and at times, unbelievable insights. I have risked a lot to bring Amber to you and this book to fruition. Opening up my heart, soul, and life to the world is unnerving and unnatural, almost scary. As you will see, the risk I took is small, nearly insignificant, compared to the tremendous suffering and loneliness that millions of people feel when they are touched by cancer. But this is not a book about cancer. It is a book about miracles.

*Embrace the Angel* is the story of Amber's journey through cancer and into the world beyond. It is an opportunity to know her, understand her purpose, hear her words of wisdom, and believe in the power that dwells in each of us, just waiting to be tapped. It is also the story of one mother who learned, through her own childhood and then the death of her daughter, the importance of harnessing the power from deep within to overcome obstacles and transform grief into greatness. Yes, there are parts of it that are sad, emotionally draining, filled with anguish, and may prompt you to close the book. Some readers have told me that they could not pick it up again. That is okay. Amber's story simply invites, it does not demand.

There are also moments of courage, inspiration, and wisdom that will change the way you see the world, your life, and the trials and tribulations in it. Most readers find this book to be uplifting, genuine, spiritually gratifying, compelling. Many have told me that, once they begin reading, they cannot put it down until they've finished. They read right through the night. It becomes an experience of enlightenment, gratitude, awakening, and a connection to the divine. Their lives are changed forever and they, too, experience the miracle of Amber's life, and especially her death... her crossing over the threshold.

She knew she was dying, as most people do, and gave me the gift of a lifetime. Her last words have sustained me during the tough times and transformed me in ways I have yet to discover. "Mom, when I die, I'll still be Amber, I'll just be *different.*" This is Amber's message to the world: Death does not delete our lives, it transforms them. Knowing that death is simply change, I did not "lose a child," she did not "pass away." She is still with me today, but *different.*

Thank God I have stayed open to "see" her in all her many forms—butterflies, a falling leaf in the woods, people—especially children—dragonflies, and Annie. Each one a container for Amber's spirit. Each one a miracle on its own. And the miracles never stopped.

For months, I spent hour upon hour scanning the negatives and photographs that chronicled my journey with Amber. I was driven to tell the story that these words alone cannot. The images, some of which I hadn't seen in thirty years, returned me to that time of power, helplessness, joy, and sadness. It was a heavy weight to bear and I was only human. I needed to get past scanning the negatives of her death, to a place of recovery and healing, to the time when we returned to the Bahamas to collect our things. I worked night and day.

Finishing the last group of negatives late one night, I sat down at my computer to review the photos. My eyes landed on one: A black and white taken the day before she died. It was a close up of the right side of her head, the side of her tumor. I was transfixed. The tumor had grown so large, it nearly obscured her head and hid her beautiful face. I was stunned, on the verge of disbelief, but *had* to believe my eyes. Cancer was real and this really happened. It could not be denied.

"There was as much *inside* her head as outside. It was eating my baby alive!" I buried my head in my hands and wept. "The horror... the horror of it all," I cried again and again. After years of holding on, I finally released the anguish of watching all that Amber went through... of watching my little girl die. "How did she do it? How did she live through this and *always with a smile?*"

When my tears had drained away, I washed my face and quietly got into bed, feeling John's warm body and hearing him breathe deeply. "He's asleep," I thought. I lay back and opened my eyes. It was autumn and the wind was swirling the leaves around as they fell from the trees. They mixed with the rain that fell from the night sky.

My eyes focused closer. On the outside of the skylight window above our bed, leaves had landed in a big "Happy Face" smile. But one leaf was missing. It was on the other side. It looked like a tear. I heard a familiar voice. "Mom, it's okay to cry. Just remember, when you cry out all your tears, you have to put the last one back to complete your smile." Amber continues to teach me with her words of wisdom... to show me the meaning of life and love.

Our tears are like liquid love.  We cry because we feel.  And we feel because we care.  Caring for someone you love is a miracle to savor... a gift from the heart.  This gift is Amber.  Hold her in your arms.  See her with your eyes.  Keep her in your heart.  For you are meant to listen, to understand, to embrace her words of wisdom... to truly know the meaning of life and your time here on earth.

*Patti DiMiceli*

Annapolis, MD

# Acknowledgments

There are literally *millions* of people to whom I owe a debt of gratitude: Those who have suffered with cancer—from the people who had... who *have* it growing in their bodies, to their loved ones who stood... who stand by their side. I can only hope that Amber's story, and my feeble attempt to tell it, can bring all of us together, to finally solve the mystery of cancer and eradicate it in our lifetime.

Without God... Allah... Jehovah... the Supreme Power... the "Glue" (as I see God), and His constant prodding and inspiration, this book would have stayed a dream (or a nightmare), never to become a reality. *HE/SHE* is the one who wrote this book. I simply did as I was told. I put myself before my computer and typed, staying open to direction and guidance.

Toby, my only child... my only son who has allowed me to redeem my heartfelt mothering instincts. Having him in my life has given me hope, gratitude, joy, and an opportunity to "mother..." to care... to satisfy the longing of leaving behind a legacy. The physical hole that was left by Amber "crossing over" was more than filled with Toby. I am so proud of the man he has become: Kind, capable, giving, loving, and a good friend. I rest in knowing he has found true love with Kimberly, a lovely young woman who will go far in life with her talent, creativity, and zest for life, all the while being a life partner with Toby. What a gift to see my son find contentment, balance, and the sweet pleasure of having an "oasis" in life.

John, my ever-loving, everlasting husband in my "second half" of life who has stood by my side, shown me the true meaning of love and marriage, and has always been willing to support me in ways both known and unknown. Having him as my rock... my solid foundation, has allowed me to dive into this project of rewriting the first edition heart first, indulge my inspiration and passion, subtract from our time together, and move forward with vigor and confidence to complete my Life Task. How fun it is to share my life with a man who loves me without conditions and, not *in spite* of my shortcomings, but because of them! Knowing he believes in me is a source of comfort, strength, and excitement.

Mom, my mom-in-law, the only mother I've ever truly known, has been an incredible source of strength, steadfastness, courage, inspiration, and flexibility. She never wavers on the principles that guide her life, while showing a youth... a newness in her advice and outlook. I can only hope that I will live the rest of my life with the optimistic joy, sense of family tradition and bond, adventure and exploration, and the willingness to invest in life while moving ever closer to "the threshold."

In-laws Ralph and Jeannette, John and Salvatrice and their extended families and friends have, with open arms and hearts, welcomed me. Never have I known such love, commitment, acceptance, and caring as I have with them. Family is not just a word, it is love in action every day and in many small ways. My new "big Italian family" is a vessel from which I draw sustenance, comfort, peace, inspiration, and joy. Celebrating holidays, sharing grief, counting on them for advice, and learning new ways of seeing the world have filled me and kept me grounded.

Gary and Todd not only stood by me through my ordeal with Amber, but cheered me on from the sidelines, endured my moods, my obsession, and the sacrifices needed to complete my Life Task. As Gary knows, he shared both Amber's life and her death. It is a bond that will never be broken and always cherished. At my side from the beginning, he supported both of us in every way so that I could focus on helping her through the various therapies, saving her life, and ultimately holding her hand as she crossed over "the threshold" to the other side. A good and kind man to the core, he is still in my life... in *our* life today.

Mrs. Barbara N. (Amber's angel), Jeff Winograd, Rich Abraham, Dr. Touloukian, Dr. Kaplowe, Dr. Manner, Dr. Cole, Dr. Beatty, Dr. Burton, Dr. Clement, David Stewart, Dr. Knowlton, The Compassionate Friends, and Elisabeth Kubler-Ross, along with thousands of others who reached out to us through the newspaper articles and television appearances, touched me in a very special way. They carried us over the hurdles, gave me direction and hope, and taught me the art of living *and* dying. Without their willingness to help... to ease our pain and burden, I would surely have been crushed by the weight. I will always be in their debt and never forget the incredible kindness, generosity, and love that enveloped us then and now.

Dr. Bernie Siegel—*"Bernie—"* went above and beyond what any other doctor/surgeon would do. He did not see Amber as a patient, but rather a person. He took us into his care, did all that he could to save her life, then gently and courageously taught us how to live *life* to the fullest while embracing death with grace and dignity.

The people of Connecticut, the state we called "home" for many years, welcomed us into their lives and supported Amber as she went through her journey with cancer. Milford became our family and embraced us as one of their own. I am forever grateful to Judy Doherty from the *New Haven Register* and Linda Bouvier from the *Milford Citizen* for going beyond simply reporting, to connecting us to their readers, to deeply caring for us.

Hospice of the Chesapeake, under the leadership of Erwin Abrams, gave me the opportunity and the privilege to help others "cross the threshold" between life and death. They cherish the process of fully living... of truly embracing life until you die. From their extraordinary training program, to their passionate professionalism, each person working there displays "love in action." They are our Earthly Angels.

The city of Annapolis, especially the people who live here, have given me what I've always wanted: A place to belong... a chance to know my neighbors. This town became my home when we landed here in 1986 while traveling in our 38' Hans Christian sailboat, Stormalong, on our way to Paradise: The Caribbean islands. It is a strong, intimate, respectful, caring community where one person *can* make a difference and does.

My neighbors have given me a sense of community, a place to call "home," and the feeling of comfort as I returned to rewrite this book. Even though I was isolated in my Studio for months on end, I always felt connected to the world outside my walls and the people who matter to me. Knowing I could reach out to them at any time, meant the world to me.

Brian and Stacy Siffel and their children, Jacob and Sarah, have invited me... invited *us* to become part of their family.

Sharing our lives and spending time together gives me so much joy and happiness. Playing with the children feeds my "childlike wonder" and keeps it alive and thriving.

The folks at Quiet Waters Park—my oasis, my place of peace, my little bit of Paradise—put their hearts into caring for the land. Because they do, I can enjoy my daily walks through the woods with Annie, balance my life, and listen to God for further instructions. It is a place filled with magic and an abundance of hidden treasures just waiting to be discovered. One of the most valuable is its gatekeeper, John A. Naegele III ("Father John") who is not only a man of God, but an awe-inspiring artist and photographer.

The trainers, especially Carl Eng, at the Apple store in Annapolis welcomed my questions and quandaries. They answered with patience, skill, and the tenderness needed to complete this project and launch it into the world. Kudos to Apple for putting people before product.

My friends—my *chosen* family—thank you for your steadfast love and support. Without you, I would be just another mother who lost a child and Amber would be a forgotten statistic. You listened to me dream, complain, create, wonder, cry, get excited, be depressed, feel anger, relish joy. You know me well and love me still.

And *you*, dear reader, you are the fulfillment of my Life Task. For in your quest for knowledge, you have cast aside your fear, picked up this book, and mustered the courage to enter the *real* world of cancer—a world most people choose to avoid until it is thrust upon them. I admire your pioneering spirit and your bravery. I am grateful for your support. You have sparked the fire of love deep within me, that did not die with Amber, but instead, was transformed into her legacy: This book that you hold in your hands.

# Introduction

Death happens to all of us. Some sooner than others. Those who are fortunate to live a long, healthy, happy life are the exception, not the rule. Knowing this, how do we react to the dying... to the death of a loved one? Do we shrink from it? Hide from it? Sink into the shadows of life, overwhelmed by the pain of the missing? Bury our grief, only to be haunted by it forever? Become outraged? Unforgiving? Fearful? Do we avoid people who have had a loved one die, afraid of saying the "wrong" thing, unable to heal the hurt... to stop the pain? Do we refrain from mentioning the person who died or sharing the memories with those who knew them? What do you call a mother who's child has died? An orphan? A widow? There is no word in our vocabulary that explains this to us... no thought as unthinkable as a child dying.

Dr. Elisabeth Kubler-Ross revolutionized the way we understand grief with her model for death and bereavement. The "Five Stages of Grief" (denial, anger, bargaining, depression, and acceptance) is a framework for each of us to experience. It is a flexible, not rigid, guide that we can use to lean on as we react to the death of a loved one. Like a fingerprint, each of us will experience grief differently; some will not experience a stage at all; others will revisit a stage again and again. There is no set pattern or timeline or deadline. Knowing ourselves and our emotions, allowing ourselves to truly feel, and being compassionate with ourselves moves us closer to the stage of acceptance. But there is something more, another way to not just endure, but transcend the experience of dying and ultimately death.

When I searched my heart for a title for this book, I wanted people to gain as much as I had from Amber. I thought of her, now an angel, and how with Bernie's help, I had come to—not only live through and cope with her dying and subsequent death—but actually *embrace* it. In this simple paradigm shift, I was able to cherish each moment, appreciate how good my life was with Amber in it, and see the reality of our life *after* her death. As a result, I am living with no regrets for what I *should* have done or *should* have said. Amber's death continues to give me reassurance, joy, and a zest for life that I may have never known.

Throughout history, man has had a basic need to find the meaning in life and death... to see how we can utilize the lessons we are taught... to move our lives from acceptable to exceptional. I propose adding another stage to Elisabeth's cycle: To *embrace* dying and death... to move beyond simply *accepting* it and begin to incorporate it into our lives... to discover the power it holds and transform it in ways that propel us to move out of the shadows and live our lives in the light.

But I am just like you. I am human. I am fallible. I am doing the best I can with the life God has given me... with my time here on earth. To be sure, watching Amber suffer with cancer was unbearable and heartbreaking. It tore at my soul and crushed my spirit at times. After she died, I was determined to stop this from happening to anyone else... to remove this disease from our lives and place it in the history books, right next to polio. But I couldn't. I was a lone voice shouting into the wind.

People continue to get cancer; families continue to stand by and watch their loved ones suffer. My hope is that this book, that Amber's life and death, will change this fact... that it will transform thinking and unite all of us to prevent, treat, and cure cancer, in that order. Although *some* progress has been made, there is still much work to do to prevent cancer from taking its toll and eradicate it from our lives.

But more than cancer, this book is about how we can harness the power of tribulation and use it to shape our legacy and empower others. For me, cancer was the catalyst for a deeper insight into the human spirit and how we transform tragedy into triumph... the depths of despair into the heights of Heaven. Amber's courage, sense of humor, willingness to endure, and priceless wisdom is immortalized in these pages. Her incredible ability to see *good* despite the massive tumor that grew to nearly the size of her head, is a memory that turned my life around, that put my heartache in perspective. Each time I asked, "Amber, how do you feel?" she answered, "Good." How can I compare my own life struggles to that? I can't.

So, why did I write this book? And, how did I know I would do it even while I was living through Amber's cancer? What forced me to keep moving forward to get it published? Why didn't I just let her die... let this book die and move on with my life? How did I re-live this time in my life, to dig down and discover the hidden feelings, motivations, fears, and emotions? Why didn't I let cancer defeat me? How did I live through my daughter dying? What gives my life meaning? How do I carry on? I've asked myself these questions again and again as I searched for the answers and found them, but only after many years and much anguish. I am now at peace and can tell you Amber's story.

In August of 1979, while I stroked Amber's hair and lulled her to sleep, I discovered the small tumor that would transform our world. Since then, I have come to understand her "Life Task" on this earth: To live with cancer and through this journey, teach the world about love, courage, hope, the reality of "Heaven," and the power we possess. My "Life Task" was revealed to me slowly and oh, so painfully. God directed me. "Be at her side. Document her journey. Learn through your heartbreak. Bring Amber's message to the world."

It has not been easy to accept my fate. I have fought and resisted every step of the way. Though I have given up many times, God has not. He gently nudged me along, guiding each step and giving me the strength and fortitude to continue this mission. You may ask why.

There are four reasons why I didn't let Amber simply die and become a statistic. First, she was an extraordinary little girl—perfect in every way—*except* for the huge tumor that grew on and *in* her head. It was very graphic; not hidden somewhere inside her body; not easy to dismiss. I couldn't forget the *sight* of cancer, the sound of Amber pleading with God to make the pain stop, or the smell of the necrotic tumor as it ate away at my little girl. My senses are still reeling as I search my soul and call up the experience to complete the rewrite of this second edition.

Second, though my daughter was dead, I couldn't ignore the millions of people who have cancer *now,* nor its future victims and their families who live with the anguish. What about them? Who will speak for them? They need a voice. What better than a child's voice? I can't let *them* become a statistic either.

Third, the "War on Cancer" that Nixon launched in 1971 has become a war amongst ourselves. The very people assigned to eradicating cancer are instead fighting with each other. As Dr. Samuel Epstein, cancer expert and author of *The Politics of Cancer*, says, "Winning the war on cancer means preventing cancer. Yet cancer is a multi-billion dollar business. Isn't preventing cancer bad for business? It is for the pharmaceutical and mammography businesses. These industries have intricate ties to U. S. policy makers, directing research funds to insure their continued profits in cancer diagnosis/treatment. It's time for reform. Congressional leaders are calling for an investigation of the U. S. National Cancer Institute for its indifference to cancer prevention, other than smoking, and for denying the public of its Right-to-Know, and for failing to inform Congress and regulatory agencies."

We are all guilty, more or less, of "turning a blind eye" to the people, especially the children, who are suffering. It is so incredibly unbearable, the mere thought of "CANCER" conjures up the most terrifying state we can imagine. It is a form of torture that no one would invite. Unless cancer is thrust upon us, we cannot invite it into our lives. As humans, this denial is a necessary tool to survive... a natural response to pain... a way to move on with our lives and truly live.

But we can't simply accept cancer and the pain and profit it produces, can we? The research community, citizen action groups, the medical establishment, business, alternative cancer groups, government, you and me; we all have some responsibility in this argument... this issue... this controversy of cancer. Hopefully, we will stop fighting long enough to listen to Amber and come together as one to resolve our differences, work to heal the wounds, and finally *prevent* cancer once and for all.

Fourth, I have no choice. I *must* complete my Life Task: To bring Amber's message to the world... to give you hope in the face of despair. It is why I was chosen. It is why I am on this earth.

I ask you now to read Amber's story. See her as your child... your friend, mother, father, sister, brother, aunt, uncle, grandmother, grandfather... your loved one who was touched by cancer... yourself as you grappled with giving up and longed to surrender to despair. Amber is the symbol for cancer but, more importantly, she is the catalyst for change. As you will see, Amber is an angel, a sacrificial lamb, a messenger. Open your heart to her love, your mind to the world of cancer, and your spirit to embrace her.

As you embark on this journey with Amber and me, realize that you are not alone. We are all in the same boat of humanity. The tide has turned and we are caught in the current of change. Don't fight it. Relax and go with it, for God is at the helm. He is guiding you through the pain and the joy, the fear and the courage, the desperation and the hope contained in these pages. In the end, your life will be transformed, as was mine. Besides, it's too late to turn back. You have been touched by her, too.

I have given birth to the miracle of Amber. In this book, she resides. Her spirit and her message will give *you* that miracle... the proof of God's existence here on earth. When she died on my 27th birthday, she gave me a gift that will sustain me forever: *I physically felt God.* And now you are feeling Him, too, through these pages, the laughter and the tears, but most of all, deep in your heart and soul.

Just like Amber *was* my little girl and *is* my angel, God is real. *He* is "The Power" that resides in each of us, just waiting to be tapped... to be used for good—for ourselves and for everyone we meet while on this journey we call "Life," a journey we take together.

**For Amber—**
**her life, her death, and the**
**footprints she left behind.**

**And...**

... for each and every one of the nearly **22,000,000** people
who have died from cancer, and the loved ones *they* left
behind, in the forty years since President Nixon declared
"War on Cancer" on December 23, 1971.

# For Amber

Amber, such a young child of four
Is moving too quickly to the final door.
Amber's parents must be asking why
Why is our child the one to die?
I want everyone who reads this, to recall
That this could happen to anyone at all.
She's too young to never have the chance
To live and grow up, laugh, love, and dance.

In this age of technology
And the advancement of man,
Isn't there someone who can lend a hand?
She's just too young to be swept away so soon,
While scientists work on exploring the moon.
They should focus on the needs of this earth
And why there are some who die right after birth
Or live for a short stretch, just to end in pain.
Is the purpose of our existence all in vain?

People, we have to think hard and find a way
To use all and everyone we know today
To put all our facts together as one,
To discover a cure together as one,
Together as a universal whole
Because we know how cancer takes its toll.
And in hopes that this disease will end
We've got to do it as Amber's friend.

In her name, we've got to try our best
As she will find peace and eternal rest.
The spirit of her will never die,
If we hope and pray and try,
And try.

—**Alicia Smith**

# An Amber

An Amber is a shining star,
A shining light sent from afar.

An Amber is a glow of love,
Sent from above on the wings of a dove.

An Amber is a sparkle, a twinkle, a glow.
Amber is the essence of love.

An Amber is a child,
Brought forth in God's love.

Amber, you are a glow of love,
A glow of light, a glow of life.

Amber, you are a precious gift
A precious love, a precious child.

You are God's gift, a symbol of
His Love, Truth, and Pureness.

Amber, you are an angel of love,
Here to remind us of Jesus and His Love.

**—Charley Savinelli**

# Your Little Sunbeam

A sunbeam is born in the morning,
a bar of gold ladders the sky,
and falling across crystal blades,
She'll defrost the images on the grass.

She rises with her mother,

and yawns across the fields,
while doe drink from the river,
not afraid of their tender friend,
Who sparkles on the glassy water.

And finding every bedroom window,
she whispers through the curtains,
To visit only for a while.

But over the horizon, the sun could see,
a cloud bearing tearful rain,
Chancing upon her little beam.

Though with all her might,
she tried to break free,
and let out a rainbow of light,
they could never reach the ground,
Only to echo across the mountains.

And though the cloud will shade us black,
our amber hearts will forever glow,
for among the stars in the evening light,
I saw a dove from my window.

**—Paul Marottlo**


Dear Amber,

My little Melissa has found a place where the sun shines all the
time and makes the clear rivers sparkle.
Melissa picks up the fish with her hands, then sets them free.
There is a wonderful Teacher there, who teaches her anything she
wants to know.
I can't go there yet, but she can come to me
whenever she wants.
Melissa wears a white gown and
has shimmering slippers on her feet.

There is a crown of sparkling stars she wears on her head.
The Teacher has taught her to ride a white pony.
The Teacher loves her, and everyone there so much, especially the
little children;
and everyone loves the Teacher, too.
No one ever cries there.
Melissa is always smiling and having fun.
She asked the Teacher if you could come there, too.
He said, "Not now, but someday soon."
Here is a picture of Melissa, so you will know her.
I will send you a picture of her on her horse next week.

Love,
Linda

## The Key to Heaven

In my little hand I hold a Key,
Clenched tightly in my fist to comfort me.
I will embrace this priceless gift of mine,
A Key so very precious to me.

This very Key that I possess,
It is the Key to peacefulness.
A Key of hope is in my palm,
With such reassurance my fears are calmed.

You see, the Key I hold is not to a box or door,
There is only one thing that it is for.
To open the Golden Gates of Heaven,
Where I will be an Angel forever more.

**—Megan E. Johnson**

# Impressions of Amber:
## Her Life & Her Journey

**From those who knew her, Amber's life:**

*Bernie Siegel, MD:* Amber's surgeon, author of *Peace, Love, and Healing*, as well as *Love, Medicine, and Miracles*, and others: "She seemed more like four *hundred* years old, instead of four. She was so wise. Whenever I sent her for x-rays or tests, everyone came back to me saying, 'She's so beautiful... so cooperative.' She made people feel good around her."

*Gary Stiewing*, Amber's true father: "Amber is with me forever. It's very hard to write about my time with Amber. So much to say. Happy, oh so happy about life. I really didn't know what to do. Every step of every moment seemed the most important. I was there to help, to support, to love. As it turned out, Amber helped me to truly understand how important every breath, every step can be if we just let go of our needs. Now I live with my children and try to remember what Amber, that angel whom I believe is holding a seat for me, has taught us all. Thanks Amber."

*Todd Stiewing*, Amber's brother: "I was just three years old when I met Amber and her mother Patti, and so my memories of that time are tied closely to faded photographs and well-worn stories. Images of sailing on Long Island Sound, exploring our (boat)yard at Brown's Marina, adventures on the beach, and living in a studio where display cases magically turned into our furniture in the evening hours.

When I look back on the brief span of time that Amber was part of my life, it seems impossible that it was only two years. For me it was a lifetime, her lifetime, and it has left an impression on me that lifts my heart and leaves a smile on my face whenever I hear her name. My first sister, Amber."

*Lil Stiewing:* "I am Amber's grandmother. Amber was a sweet, polite, and beautiful little girl, very intelligent and she just loved to dress up and be *so* pretty! I was very proud to know her and love her. Amber didn't have a care in the world. Only happiness and beauty seemed to surround her always. She just loved to have playmates over and just have a lot of fun! She was a child everyone would love. She loved life. Amber was very adult for her age.

This all changed when the sad news came: 'Amber has cancer.' She would tell everyone about it. I just can't believe how well she accepted this news. Amber was a beautiful child and she was strong and understood all about this dreadful disease and went on with her life. Amber knew and had the idea she was going to Heaven to meet God and he would take care of her forever. Yes, she did accept this. Amber had the beauty of an Angel and the inner strength of her God. She was loved by everyone that met her and still is. She truly was an 'Angel'."

*Patti Reid,* my sister-in-law: Amber was a beautiful sweet little girl. She was always happy and loved to dance. I remember her always picking flowers and giving them to Patti. She always liked to be naked and enjoyed going to the park, too!

*Arla Amara:* our guide at The Clinic: "Amber taught me that a person doesn't have to be big to be courageous. A person doesn't have to be big to be strong. *Love* has to be big, though, and love can come in very little people."

*Jane Bristol,* our refuge from the storms of life: "I loved Amber like my own daughter. It hurts to think of her, even today, but I have so many good memories. One of my favorites is her running, stark naked, in the fields around my house, giggling and laughing."

### From those who read the book:

*Elisabeth Kubler-Ross,* author of *On Death and Dying, On Children and Death,* and others: "I just discovered *Embrace the Angel.* I read right through and through all over again. It's beautiful and very touching; especially her dreams and her courage and wisdom. You need to share this with the world—for Amber and Chad and all the many parents who need to *know.*

Thank you, thank you, thank you for the lovely and moving Amber book which needs to be read by every healthcare giver, parent, sibling, etc. of any child with cancer.

Yes, Amber is (was, will always be) an old wise soul and a terrific teacher and you have been blessed (like many) to be her mother!!"

*Samuel Epstein, MD,* author of *The Politics of Cancer* and *Hazardous Waste in America:* "Thank you for your letter and manuscript. This was very touching and moving... I wish you success with its publication."

*Elizabeth O'Neil,* managing editor of *Connecticut Magazine:* "Your story of Amber is one of the most moving manuscripts we've read... It's an intolerably sad, beautiful, wrenching, uplifting— words fail—tale. Amber was an extraordinary child. You're an extraordinary woman."

*Carol Dumbach,* assistant to Joe Graedon of The People's Pharmacy: "We received a copy of *Embrace the Angel* a couple of weeks ago. We have shown it to several people, all with the same response. It is the most moving statement I have ever seen on cancer. It is certainly a wonderful movement for your daughter's memory and something everyone should be able to share, as everyone is somewhat affected by this terrible disease."

*Marge Cohen,* my friend, who followed Amber's story from the beginning and never forgets to remember her now. "October 30, 1980- Amber's death day.  Who is Amber? Who is her mother, Patti? Having done bereavement counseling for 12 years, I know one thing - there is NO loss worse than that of your child. How do parents survive? Patti has shown us how. She is AMAZING! Amber was a MIRACLE and Patti, her mother, has "inherited" her MIRACULOUSNESS."

*Kimberly Carr,* graphic design student and Toby's sweetheart: "*Embrace the Angel* truly touched my heart. This is a book you can't put down! It made me appreciate the people I have in my life because you should never take them for granted!"

*Doris Storm,* Jacoby/Storm Productions, Inc.: "I cannot imagine the strength it took to write *Embrace the Angel.* I only know that it's a powerful and extraordinary piece of work. We all wish you Godspeed and hope that people will listen to the important message you bring them."

**Ann Cinquina,** executive director of International Association of Cancer Victors and Friends: *"Embrace the Angel* will remain in my heart for a long time."

**Paula D'Arcy,** author of *Song for Sarah:"* "I was deeply moved by Amber's story. It is brave and courageous. It is frighteningly real. You gave me a view of cancer I've never known before."

**Argo Duenas,** owner of Back to Nature: *"Embrace the Angel* is the embodiment of Patti's growth and development of her soul. I believe that Amber's connection to the divine and her childlike faith inspired, encouraged, transformed and touched the very heart and soul of everyone she embraced. This book is informative, inspiring, and enlightening. I have shared and passed this book on to many clients and friends, especially those who have been challenged with cancer. I am eternally grateful to Patti and Amber for being channels of Light and Love. Thank you for showing us the Way."

**Tamara Trujillo,** owner of Hands on Health: "Amber's story touches my soul and opens my heart. I am inspired to ask the questions, look at all possibilities, and use my intuition and God's love in making life's choices."

**Maria Sinagra,** my mother-in-law and the BEST mother in the world:  "Reflecting, after reading *Embrace the Angel,* I am astounded on the resilience of human nature, when faced with the most difficult task, a mother saving the life of her child.  A mother will spare no sacrifice, face any hardship, go to any length at the expense of herself, to achieve this undertaking.  I now understand why she became the person she is.  There aren't enough words to applaud such a person as this, my daughter-in-law, Patti."

**Pam Scarbro,** my compassionate friend, accomplished woman, and caring mother: "Sometimes the English language has a word for those who have experienced devastating loss. Unlike 'widow' or 'orphan,' there is no title for a mother who has lost a child. Patti's book chronicles her journey from childhood to motherhood to childlessness to having outlived her daughter—a most unnatural life progression. As one who knows, burying a child is the greatest fear and the deepest pain. The story of losing Amber gives strength, courage, hope, and inspiration to mothers who have walked the same path and born the same pain. Her message is clear: Persevere on the journey, endure the pain, and embrace the angel."

*Susan Craig,* longtime friend, trusted confidant, and wonderful mother: "Patti came into my life when Chloe and Charlotte were young. Like a whirlwind full of energy, she bounced into my life. We have remained friends ever since.

When I read *Embrace The Angel* back in 1996, it showed another side to Patti. That side is not often discussed. I remember being addicted to the book, wanting a happy ending, but knowing that was not to be. I admire a person who has continued to be a beacon of light, brought joy to everyone, and has given to others.

For me, I see my children and I think of Patti's loss. Every time I see a butterfly, I stop, think, and smile. I'd like to think it's Amber, free on the wind, continuing to bring joy and love to all who knew her and to those that were denied the privilege."

*John DiMiceli,* my husband, my rock, my partner in life: "I remember the first time I heard a recording of Amber's voice. Tears welled up in my eyes. It was as though I was meeting someone for the first time, someone that I knew did not have long to live. Her voice proved that she lived beyond Patti's recollections.

I have felt the loss of loved ones that have died, but now I feel the loss of someone whom I'd never met. What would she have been like as an adult woman with a husband and children and...? Like the lyrics to Elton John's *Candle in the Wind:* "I would've liked to have known you, but I was just a kid. Your candle burned out long before your legend ever did," I felt a yearning to know this person so central to Patti's heart and life.

Through Patti's painstaking efforts to record Amber's life, we *can* get to know her. Amber—the real person—lived and breathed and gave joy to those around her. This book helped me to get to know the child who gave so much during her short life."

# Chapter 1

## *Discovery*

*"When we are dreaming alone it is only a dream. When we are dreaming with others, it is the beginning of reality."* —Dom Helder Camara

For as long as I can remember, I wanted a little girl. "The Dream" was clear in my mind and I played it over and over throughout my childhood. She would be cute and sweet. Long, dark, curly hair flowed to her waist. Her big, blue eyes were framed with thick lashes, and they betrayed the wisdom she radiated from within. Everyone would be dazzled by her and it wasn't hard to see why. She would be easy-going and quick to laugh, loving, caring, obedient, smart, and giving. Sent down from the heavens, she was the perfect angel... she was *my* perfect angel.

Her brother would be exactly three years older and very protective. Instantly, he became her best friend and playmate. No sibling rivalry in *this* family. The bond they created would never be broken. As they grew into adolescence, his friends would date, perhaps marry, her.

Their father—the "Man of My Dreams"—would be handsome, kind, and sensitive to my every need and desire. He would be involved, cultured, sophisticated, generous, and playful, my partner in life, my confidant and trusted companion, my best friend. He would cherish, maybe even *adore* me. Our love would be so strong and enduring, that we could survive anything. Of course nothing devastating would ever happen to us. Those things only happened to *other* people. Our perfect life would protect us from harm, tragedy, or anything unpleasant. Thinking and dreaming this life would make it so. I was convinced.

We'd live in this great, big, fantastic house set high on a hill, overlooking the ocean, surrounded by lots of trees and land. Our vacation home would be in the mountains, deep in the woods, with a stream that we could see from our living room and listen to from our bed. A big skylight opened up the universe as my husband and I lay in our bed, wishing on the falling stars that whispered across the velvet backdrop. I could feel his arms around me, the warmth of his body next to mine, and treasured the thought, "I feel so safe... so secure... so truly loved." My pleasant thoughts held me as I drifted off to sleep.

Of course, money would be no object. I'd have my career as artist/teacher; he'd have his as dynamic executive. We'd have a four-wheel-drive truck to plow through the snow and the back country and a luxury sedan for our forays into the city to soak up the cultured life. My closets were filled to the brim with totally coordinated outfits that complemented my totally pampered and toned body. I was on a first name basis with the staff at the local first class spa where my personal trainer set his schedule according to mine.

When I'd return home, exhausted from my shopping spree, the house would be clean, my husband would be romping on the living room floor with the kids, and dinner was waiting on the perfectly set dining room table. The housekeeper greeted me with a smile, then set about serving dinner. My family, my home, my health, my good fortune, all of this waited for me in my future.

Here, in our happy homes, we'd watch our children grow as we grew old together; still deeply in love after all those years. No problems, no worries. And so my life would go. I truly believed this, until that August evening.

It was a typical Connecticut summer evening—hot, still, and humid. As I gazed out our bedroom window, I could see the day turning to night as the sun was just beginning to sink behind the trees. After working as a construction laborer all day, my body wallowed in rest. Having finished our daily routine of dinner, bath, and story, I was ready to succumb to sweet slumber. A slight cross-breeze brushed against my skin as I lay next to Amber. She was exhausted from her long day at day care and somewhat sleepy. I felt drowsy, almost dreamlike, as I eased her to sleep, singing the Irish lullabies my mother used to sing to me. Her breathing slowed down; her muscles relaxed. I knew she'd be asleep in a matter of minutes.

As I gently stroked her, my thoughts turned to us. Our life together was a struggle with very little time for rest, but we had each other, our health, a roof over our heads, and this nice room to sleep in. Raising a child alone was not part of "My Dream." Though I tried my best to achieve it, I knew in my heart it was just that—a dream. *This* was my reality: I had my angel and she had me. We were alone in the world. Amber was my family, my *only* family. The mother I *wanted* as a child, I had become. I remembered my needs, wants, and dreams of my childhood, then set out to fulfill them with Amber. She was me; I was her. It was easy to put myself in her place and see the world through her eyes. The exchange was seamless and true.

As she lay on her belly, I could hear the rise and fall of her breath; my hands traced the map of her body. I knew it well. "How perfect she is. Her skin is so soft... stubby toes like mine... legs, with this beauty mark just above her knee... cute buns... strong back... chubby arms... I *love* it when her arms are around my neck... silky, soft hair... mmm... I wish *I* had these curls. She's *so* beautiful and perfect and...

**"Oh, my God!!!"**

I quickly pulled back her hair. Behind her right ear, a small, hard lump grew. *"CANCER!!!"* I screamed inside my head. It was loud, long, and empty. My body trembled, my mind raced, and I fought to stay in control. I had no reason to think it was cancer; no experience with cancer at all. Though I desperately tried to reason, I couldn't explain the thought away or find peace in a silent comfortable void. The words would not stop.

"Oh, my God, *IS* this cancer??? *It's cancer!* No, *kids don't get cancer!* Only *old* people get cancer. It can't be..." I silently rattled on and on. I didn't want to wake her up. I didn't want to frighten her. She was enjoying my touch and drifting off to sleep. "She's nearly there." I kept stroking her, straining to slow down my pace, control the panic that was rising within, praying for her sweet sleep, trying to avoid the area behind her ear. But I couldn't stop myself. I was desperate to examine it.

My hand pulled back her hair from the lump; my fingertips touched it. I was wide awake now, not dreaming. I stared at the nightmare. Like a bright light in my eyes, it stared back at me. It hurt. I blinked. My eyes were wet and burning. My mind began to race and then I heard it: A voice... a vision, "It's not *you* who will die, it's *Amber*." The voice was calm, almost reassuring, but I refused to accept it and fought back. *"No!!! It can't be!!! Not Amber!!!"* I was losing my mind. "Oh, God, *please.*"

I looked around the room. There was no one else but us. Her sweet sleeping body—so beautiful, so innocent—and me. Oh, how I wanted her... tried for her... did my best to create a good life for us. What I saw with my eyes, betrayed what I knew in my heart. Amber would die and I would have to endure it—even surpass it—and carry on her message to the world. *"God... NO!"* Without words, my entire being implored the silent space that surrounded me. And then there was silence, a loud crashing silence. I scrambled for answers.

Everything fell into place. My life became a movie and I watched it in my mind. Hours after Amber's birth, I had a premonition: I would die before she was six. "Mother's instinct" told me this was true and I lived my life accordingly. I began to document our life together so that she would know me after I died. If I couldn't stay behind, the movies, tapes, photos, and my journal could; they would be our "link." It was crucial that she'd have the tools to know me and relive our time together. She could see me living and laughing with her and know that she was loved and cherished.

Ever so gently, she turned over and let out a sigh; blissfully ignorant of the nightmare I was living. Lost in her world of dreams, she was relaxed and confident that I was there to care for her. "Oh, God, how I love you, Amber." My thoughts became a plea. I didn't know or care who was listening to my thoughts... who could see into my heart and soul. I just wanted her to live, not die.

Returning to the scene, I saw The Lump, my life, our life, Amber's life, and her impending death. I tried to talk myself out of this nightmare; tried to convince God that we didn't deserve this. Our life had been too difficult already. We needed some peace and comfort and joy. I was sure "The Dream" was not too far away now. It was just around the corner and I needed some time to achieve it.

I was desperate. No matter how much I wanted to change this reality, the scene began to escalate. I was a spectator and this was a horror movie. In a flash, I found myself in a courtroom— God's courtroom. It was packed full of people, though I couldn't see their faces. The jury walked in. The verdict was delivered. I sat in front—helplessly human—unable to stop it.

In one voice, they spoke. "She will die." The people vanished. God and I remained. I begged for her life. "Oh, God, *please!!!* I don't want her to die! She's just a baby... hasn't had a chance to live. She has so much to give to the world. Please don't take her from me. She's all I have! I can't live without her! I *WON'T* live without her!" He reassured me. "I am here. I will guide you. Open your heart... listen... follow."

The movie faded. Before me, my beautiful daughter lay sleeping. "Is she... breathing? Yes... breathing. She's alive." The sun was down. The room was dark. I could only see the silhouette of her... of our future... of my hope. Illuminated by my fear, The Lump glared back at me. I wanted to erase it, pretend I never saw it. I blinked it away. It remained.

Amber was in a deep sleep now, so I touched it. I probed the area around it, hoping to change the diagnosis. "It doesn't feel like a mosquito bite, it's too big. Could it be a spider bite? Maybe she bumped her head. Yeah, kids are always bumping their heads. That's it." I wasn't convinced. My thoughts were in vain. The Lump was there. It didn't move. Hard like bone, it was there to stay. Nothing I could do, say, dream, or plead would make a difference. Like a prediction made in stone, it would change our lives forever.

My life seemed like a bad soap opera. No matter how hard I tried to make "The Dream" become my reality, happiness and contentment eluded me. Obstacles grew like weeds. As I plucked them from my "garden," others would spring up without warning to take their place. There were so many weeds and I was so tired of pulling them. Looking back, I can see they took root in my childhood and then grew, unchecked, throughout my life.

# Birth Certificate

This Certifies that

Patricia Anne White

was born in

## Queen of Angels Hospital

Los Angeles, California

at 9:47 A.M. Friday the 30th day of October A. D. 1953

In Witness Whereof the said Hospital has caused this certificate to be signed by its duly authorized officer and its Corporate Seal to be hereunto affixed

Sister M. Raymond
Superintendent

Louis J Smith M.D.
Attending Physician

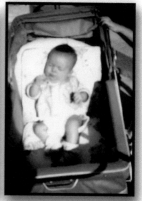

# Chapter 2

# Finding Hope in Hell

*"The greatest oak was once a little nut who held its ground."* —Author Unknown

I was born at 9:47 am, Friday, October 30, 1953 in Los Angeles, California, at the Queen of Angels hospital. I was the second daughter; my sister, Kathy, was born three years earlier. From the day I was brought home from the hospital, she considered me an intruder who was stealing the spotlight from her role as "princess of the family." "Can't you bring her back?" she asked my mother upon arriving home with me in her arms. That set the tone for our relationship that would last a lifetime.

Before Kathy was born, my parents fled their hometown of Paterson, New Jersey. My father, thirty and still married, had three other children. He left them. According to the times, a pregnant, unmarried seventeen year old girl brought shame upon her family. Under a cloak of secrecy, they fled and headed to Philadelphia. For three years, they were invisible. No one heard from them. On June 5, 1951, they left the east coast and flew to California, settling in Echo Park, a city on the outskirts of downtown LA. That date would come back to haunt me.

When I was a toddler, we moved to Monterey Park. A small house tucked behind a larger one would be home for the next few years. My memories of this time bring back good feelings: chasing my sister around the back yard with a grasshopper in hand, going topless in the wading pool, playing with the kids in the neighborhood, hitting the kid next door over the head with a brick to make my point. We didn't have much, but I cherish the innocent and simple life we led.

I was two when my brother, Joey, was born. Three years later, Harry was born. The tiny house grew smaller, so we moved to a three bedroom house in San Gabriel. My family life began to change. At first, it was hardly noticed by me. It started off as bickering, grew to fighting, then escalated to violence. Hearing my parents scream obscenities and watching them attack each other was more painful than I could express. They used beer bottles, ash trays, shoes, knives from the kitchen drawer—anything nearby that they could pick up and throw at each other and at us. "If this is Hell, I am living in it," I secretly thought, but hoped things would get better.

To everyone in the *outside* world, we were a typical family. Mom and Dad worked their factory jobs. The four of us went to school, did our chores, and played in the street with the neighborhood kids. *Inside* the walls of my house, life was very different. I lived in a sealed tomb of sorts, one that was filled with the stench of cigarettes, beer, and filth. The windows were always closed; the shades were drawn; no one from the outside could ever come inside. *No one* could ever know the truth.

The fighting between my parents was vicious and intense. My father would lash out at anyone in his way; cursing, yelling, hitting, even spitting. No reason was needed, only opportunity and a victim in sight. My mother would join in the fray and together they would scream names and words and phrases I could not understand, hurling them like shards of broken glass. Terrified, I would hide; any place deep enough to shut them out. Under the bed, in the closet on the back porch, or at the bottom of my bedroom closet, under the dirty clothes. I'd try to soothe and calm myself, stop my body from trembling, afraid they would find me. "Don't shake. They'll see the clothes moving. They'll find me. They'll kill me."

Tired, weary, and desperate, I wanted to stop being afraid and live in a home filled with love, caring, and tenderness. I alone would have to design my fate. Unwilling to wait and unable to leave, I needed a way out of this hell. Determined to push my fear aside, I decided to defend myself, risk my life, and speak out. This split-second decision changed my life forever. Though only a

8

small child, I discovered my "Power Within." It would be my saving grace in a world of chaos.

They were fighting in the kitchen. My mother stood at the ironing board ironing my father's khakis, as I stood underneath it. I must've been three or four years old and just about waist high. As my father lurched toward my mother, I stepped out and confronted him. I can't remember my words, but I do remember my feelings. I was brave. I was righteous. I was powerful. Finally, I was not afraid.

I defended my mother with a vengeance. My father looked down at me, his face flushed, his eyes glaring, completely startled. *"You little bitch!"* his words were low, slow, and long as he gritted his teeth and shook his head slowly. His eyes were like lasers and tried to pierce my soul. Defiantly, I looked back without wavering. I saw hatred and envy and regret. From then on, I knew: "I am alone... alone in this family... alone in this world. I must survive... live. I can't trust anyone. I am a bitch. That is bad. I am bad."

Looking back, I see that my parents never realized their own power within. Even though they created their own set of circumstances, their own private version of Hell, they believed they were victims, always victims. They were victims of their bosses, their neighbors, their few friends. Unwilling to take responsibility for their actions... to change the course of their lives, they saw themselves as innocent and the rest of the world as guilty. Convinced that they simply had no choice, their life became a series of dramatic happenings; things happening *to* them, not the other way around.

Because of this mindset, they did not have the skills nor the resources to make their life worth living. So, instead of choosing life, they chose death. Life as they knew it was too painful. Without pulling the trigger, they would spend their whole life trying to die. Anyone around them that seemed to be living and enjoying life—and that included me—had to die with them. If they couldn't kill my body, then they would certainly doom my spirit and soul. Thus began their campaign to ensure that I would follow in their footsteps.

Fired from his job in 1962, my father had a "nervous breakdown," a luxury he couldn't afford. Our family suffered from his self-imposed exile. Night after night, he paced the floor and drank to ease his pain and erase his reality. That's when "The War" began. Our house became a "war zone" filled with "bombs" (any object near enough to throw) and "casualties" (us). My childhood was spent trying to escape the "prison camp" (my house) and trying to overthrow the "dictator" (my father). I secretly wished he'd die, or leave, or my mother would leave, or I *could* leave.

One evening, in the middle of a battle, we were told to take our mattresses to the washroom—a separate room behind the house where the wringer washing machine was kept. The next morning, we dragged one mattress for me and my sister, one for my brothers, and one for my parents, out the back door and stacked them; throwing clothes on top to disguise them. When I returned home from school, I walked into an empty house. Everything was gone. My footsteps and my thoughts echoed throughout the barren rooms. They took everything, everything except the hidden mattresses. We had gone bankrupt.

Ironically, it was the happiest time of my childhood, for we had nothing but each other. We purchased a small styrofoam cooler and a single-burner hot plate. Crates became our furniture. Dinners were mostly canned tomato soup and lunches, a peanut butter and jelly sandwich. Our entertainment was a deck of cards; no TV, no radio. For the first and only time in my memory, we talked—*really talked*—to each other. Despite the dire circumstance, my imagination soared. "We're finally a real family," I thought, and filled my mind with other wonderful fantasies. But the reprieve did not last long. Within weeks, we returned to the "battlefield."

The world outside my house became my redeemer; my elderly neighbors, my family. I was special and they cared for me. I would visit. I would pretend. I would be their only child. Their homes were so neat and orderly, filled with knick knacks and pretty things and happy memories. In their homes, I felt safe, loved, and protected. I was fascinated and somewhat bewildered as I observed their relationships. They treated each other with genuine love and respect, laughed often, and embraced this neighbor child. I learned: "It *is possible* to be happy, fulfilled, and hopeful. I *can* find hope in Hell."

For no reason I could name, I just felt different, unusual, mismatched to the world around me. Though I knew from a very early age that I was chosen, I wouldn't know why until decades later. "Someone" was speaking to me inside my head and it wasn't me. I was directed and encouraged, given understanding of bewildering circumstances, and could see the true spirit in everything. Prodded to make a certain choice, I listened and obeyed. Someone was looking out for me and I wasn't sure just who. At times, I was scared and other times excited. And always, I wondered, *"Why me?"*

In first grade, my spiritual journey began. I attended the day school at Maryvale Orphanage that is run by the Sisters of Charity. Their swooping white hats, long black habits, and orderly appearance were a stark contrast to the chaos in my life. As a child, I was mesmerized. They were strict, yet kind; disciplined and fun; caring and willing to show me. Their daily devotion to God was magical and somewhat mysterious. I wanted to know more.

When I went to school each day, I was surrounded by goodness; it was a world away from what I left behind. The nuns seemed liked saints, the classroom a place to excel and be noticed, and the tiny chapel was my safe haven. "No one can hurt me here; this is God's House." I thought I'd found Heaven; a solace from my secret Hell. The girls that lived in the orphanage—though parent-less—were loved and cared for by the staff. I longed to live there, too. Oh, how I wanted to belong.

It was here that I discovered the presence of a power much greater than myself yet easily accessible—my own personal God. He was with me always as I soon discovered. He was the Father I longed for; someone to turn to in my times of sadness and confusion, but I needed physical affection. "If only I could *see* Him and *feel* His arms around me." I prayed and begged and pleaded that He, or at least the Virgin Mary, would appear to me. I was certain that they would; it was only a matter of time. At night, after the lights went out and Kathy was fast asleep, I'd secretly summon God for a conference. "O.K., God, You can come out now. You can appear to me. C'mon, God, *please!* No one's looking." I'd fall asleep praying to be blessed with a miracle, not knowing it would take decades to come.

One morning, Kathy told me, "I woke up in the middle of the night and looked over at your bed. I saw a cross above it with blood dripping down on you!" I didn't believe her but I wanted...I *needed* a miracle in my life. I knew I was special... chosen by God and that He put me on this earth, in this family, for a reason. I was being prepared for it. Perplexed and confused, I wondered again, "What *is* it and why *me???*" Without answers, I moved through my days with a sense of purpose and hope for the future.

Despite my determination, I was simply a child, and my home life was taking its toll. My mother had joined my father in his misery and now they drowned their pain together. The pattern never varied: drink, fight, pass out, get up, go to work, stop at the bar, come home, drink, and on and on. My sister and I—the "women" in the family—became the parents. We cooked, cleaned, ironed, did everything except drive the car and pay the bills. It was nearly impossible to keep up the house and clean up after them. Beer bottles, shoes, cigarette ashes, stains, and tattered furniture littered the landscape. The foul smell of cigarettes and booze hung like a gray cloud over everything. My room was my hideaway, but not my fortress.

When I was eight, Kathy and I had gone to my mother with the news that their friends, "Aunt" Dee and "Uncle" Gabe, were touching us. She didn't believe us, but told my father anyway. In the middle of the night, my bedroom door crashed open, the light switched on, and I could feel blows from the belt and my father's fists. "You little whores! You fucking whores!!!" Those words went on forever. I was terrified and bewildered. Between the blows and the pain, I wondered, "What is a whore? Why is he beating me? When will he stop?"

Money was scarce. Most of it went for bills, rent, beer, cigarettes, and their bar tab. They bought food with whatever was left. Toward the end of the week and before "pay day," we went to the "bank—" the row of kitchen cupboards that were set aside to collect the 70 or 80 "empties." We'd fill cardboard boxes with empty quart bottles of Eastside Lager Beer, load the car, and return them to the store for a nickel apiece. That would buy enough milk and bread to last us until Friday, when the cycle would repeat itself: Get paid, cash the check, go to the bar and get drunk, come home, fight until the wee hours, wake up at noon, watch TV while drinking beer and smoking all day, until night. By the time Monday came, the money was nearly gone and they dragged themselves to work to earn more... to repeat the cycle.

Sandwiched between the bad memories and the ones I could never understand, I have some very good memories. Most of them are of me, independent and alone, or us kids away from our parents. We'd pack a lunch of peanut butter and jelly sandwiches and Koolaid then strike out on an adventure for the entire day. We'd hike in the fields that surrounded our house, get big cardboard boxes and turn them into sleds, then slide down the hills that were covered in tall, dried grass. Always on the lookout for a new home, I built many "forts" in the bushes, caves, and trees. This gave me the chance to have a sense of control, rearrange my life, and develop the skills I'd need to create a loving home in my future.

I spent as much time as I could alone. The giant trees that lined the sidewalks were the perfect loft. I'd climb as high as I could into the dense branches, chew bubble gum, and spy on "normal" people as they went about their daily lives. These times provided hours of endless fascination and my only way to learn another way to live. I relished the sense of freedom and dreaded the thought, "Time to go home." My only hope of survival was to escape or be rescued.

I dreamed of the day when someone would discover me, free me from the torture, and I would live happily ever after with *them.* Each adult or family I saw would be evaluated for possible "new parent material." I was certain they would adopt me, "If only they could see how *good* I am." My brightest hope lay with Ronnie.

She was a woman in her forties, who lived in a small trailer in the middle of acres and acres of orange groves on a large piece of land in La Puente. The fairy tale was enriched by the hundreds of peacocks, chickens, and geese that roamed free throughout the property. My mother would wake us up very early in the morning, rush us into our clothes, and then drop us off at Ronnie's, our babysitter. The school bus picked me up at the end of the long, dirt driveway, and as we drove away, I'd brag to the kids, "Oh yeah, I live in a BIG house... *HUGE*... but you can't see it 'cuz it hidden behind the orange trees." If my life wasn't what I wanted, then I'd simply reinvent it in my mind and try to convince everyone else it was true. At the end of the day, I could count on Henny Penny—a huge, white hen—waiting for me to get off the bus at the end of the road. "Oh yes, *this* is my home... I wonder if Ronnie will adopt me." She didn't, but I could still pretend. My imagination soared.

My good memories are blurred by the ongoing fights and struggles that continued throughout our brief stay in La Puente. I felt ashamed, since the neighbors could hear the battles, and couldn't understand why they wouldn't help me get away. They knew and they wouldn't help me. We returned once again to the little house on Kelburn Avenue in San Gabriel.

From fifth to eighth grades, I attended St. Anthony's Catholic school. Aside from trying to cope and survive, my energy was spent trying to prove myself. I was invisible at home, but at school I was *somebody*. I realized that I could manipulate my "image" by what I accomplished and how I treated people. I was an actor and this was my stage. My role was a good student, friend, volleyball player, school treasurer, teacher's pet. It was an image I would fight to the death to maintain. But there were cracks in this facade, and my home life kept seeping out, threatening to blow my cover.

In sixth grade, my parents decided that they couldn't afford the $8 a month tuition. "If you want to keep going to this school, you're going to have to work it off." They made arrangements with the nuns that I should work on Saturdays cleaning floors and desks and covering books. My classmates would sneak up to the classroom windows and taunt me. I was trapped. First, at home, now at school. Only my spiritual life, my private and precious relationship with God, was untouched. This was the hinge upon which my life hung.

Unexpectedly, I tasted freedom on the back of a horse. My parent's friend owned a piece of property in the desert on the outskirts of LA. We were invited to spend the weekend. The house was small and rundown but the corral that held a couple of horses was perfect. I sat on the fence rail watching them live. "Wow! They're beautiful and wild and free!" One came over to me. We were both curious. I stood up and slipped my leg over his back. Before I knew it, he bolted towards the far fence at breakneck speed. Without hesitation, I grabbed his mane and pushed my legs into his sides just in time for him to leap over the fence and into the desert where freedom awaited. He took long, deep strides as I hung on for dear life. Within moments, we found our rhythm and our bodies moved as one. Racing through the hot desert wind, we were free from our tethers: He from his corral; me from my "prison camp."

At thirteen, my parents decided it was time I got a job to help pay for my "room and board." They got me an interview for a dishwasher at Paul's Diner. It was owned by one of their bar buddies who was a "bookie" on the side. I got the job at $1.50 an hour, a fortune for me. Each Saturday and Sunday morning, I'd get up at four, walk the two miles to work, past the bars and the drunks that slept in the doorways. I'd hurry by, avoiding their eyes, afraid I'd see my parents there and smell the same foul odor of alcohol and cigarettes that pervaded my house. After washing dishes all day, I'd head home, tired but very pleased with myself. By this time, the drunks were gone and I had money in my pocket. Sunday afternoon my mother would be waiting—hand outstretched—for the $25 I owed for my "keep."

The War continued. Many nights I wanted to die… I prayed for death to come. "At least it's freedom from this constant torture. I just want it to stop. If I can't stop *them,* I can stop me from having to listen to them." I put my pillow over my head and cried so hard I tried to implode. There was no escape. I could share this with no one on earth, only God. "I feel so alone. I'm ashamed of my family. I'm sure You made a mistake. I know You meant to put me in another family not *this* one, God." I was different, not like the rest of them, and it was beginning to show.

I wouldn't—I *couldn't* believe their brainwashing. The constant barrage of negative comments, name calling, cursing, and berating, were fought with my own positive, constructive, optimistic, and enriching thoughts. I looked at them, at everything they said and did, as the perfect example of what *not* to be. Although I had no control over what was happening to me, I *could* control my attitude towards it. "When I grow up, I won't do this to my child." I held on to my dignity and my mind while taking mental notes on what I needed and would never get. I locked them away in my memory and decided what kind of mother I would be: The opposite of my own.

By the time I entered high school, I was a master at hiding my secret life. My friends were not allowed to come over or call, my parents never came to my school, my teachers never questioned, my dates would drop me at the end of the driveway, not walk me to the door. I *was* who I *wanted* to be. I was popular. I was pretty. I was loved. I was accepted. I belonged. Nothing was wrong. Everything was perfect. "God help me if anyone finds out the truth."

At home I was tolerated, not noticed. Most of the time I was overlooked, except when they needed a target. The constant drone of the television could be heard from the moment they woke up until the moment they went to bed. Until then, they sat in their respective chairs—a table between them—drinking beer, smoking cigarettes, and watching TV. The table was "set" with an ashtray, a lamp with a clock, a bottle of Excedrin, a pack of cigarettes, matches, and a cold, always full, glass of beer. When I passed through their direct line of vision to the TV, my father barked, "Hey, Shorty, get me another beer... When are you gonna clean up that kitchen?... Hey, Fat Ass, move out of the way!" Aside from the necessary chatter, I didn't talk to my parents, and I *never* talked *with* them.

Throughout my high school years I fine tuned my two lives. As soon as I stepped on the bus and headed to school, *I* was in control, no longer a victim... no reason for shame. Just as I rode bareback on that wild horse in the California desert when I was eleven, I now climbed on the back of life, seized the reins, and rode it for all it was worth. I was Patti White. I was liked. And to prove it, I got elected to Student Congress, became a Junior Varsity Cheerleader, a Homecoming Princess, and a Song Girl. Outside of my Hell... outside of my house, I was living every girl's dream. Best of all, I was in love.

My friend, Teri, was going out with Bob Adams, a wonderful guy from England. Occasionally, we would ditch school and drive down to Newport Beach where he lived with his brother in the guest house behind his parent's home. It was during one of these jaunts that I met Jim. From the moment I saw him, I fell deeply in love. He was a struggling artist, but ambitious and very talented. Tall and lean, with soft brown eyes that saw through my facade to my soul. I knew I had met my match. The allure of dating a *man* (he was twenty-one) while I was still a girl (sixteen) swept me up before I could stop it; besides, I didn't want to.

We dated for a year or so. With Jim, I felt—*for the first time in my life*—truly loved and cherished. I wanted him to fulfill my fantasy… to fit my image of the "Man of My Dreams." I prayed he would love me forever, though I knew it wouldn't last; our lives were worlds apart. I saw how far one night.

We'd just come back from a nice dinner in Hollywood. It was very late and, as usual, I had the feeling of dread as we drove closer to my house on Graves Avenue. My dreams slowly dissolved as we pulled into the driveway. There were eight houses on one lot, all of them dumpy and dirty. There was no grass, no flowers, no love here; only cars, and garbage, and broken things, the tell-tale signs of broken homes and broken dreams. The night was black and I was grateful that they left the porch light off. The darkness made the scene before us look more like a *shadow* of reality, or so I hoped. I wanted to disappear; dissolve like Cinderella; make my exit gracefully. We stood on the porch saying good night, clinging to each other, unwilling to part. And then, like a flash from a bomb, the porch light went on, the door swung open, and my father stood in front of us, drunk and naked. He yelled and screamed; what he said, I can't remember. I buried his words, but not the memory and not the sight of Jim, embarrassed for me, quickly walking down the driveway to leave. Soon after, we went our separate ways.

There was little I could count on except myself and "the cycle," their weekly routine. During the week, they'd have fights, but every weekend, there would be "blowouts." It was during one of these blowouts that I learned what some of the code words meant. "Dad's on the warpath," my mother would say. Which meant "Stay out of his way. You never know what he might do. Danger is imminent." We followed this unspoken advice and always left the scene quickly, running if we had to save ourselves.

My brothers and sister were out of the house. My parents were yelling back and forth, screaming and hitting, cursing and spitting, blaming each other for all of their heartaches. "Go ahead! Tell her you fucking bitch! *Tell her!!!*" My mother refused. "Tell me *what?*" I cried through my tears. *"Tell her!!!"* Defiantly, she held her ground. He grabbed her by the hair and pushed her towards me. She finally relented. "Your father and I aren't married." "What do you mean 'not married'?!" *"We're NOT MARRIED! We never got married!"* "Then what was June 5th? You said it was your wedding anniversary!" "That was the day we left Philadelphia and flew to LA." "You mean... I'm... *illegitimate?!?"* My world began to spin. I looked at them as though they were aliens, not people, and certainly not my parents. I had to get out. I called my friend, Jan, and asked her if I could spend the weekend, then I fled.

Not only was I "bad," now I was a "bastard," too. In a time where the stigma was a curse, this was more than I could take. I just *had* to find a way to flee. It became a full time job to keep up my facade, but deep inside, I knew if I stayed I would die. The line between my fake life and my real life was becoming blurred. The hope of escape was more than my lifeline, it was my life. I was shipwrecked and drowning. I was feeling myself slip away.

A life ring and an opportunity to live came suddenly. It was a typical Friday night: drinking, fighting, etc. My father was beating my mother and, as I tried to break it up, he lashed out at me. I tried to get away. He picked up a watch and threw it across the room, splitting my head open. I ran, crying and bleeding, to the phone booth on the corner and asked Teri if I could live with her and her dad. Although her parents were divorced, they didn't seem to harbor the hostility and terror I had grown accustomed to. Debbie, Teri's sister, lived in Newport Beach with her mom, and Timmy, her brother, was away at school. The Malcolm's rescued me. They took me into their home, into their hearts, and made me part of their family. At last, I could let the facade fade away. Finally, I felt normal, proud, and free to grow up in my new home.

I spent my time going to school, cruising down to Newport on the weekends with Teri, or up to Bass Lake to water ski and party. Life was good... so good. Perhaps there was hope for me after all. The many years of brainwashing had taken its toll, but, deep down, I was clinging to the belief that I was good, kind, giving, and lovable. I could see that my stubbornness, my strength, my unwillingness to yield, was simply my instinct to survive. I had finally escaped the "prison camp." I made a lifelong vow: "I will never live in a home filled with hatred, rage, yelling, and screaming *ever* again. My home will be my oasis... my refuge from the storms of life."

After I graduated from high school, Jan and I found a small house and moved in together. It was in the hilly section of Eagle Rock, near downtown LA. During this time, I did my experimenting and soul-searching. I pushed life to the outer limits, then pulled back, afraid to tempt fate. Jan and I held down jobs during the week and on weekends, we combed the cities and beaches, countryside and mountains, looking for a good time and a bit of irresponsibility.

By chance, Jan ran into an old high school buddy, John Jarvis, an incredible piano player. He was living in a tiny house, high in the Hollywood Hills with another musician, Stephen Bishop. One thing led to another and we paired off—John and Jan, Stephen and I. Since he was trying to break into the music business, our dates consisted of "being seen" at different events while Stephen schmoozed, driving around Hollywood, or hanging out at home listening to him play his guitar and sing his latest songs. I cared for him, but knew our goals were different. He wanted fame, I wanted My Dream. I let the relationship die on its own, but took the "Life Lessons" he taught me with gratitude. "Keep your vision in focus and never give up." He went on to produce several albums and wrote the opening song "It Might Be You" for the movie "Tootsie," along with several other movies and hits. Each time I heard him singing—whether in the grocery store or on the radio or in a movie—I was reminded of the good memories we shared, along with his talent and tenacity.

For another year, I continued to plod along in my factory job with an electronics firm until I could take it no more. Jan and I planned a cross-country car trip during the summer of '73. Our destination was Vermont. Nancy, her sister who was my high school classmate, lived there and was nearly ready to deliver her first baby. For three days and nights, we drove straight through to Washington, DC, then headed up the East Coast. We arrived just in time. In a matter of days, Sarah was born, and we were there to share in the joy.

To celebrate Sarah's first days home, we gave Nancy and her husband, Michael, a party. Many of their Bohemian friends arrived to celebrate and socialize. Candlemakers, nurses, farmers, and musicians were only part of the very large gathering. "Sex, drugs, and rock & roll" was the theme. It was wild, crazy, and fun —the last place I expected to meet The Man of Dreams.

Harry, my mother, Kathy, me, and Joey

8th grade
@ St. Anthony's

As Student Body Treasurer, I was beginning to find my way in the world, a
way to not only survive my miserable life with my family, but
thrive because of it. This was my training for what was to come and I learned
well. Instead of believing the negativity from my parents,
I was motivated to look beyond them... to see the best in people,
including myself. I discovered my own "Power Within."

Just like the paintings on the wall, the quart bottle of Eastside Lager beer with
full glass, Herbert Tareyton cigarettes, ashtray, Excedrin, and used hankies
tucked in the sides of my father's chair were fixtures. I knew it *could* be
different and vowed never to live in chaos again.

My early high school days were filled with wonderful memories:
Becoming a Junior Varsity Cheerleader, going to the "Backwards Dance,"
and spending time with friends.

# SONG

Lynn

Connie

Sue

Patti

Niki

Sandi

*ROW 1* (bottom): Sandi Wood, Connie Hulin, Nike Escobedo. *ROW 2*: Sue Emlay, Patti White, Lynn Christensen.

Patti White
Princess

I reached my high school pinnacle when I became a Song Leader and
then a Homecoming Princess. It was every young girl's dream
at the time and I was actually living it. It felt oh, so sweet!

Jim Adams, Teri, Bob, and Bass Lake

# Chapter 3

## *Creating Amber*

*"The whole difference between construction and creation is exactly this: That a thing constructed can only be loved after it is constructed; but a thing created is loved before it exists."* —Charles Dickens

From across the room, I saw him. Our eyes met, then locked together in an almost uncomfortable stare. He moved in my direction as the rest of the room fell away. Dark curly hair, big blue eyes, and a voice that was soft and sexy. "Hi, I'm Michael." I instantly fell in lust. "Finally, I've found him: the 'Man of My Dreams' " I thought. For the next two weeks, we were inseparable. I was *sure* this was love, not lust, and no one could tell me differently.

Vermont was the perfect backdrop for this perfect romance. It was August; the days were warm; the nights were cool. We walked through the fields and apple orchards, picking flowers, holding hands and talking. I can't remember *what* he said and besides, who cared? The important thing was how his mouth moved when he spoke; the way his dreamy "bedroom eyes" glanced at me; how his hair danced when he shook his head in laughter; how good his butt looked in his jeans or out. I was awestruck and sure *this* was the true love I'd been longing to know. Confident it would last, I wanted this man's baby.

In December, Michael and George, his roommate, moved to California and in with Jan and me. We all lived in a big house near the foothills of the Sierra Madre Mountains in Altadena. From the beginning, there was a personality conflict between George and me, though I never understood why. A few months later, Michael and I moved to a small cottage to begin a life of our own.

We both had jobs selling Kirby vacuum cleaners door to door. Despite our efforts to build an ideal life, strife began to creep into our relationship. Part of it was immaturity, part of it was different personalities, and the rest was my warped view of family life. I had learned to "look at the bright side" or "ignore the ugly reality" depending on your perspective. If my world was not perfect, I would create one that was, even if it was only in my mind. Reality could've jumped up and bitten me and I'd still refuse to see it. It was a survival skill I learned in "prison camp." Never see the "ugly" in reality or it will be true.

After a period of calm and closeness, Michael asked me to marry him. I didn't hesitate. I was sure I wanted to have a family with him. I knew I would give birth to Amber. On December 22, 1974, we were married in a simple, outside, "hippie-style" wedding at the church we attended, Altadena Baptist Church. The previous week, Michael and I had sold a couple of Kirby vacuums to pay for our wedding and reception. It cost less than $200. Our honeymoon was spent in the back of our 1966 Chevy Impala station wagon at the local drive-in movies.

Marriage was not the magic solution that I hoped would transform us... hoped would create the perfect relationship I longed for. In spite of the frequent fights, his "wandering eye," and threats of leaving, I still wanted his baby. "You can leave, just get me pregnant before you go," I'd say. He didn't want a baby; he already had a four year old daughter, Krissy, from a previous marriage. "Well, if he doesn't want a baby, let *him* do something about it," I thought. But in my heart, I knew he wouldn't. I stopped taking birth control pills and began to manipulate him into making love with me. I was certain that if he *physically* loved me, then he *truly* loved me. How could I know the difference?

We couldn't depend on our sales commission selling vacuums. I wanted... I *needed* more stability. I decided to get a steady job with a reliable paycheck and applied for a job as a glassblower for Glass Instruments in Pasadena. Several people were considered, but I was chosen. Little did I know that the job had... the job *has* the potential to kill me.

For the next six months, I learned and mastered the art of blowing glass. My main job was to fuze two glass tubes together to form a vacuum that would test the ultra-violet lamps for leaks. With short puffs into a rubber tube, I would blow air to keep the tubes open, while heating up both openings, then connecting them. My workspace was always clean and tidy; the white boards and work surfaces free of the white dust that continually coated them. Years later, I would learn how deadly the powder was. It was asbestos. My work area, my gloves, even my apron, which protected me from the molten glass, was pure asbestos.

Our married life was just as rocky as before, but I was determined to make it work. I began to turn myself into the person I thought would make Michael happy. Besides, I didn't know who I was anymore and even if I did, who on earth would love *me?* It didn't make a difference; the fights continued. "Maybe a change of scenery will help." In July, we moved to a tiny house in Long Beach. The tension between us was immense, but it was familiar... it was family. If he fought with me, he apologized, he paid attention to me, he cared about me, he loved me. And we always made love when we made up.

Within weeks, my body began to feel very odd. "Could I be...?" Hope in hand, I went for a pregnancy test at the local clinic. The results came back. "Positive," the nurse said. "It's *POSITIVE?*" I was overjoyed as I hurried to Michael's work to break the news. I was certain that once he knew we were going to have a baby, he'd be thrilled. I believed that this new life would resurrect our own.

He was a mechanic for a paving company and covered in dirt and grease when I drove up. I opened the car door and ran into his arms. "Michael, Michael, guess what? I'm pregnant! You're going to be a *father!*" I waited for his reaction. A cold wave of shock and disappointment covered his face. I could feel his body tighten and pull away. My heart sank but I tried to overlook it. He realized his obvious slip and quickly faked a smile. "Oh... good," he strained. At that moment I knew, but buried the knowledge, that he would not love this baby as I did. Again, I was on my own.

My belly began to grow and the life within me stir as I meandered through the myriad of emotions that began to rule my life. Although I was now four months pregnant and married, It was hard to feel stable and grounded. Like a see-saw gone berserk, my hormones dictated my mood swings. I couldn't explain what was happening to myself *or* to Michael. He had little patience for the changes that were taking place; he seemed to *want* to argue, to engage me in another fruitless struggle. I just wanted peace. Many nights, I'd leave the house and drive down to the beach for a walk; unwilling to participate in the dispute, unable to sleep. I desperately wanted to leave him but was afraid to be on my own... on my own *and pregnant.* And so I usually walked and walked and as I did, talked myself into staying. "It really isn't *that* bad. Maybe I am doing something to *provoke* him. How can I change to make our life better? Maybe Michael will change. If I just stick it out, everything will be okay..." On and on I went, walking and talking until I was exhausted, then drove home. Despite my temporary reprieve, the drama would only get worse.

After one of my late night beach walks, I returned home. It was two in the morning. Michael's breathing was slow and deep. I prayed he was asleep. Carefully and quietly, I crept into bed and, with the utmost care to keep the bed from moving and possibly wake him, I lay down to sleep. He woke up. He was enraged that I'd left in the middle of an argument earlier in the evening. All my life I had to listen to people fighting; I simply didn't have any "fight" left in me. I just couldn't return the "volley" or take the bait. I didn't fight back. I surrendered. I did my best to soothe him, to pacify him, to fake it if I had to, just to stop the yelling and keep my integrity intact. My body was stiff with fear as I lay on my back, my eyes squeezed close, hoping he would tire of listening to himself rant and rave. I couldn't block him out. Suddenly, I felt the impact of his fist on my stomach and it knocked me off the bed.

I was too stunned... too paralyzed to speak. I clutched my stomach and mumbled. I cried, then screamed at the indignity. He not only hit me, but my baby who had barely begun to live. I grabbed some clothes and left. "How could he..." I know *now* that I should have left for good, but my need for a family far exceeded any thoughts of danger. "This *has* to work," I told myself again and again. I suspected the relationship was dead but was determined to revive it. "I am powerful. I can do this. I can resurrect the *dead,* even if it is only a dead relationship." My irrational thoughts ruled my reality.

We moved to Whittier, closer to work, hoping to make another fresh start. I was now working as a bookkeeper at the same paving company as Michael. To take the focus off us and our problems, we decided to expand our family. We went to the dog pound and found a couple of dogs. I chose Tara, an Irish Setter/Golden Retriever mix; Michael chose Wimpy, an old German Shepard who had an insatiable need to be free. To escape, fences were meant to be eaten. As a result, he had little white stubs, all that was left of his teeth.

Our life seemed normal enough to the observer. Go to work. Come home. Work to fix up the baby's room. Go to church on Sunday. Socialize with friends. I truly wanted a "normal" life... a life filled with respect, trust, honesty, fun, and deep abiding love. But my desperate need to have this be true, cloaked the truth. "Red flags" were everywhere and I refused to see them. Our life together was yet another facade I helped to create to hide the *real* world we were living. A secret, seething tension pervaded our lives.

According to My Dream... my childhood fantasy of the perfect life, I was going to have a boy first. "Maybe Michael will love our baby if it's a *boy."* My mind said, "Boy." My heart said, "Girl." I knew this was Amber, though I didn't know her name. I talked to her in my journal, I painted her picture—a chubby little girl with dark, curly hair and big, blue eyes. She looked like an angel.

I worked up until the day she was born. The pregnancy was normal and healthy; the labor was, too. In my heart, I knew she was a girl. I named her Jennifer until the day I gave birth. On our way to the hospital, I stopped at the store for some magazines to read during the long hours of labor. While standing in line, I heard my inner voice. "Amber." It was then that I knew *who* she was. She now had a name and was not simply "my baby."

Her birth was miserable beyond belief and almost surreal, like a bad acid trip. To speed up delivery, the doctor induced me with Pitocin and then gave me "twilight sleep." I remember only pieces of the nightmare... scenes that didn't connect: The ceiling lights whizzing by as they wheeled me to the delivery room, the doctor yanking and pulling and tugging at my body—at *her*—with forceps as if he was in a hurry, the nurses removing something from my body and taking it away. I passed out after that and woke up at four in the morning in my hospital room, bewildered and afraid. I struggled to reach the button to call the nurse. "Where's my baby?"

The nurse brought her to me. I expected to feel the "motherly bond" I'd read so much about, but didn't. I searched the depths of my feelings, but still found nothing. I brushed it off. "It'll come later." I looked at this tiny red creature as I held her in my arms. Bruised and battered, helpless and dependent, she depended on me for her very existence. She needed me to live and, as I would find out later, I needed her to *truly* live. And this was our bond: I gave birth to her body. Amber gave birth to my soul.

"You will die before she is six." I dismissed it as quickly as it came. "Of course not. I'll always be here for her. I'm her mother." I couldn't control the feeling of doom that hovered over me like a cloud. A deep sadness lingered just on the edge of my joy. I made up my mind to record our life together, just in case it was true.

Giving birth had taken its toll. I felt battered and beaten. Recalling the delivery made me recoil. To heal my body and soul, I went into the privacy of our backyard, lay naked on a blanket, and basked in the warm sun with Amber at my side. "Oh God, it feels *so good* to be relaxed, at peace, and feeling Your warmth." Many days, we would picnic, play, and swing from the huge walnut tree that dominated the yard. It was a good life punctuated by periods of torment and anguish. "Finding the balance" continued to elude me so I was determined to focus on the good and ignore the bad, hoping it would resolve itself.

Michael seemed happy to have Amber in our lives and we both enjoyed watching her grow. The 8mm movie camera, that he'd gotten me for Christmas during my pregnancy, was used to capture our life on film... to document our time together. I wanted her to know me after I died—how much I loved her, all of the fun we had, and that she had a "normal" childhood. I'd forgotten my "thought" in the hospital until she was two months old.

Throughout my pregnancy, I smoked. I had no intentions of quitting, until I felt sick. Reluctantly, I went to the doctor. He suspected tuberculosis, tested me, and told me to stop smoking. "I can't." He gave me the name of a program that would help: The "Five Day Plan." I drove away in terror... my "thought" was coming true.

As soon as I got home, I called to get information and directions to the next meeting. It was an educational program. Each evening, smokers met to learn about smoking—what it is and how it affects your body. They brought in lungs from cadavers. The smoker's were black and full of holes; the non-smoker's were pink and full. I imagined my own lungs and knew I needed to live... to be Amber's mother, not die. The premise of the program was clear and powerful: Once you know... you actually *see* what smoking is doing to your body, you make the conscious choice to quit.

On the third evening, I brought Amber. She lay sleeping in her car seat at my feet, while we watched a movie about a young mother who smoked, as seen through the eyes of her child. It began with the child in the womb, talking to her mother about what her smoking felt like, and followed the little girl throughout her childhood; all the while her mother continued to smoke. I glanced down at Amber. The last scene was much too close to home. The girl, now a teenager, entered her mother's hospital room. The image of a woman cut down in the prime of her life, suffering and dying from lung cancer, and her daughter distraught at her side, sent chills down my spine. "Mom, why didn't you quit smoking?" she pleaded. I saw Amber. I saw me. I decided to quit smoking. I didn't want to die of cancer and leave my daughter behind.

The arguments with Michael continued; many of them ended with him leaving and going to the local nightclub. "At least it's peaceful now," I told myself. But I wasn't ready to let my marriage—My Dream—die. Something inside told me to hang on. "It will be different," I convinced myself. We asked Pastor George, our pastor at Altadena Baptist Church and the man who married us, to help us sort out the difficulties in our marriage. We learned a lot but we were too immature to take his advice to heart. Hoping a change of scenery would be the catalyst that would save our relationship, we moved again.

Michael got a job at a car wash for a couple of months so that we could save enough money for the trip cross-county to northern Connecticut, near his hometown of New Britain. "Maybe moving closer to your family will give us the support system we need," I told him. Krissy, his daughter by his first wife, lived there, along with his father, mother, brother, sister, and cousins. We needed to bond with them... to have them know Amber and vice versa. Growing up without a close family of my own, I welcomed the move.

When Amber was nine months old, we sold most of our belongings at a yard sale, packed up a U-Haul trailer, and headed Back East. Since this was before car seats and even some seat belts, we tried to set up the back so that she would be safe and comfortable. We removed the back seat of the Ford Galaxy 500 that we had restored, put Amber's crib mattress in, lined it with lots of pillows and blankets, and we were off. Since Wimpy had escaped, never to be found again, we only had Tara. She and Amber made themselves comfortable in their backseat world as we drove across county heading for another chance to make our marriage work... to keep our family intact. With hope in our hearts, we moved forward and didn't look back.

It was November and the leaves had fallen long ago. Growing up in California, this was my first experience with the change of seasons. The biting cold was refreshing. I was amazed at how stark and naked everything was: No leaves, no grass, no animals. "Where is everything?" I was curious and wanted to find out. Since we didn't have money for winter clothes, I made do. I put several pairs of socks on my feet to fit into Michael's rubber boots and donned layer upon layer of shirts and pants. With Tara at my side and Amber in a backpack, we ventured into the woods to explore... to find peace... to restore my sense of balance.

Growing up in California, I'd never known "woods," only housing developments—one after the other—and rolling dried hills. Nature held a special fascination for us. Each day, after Michael left for work, I would put on my layers, load myself up with water, our lunch, a blanket, and Amber, call Tara to my side and off we'd go on another expedition into the surrounding woods. We marveled at the icy streams, hiked through the thickets, and climbed to the summit of the nearest hill. Finding a dry place in the sun, I'd spread the blanket and unload, happy to be away from the world and encircled in peace. After lunch, we'd lay on our bellies, dig down through the layers of snow and soil, and wonder at the life that existed there. We were students of life, learning together. Each time we discovered a new bug or creature, our eyes would meet, then lock in happiness and joy. We didn't need to speak. We gave ourselves up to the bliss... to the spiritual world that lay beyond what our eyes could see.

As the snows began to fall, our daily adventures continued; each one wild and wonderful. The soft sounds of my feet walking on snow, the flight of a bird startled from its hiding place, the blue sky, the gray sky. Each day was different and each day I grew closer to God. In the woods, I could actually *feel* Him... hear Him... pour my heart and soul out to Him. It was like being in church. I was walking amongst the divine. Sharing these walks with Amber was our special bond, a bond that would never be broken.

Our adventures took us far and wide into the countryside. At times we'd get lost, then find our way home again. Our beacon was the trail of smoke from the Bristol's big, black, potbelly stove, that snaked up and over the hills. Bob and Jane Bristol were in their 50's; a couple of bookends; so well suited to each other. Their families had lived in the Canton area for generations and the eighty acre farm they maintained, passed on from hand to hand. They were just down the road and around the bend.

As we rounded the corner, passing fields that were covered in snow, I'd point out an incredible sight to Amber and she would do the same. "Hey, look at those cows over there!... Did you see those geese?... Amber, here's a new bud. Here, hold it. No, don't pick it, let it bloom." I could feel her warm body on my back and her arm hugging my neck as she tenderly caressed the bud with a certain reverence. We were in "God's House" and she knew it.

From the crisp, cold winter air, we stepped into the warm, cozy kitchen of the Bristol's farmhouse. They helped me unload and gave me a long tender hug. While warming ourselves by the stove, Jane would pour us a much-welcomed drink: Hot cocoa for Amber and coffee or homemade wine for me. I gladly listened while Bob told me about his latest project: Stamps, pyramids, the new crops for spring planting. They were the parents I never had and they cared for me and Amber. I always felt welcome in their home and never left empty-handed. They tucked something under my arm—baked goods, veggies, or a book to read. Our friendship endured through the years.

As winter turned to spring, I was astonished to watch while God orchestrated His world coming to life. Buds replaced barren branches. The smell of flowers filled the air. Warm breezes were now blowing, not the cold, icy wind. "Hope springs eternal," was a phrase I repeated. I had hope that our family would endure, despite our differences and the buried tension it produced.

Many times, as we embarked on our hikes, we'd see Bob Bristol out in the fields planting his crops. Shallots were his favorite, but just the act of farming instilled such joy in him that it was obvious at first glance. Tanned face, baseball cap on his head, weathered hands, and bare feet, he'd be bent over and hard at work. As Amber and I approached, he'd look up with a broad grin and always a warm greeting. New to farming and growing things, I peppered him with questions and curiosity. He enjoyed sharing his knowledge and I enjoyed learning.

Jane would be tending to her horses as a mother would her babies: Stroking them, talking with them, feeding them. Her love was obvious, not hidden inside. It was there for the asking without regard for getting anything in return. The more time I spent with the Bristol's, the more I could see what a loving relationship *should* be. They accepted each other, laughed with each other, looked at each other with true and abiding love. It was the first time in my life I finally saw the meaning of love in action and I wanted that, too.

The tumultuous relationship that Michael and I shared did not resolve itself, no matter how hard we tried. We fought more than ever. The spring and summer came and went, but it didn't get any better. The more I experienced peace in the woods, the less I wanted to fight. I just wanted to live in a home filled with love and happiness; to give Amber a childhood that was different... that was more tranquil and harmonious than my own.

Unfortunately, the similarities were striking. I could see myself in her. At times, I *was* her.

Michael and I were fighting, just as my parents had; about what, I can't recall. I was pleading and begging and trying to reason with him. He was pushing me down the hallway, kicking me into submission. I looked down at Amber, struggling to hold on to my leg as she dodged his blows. Her face was flushed red; her eyes were swollen with tears. She screamed, "Mommy! *Mommy!*" In an instant, I traveled back to my own childhood. "My God, that's *me!*" I picked her up and ran into the bedroom, locking the door behind me. "I can't do this to Amber. I *won't* do this to Amber." And then the realization hit me: "This marriage is dead."

I returned to my childhood... to that moment in the kitchen: The day I saw the injustice, realized my "Power Within," and challenged my father as he beat my mother mercilessly. That moment changed my life forever and I saw it all over again, but it wasn't a memory; I was living it. I knew what I had to do and finally, I wasn't afraid to do it. Though I worried about *how* we would make it on our own, I had no doubt that we *would* be on our own, without Michael and without the constant strife. Struggle I could cope with; strife I could not.

The next morning I woke up, put my feet on the floor, walked to the dresser, and turned to Michael. He was just waking up and looked at me with expectation in his eyes. "It's over," I said as I took off my wedding ring and put it on the dresser. "My home will be my oasis, not my Hell. I won't live in Hell ever again." I then took the first step towards my new life; one that would never again be filled with anger, bitterness, fear, and fighting.

I picked up my robe and wrapped it around myself; it felt like a cloak of confidence, reassuring and comfortable. I wanted to linger but was pulled forward towards Amber's room. Carefully, quietly, I turned the door knob, hoping she was still asleep. Walking out of my life of pain with Michael and into a warm, welcoming world, I entered her room a transformed woman. I stroked her hair as she slowly woke up, unaware of the changes ahead. From that moment on, it would be just me and Amber, the one person in the world that mattered.

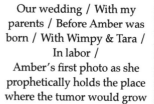

Our wedding / With my
parents / Before Amber was
born / With Wimpy & Tara /
In labor /
Amber's first photo as she
prophetically holds the place
where the tumor would grow

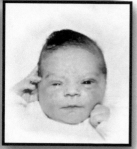

Crossing the
country /
Walking on the
Bristol's farm
with Krissy /
Bob & Jane
Bristol / Our
last days with
Michael

38

# Chapter 4

## Coast to Coast

*"Success is not final, failure in not fatal. It is the courage to continue that counts."* —Winston Churchill

From that moment, I knew we would part, but I was worried about how I would make it on my own. Just to be sure about my decision, I went to see a counselor. "Patti, how much of your time do you spend being unhappy and miserable? If your waking hours are 100%, what percent do you spend in misery, and what percent reasonably happy?" I never thought about my life in that way before. I paused to evaluate it. I knew I spent a great deal of my time feeling bad. "I guess 90% feeling bad, and the rest feeling pretty good. Usually, the good thoughts come when I imagine our life without Michael." I listened to myself speak. There was no other way.

We lived in the country and quite a distance from civilization. Michael kept the car, since he had to get to work, and agreed to buy me a used car so I could get to the store. He packed his clothes, took Tara, and went to stay with his brother. Alone and isolated, I was scared to death. But, strangely enough, for the first time in years, I began to feel alive. With some effort, my fear could easily turn to excitement. I felt peaceful, unsure, confident, afraid. It was a mixture of feelings and emotions.

Two weeks went by without so much as a word from Michael. Though I knew he was angry at me, I thought he would want to see Amber. I called him to see if he wanted to see her and to find out about the car. "I bought you a Rambler. I'll come by tomorrow and leave it in the driveway." For $100, it was clean but eaten away by rust. You could see the road through the floor if you lifted the back mats. Regardless, I was thrilled to have wheels. This was our ticket to freedom!

It was December and winter was quickly approaching. I needed to find a way to support us. "What do I know? How can I earn money? Dishwasher... waitress... factory worker?" I scoured my past for a talent, a skill, a way to support us. I remembered my "lessons" with my old boyfriend, Jim Adams, and his friend, Gary O'Gara. On our dates, while they worked at making signs or painting, I learned. Early in November, I read about an upcoming art show to be held at the local armory. Eager for my big break into the art world, I decided to rent a booth. For the next three weeks, I worked feverishly day and night, preparing my paintings and sketches to sell at the show.

Finally, the weekend was here. I asked Michael to take Amber overnight Friday and Saturday. In the morning, I loaded down the Rambler—inside and out—tying the displays to the roof with rope. I set off down the road with a solid sense of hope and optimism, listening to Bing Crosby sing "White Christmas." The thermometer read "20 degrees," the countryside was covered with snow; cows were huddled together to brace themselves from the cold. "Oh, yes, winter is here!" Undaunted, I drove to the armory. "I'll sell nearly every painting... I'll be rich! Then I can give Amber everything I never had: A nice home, lots of room and freedom, plenty of shoes and clothes, maybe even a dog."

The weekend was long and got longer each time someone passed by my display with barely a glance. I created a game with myself to keep my spirits from sinking. "Oh, they'll be back, once they see the other paintings... He just wants to look around first... They're just looking today, they'll be back tomorrow to buy..." I'd try to catch their eye, hoping to connect, perhaps telepathically beg them to buy, but they wouldn't even look. Just before the close of the show on Sunday, a man bought a sketch for $10. I slowly packed everything up, all the while trying my best to think positive. "That's O.K., all artists struggle in the beginning. You have to pay your dues before you get discovered. Maybe another show in another city another time." I picked myself up, dusted myself off, and tried to talk myself out of failure.

It was dark now and a fierce winter storm made the drive home black, windy, freezing and cold. The wind and ice whipped up through the back floor mats and the displays pounded on the roof. I stopped often to re-tie them and then resume my slow crawl to my safe haven, my home. I thought about giving up, freezing to death, crashing the car into a pole, pulling over and waiting for someone to rescue me. And then I thought of Amber. She needed me. Too weary to cry, I drove on. It was one of the darkest times of my life. I felt incredibly desperate... alone... defeated... ready to relinquish my strength to whoever came along. "I don't think I can make it," I cried out loud. Somehow, I did. Someone was pulling me through the night, moving me forward, inch-by-painful-inch.

Exhausted, but driving myself to go on, I carried my artwork and displays up the steps to our second-floor apartment, and repeated this until the car was unloaded. My mind said, "Collapse." My body refused. Robot-like, I got back into the car... back into the storm... and drove the fifteen miles through the winding country roads to get Amber. It was nearly midnight and she was sound asleep. I wrapped her in blankets, put her in the car seat, and gathered the strength and courage to go home. I wanted this night to end.

As we got to the driveway, the car sputtered, then died. It was symbolic of my spirit that cold winter night. I coasted the final ten feet to my parking place. Sheltering Amber from the wind and snow, I carried her up the stairs. She was limp and heavy with sleep. Halfway up, the phone rang. I dashed to my room, gently laid her on the bed, and grabbed it.

"Hello?" "Hi, honey, how're you doing?" It was my mother. A flood of tears came pouring out. I felt drained and trying to stop them took my last bit of strength before I was empty. I surrendered. Between sobs, I told her what happened. "Don't worry, it'll be alright. Why don't you pack your things and come back to California? You can live with us." Her voice was so soothing... so familiar... so comforting. I forgot my painful childhood and resurrected my "perfect parents" on the spot.

Although I was sad to leave my life: Michael, my home, the Bristol's, and my magical walks with Amber, I knew we could not survive living out in the country with a car that was unreliable. I needed to count on transportation to carry us through this crisis and into a life that would sustain us. Monday morning, I called Michael at work and told him that Amber and I were moving to California. Of course he was shocked, but he didn't beg me to stay... didn't ask about Amber. I needed his help. "Will you store some of my things, sell my car and send me the money, and take us to the train station in Hartford?" Silently, I begged him, then waited in anguish for his answer. "Yes."

I was grateful and regretful that we couldn't—not *wouldn't* —work everything out. We were two very different people on two divergent paths moving in opposite directions towards goals that each of us held dear. I wanted peace, true love, acceptance, and harmony, with my home as my oasis; Michael wanted something different. Not sure of what that was, I was willing to let it go without ever knowing. Although I could understand his anger towards me for leaving him, but I could not understand his indifference towards Amber. I could never understand how he could say he loved me and yet do everything possible to make my life difficult; watching with delight as I suffered. "Is *this* love?" In my heart, I knew it was not.

I packed everything I valued into a 2'x2'x4' box: All of our movies, photos, documents, and lifelong treasures. I also packed my opaque projector to help me launch my art career once we got settled. I was certain that my life in California would be easier than this. As we drove away, I turned around, one last time, to see my home and my hope for a perfect life with Michael disappear. "Gone," I thought as the house disappeared around the bend. "Finally gone." I felt sadness at what I left behind and anticipation at the thought of the adventure that lay ahead for Amber and I. My plan was to take the train from Hartford to New York City, the Long Island Railroad to my sister, Kathy's, house, stay two days to visit, take a train back to The City, then board a Greyhound bus for the three day trip to California.

Leaving Michael was easier than I had imagined; walking away from the hope of a family was not. Amber and I checked our bags then walked over and hugged Michael. I wanted to feel a twinge... a possibility... a need... a hope. I felt his body, but not his soul. We looked down at Amber. Jumping up and down with glee, she gave him a quick hug and kiss, then we boarded the train.

We found our seats and looked out to find Michael in the crowd. My thoughts rattled on: "I can't believe I'm doing this... It's done... Am I doing the right thing?... It's wrong to stay... Should I get off now, run into his arms, and beg his forgiveness?" A jolt from the train transformed my thoughts. We were moving. "Yes, we're moving forward with our life." Amber was talking nonstop and waved joyfully at her father. As our eyes met, I could see he had his doubts, too. And then he was lost in the crowd, which shriveled, then disappeared into the wintery background.

I sat back and sighed as I watched the buildings and streets... watched this phase of my life roll by until everything became a blur of color and movement. Beside me, Amber was babbling, "Mommy! Look at that big building... There's the conductor, can I give him our tickets?... How big is the train?... Can we walk around?... When are we gonna get to Auntie Kathy's?" I thought, "My God, she's so adaptable, so innocent. She just rolls with the punches... goes with the flow. I wish I was like that."

After our visit with Kathy, we returned to The City to catch our bus. We arrived at the Port Authority just in time, bought our tickets, and ran downstairs to the departure gate. I could see our bus in the distance pulling out of the station. My mind and body drained, I sat down on my bags and cried. Amber put her arm around me. "Don't worry, Mom. I'll take care of ya. It's alright we can get the next bus." I looked up to see my reason for living. "You're right, Amber. Let's find a locker to put our bags in and go explore New York."

After dinner, we caught the next bus. We set up our seats, our home for the next few days, then turned our attention to the world outside. As our bus rounded the onramp to the highway, we admired the view. It looked like a ride in Disneyland. The sun was setting behind the skyline of New York. A blaze of orange and red and yellow, it lit up the sky like a glorious backdrop; the silhouettes of buildings cradled the lights within and twinkled in random harmony. The City was slipping into darkness and the bus just rolled along I-95 leaving it all behind. I burned this picture into my memory.

For most of the trip, we had our own seats. I could only afford one ticket and each time we stopped, I counted the spaces on the bus and people who were ready to board. When the people outnumbered the spaces, Amber moved onto my lap. At 20 months old, she was heavy and active. I tried to keep her occupied but announcements, stopping, starting, and people moving on and off was wearing. It was a very long trip, a lot longer than three days and nights.

My parents met us at the El Monte bus station. I embraced them and the hope that their lives were transformed for the better. "Oh, God, I pray things have changed." But they still looked the same: Stuck. Stuck in their self-imposed prison of past regrets and lies. We loaded our bags into the dumpy old blue Valiant that had been on its last legs for years. I tried my best to be upbeat and optimistic. I kept pushing any thoughts of my past, my childhood, my pain, out of my mind. "Things are different now. I *know* they are."

We walked in the door of their house. It was the same house that I grew up in, the same one in my nightmares: The house on Graves Avenue. My mind raced. "Oh, no, it *can't* be. Please... *please, this can't be true.*" Everything was the same. It was as though I'd never left. The same dirty, dumpy, worn furniture; the stench of cigarettes and beer; the evidence of wild drunken fights; the shame I felt growing up was still there. Nothing had changed. Nothing.

I shoved back the thought and any others that threatened to spoil my illusion. "But it *smells... it looks* the same." I glanced around the room. The same two dilapidated chairs stood there with dirty hankies tucked in the cushions. The same table stood between them and the arrangement on it was untouched: Lamp, clock, ashtray, "Herbert Tareyton" cigarette pack, matches, TV guide, bottle of Excedrin, big glass of beer, half empty. My father picked it up, walked to the refrigerator, filled it, and took a long drink. I was back.

I brought our bags into my old bedroom. It was a wreck. "Oh, God, the memories. It'll take me forever to get this room clean and livable again." But I was desperate. Amber scampered in. "Hey, Mom, is this gonna be our room?" Without thinking, I switched modes. "Yup! It'll take a little bit of 'elbow grease' to clean it up. Wanna help?" And we began to clean, mop, scrub... to reconstruct our lives.

The next two weeks were Hell. Yes, I *was* back... back to the fighting, cursing, yelling, hitting, throwing, filth, disgust, glaring, threatening, pain. The feelings I long ago buried, now came to the surface once more: Embarrassment, frustration, shame, and helplessness, that suffocating feeling I'd forgot. Each night we went to bed listening to the blaring TV, the refrigerator opening and closing as my parents refilled their beer glass, and the constant yelling and screaming. Each night we fell asleep exhausted from the fear and terror. Two weeks went by. "Oh no, I can't put Amber through this."

I called my sister-in-law, Patti, my brother Joey's wife. She had always been a good friend as well as sister-in-law. I needed her now. "Can we stay with you until I can get on my feet?" She'd talk to Joey and let me know. The next day, we moved in. Once more, I was rescued. I had hope. I escaped from Hell again.

Our life began to come together. At the local thrift shop, I bought a bike, with a seat on the back for Amber, for only $13! "Wheels, again!" Reluctantly, I applied for welfare, to help until we got established and I got a job. Since Greyhound lost my box with all my valuables, I scrambled to find a way to earn money. I pounded the pavement with my homemade portfolio; it was filled with sketches and examples of my work. I kept hoping that someone would give me my big break. I sold a few paintings, but couldn't make a living for us. Still, at least I was feeding Amber and myself, and we had a roof over our heads.

We'd spend our days going to the library, the park, uptown window shopping, or walking around the college across the street. Daycare was too expensive to afford and I couldn't find work to support it. I'd walk the streets with my portfolio, going into each shop, hoping to sell them a painting or an idea. When I had an extra few dollars, I'd take her on a shopping spree to the thrift shops. As we walked along the streets, I studied our reflection in each window we passed. "She is *so* beautiful! I really think she could be a model. I wish I could give her more. I know she deserves it." I wanted to stop struggling and give her a better life: Her own room, a yard, friends in the neighborhood. "A simple life, that's all." That's all I wanted for Amber and I.

I waited and waited to hear from Michael. "Doesn't he miss Amber? How can he just forget her? Forget us?" A month or so went by and I received legal papers. He was filing for divorce and asking the court not to award any child support. *"How could he?"* A short time later, the divorce was final. I received the decree. The judge had ordered him to pay $25 a week for child support. He put my Rambler up for sale, sold it for $125, and finally sent the money and a letter for Amber. "He *does* care. He really does," I thought.

Day by day, I watched her grow. I did my best to shield her from the pain of rejection that I'm sure she felt from her father. No matter how hard I tried, I could never understand or accept the way he treated her. His indifference was painful beyond belief. I was certain that once she was born, he would grow to love her but I was wrong. I was wrong and it cost us… it cost *her.*

Amber was so extraordinary... so beautiful inside and out, that I knew I had to share her with the world. I made plans to get her into modeling and asked a friend who had a camera to take some photographs for her portfolio. I intended to take the bus to Hollywood with photos of Amber in hand, and look for an agent or modeling studio to represent her. She was very talented, lovely to look at, and funny to listen to. Her mannerisms constantly made me smile. For a two year old, she had a great command of the English language, and her vocabulary was extensive. She even created her own words: Babinsuit (bathing suit), swamwich (sandwich), boison (poison). Sometimes, I'd step back and study her, thinking, "Who *are* you, Amber? Where did you come from? I don't feel like your *mother,* I feel like your *guardian.* God must've sent you for a very special reason. I wonder what it is."

I had plenty of determination, but little money. The movie "Rocky" was being filmed in uptown Whittier. "Ah ha!" I thought, "Her chance to be discovered!" I dressed her in her prettiest dress, fixed her hair, and strapped her into the seat on the back of my bike. We rode to the set. A large group of people with cameras and cables and lights formed a semi-circle around the local drugstore. "This is our chance." I aimed my bike at the outskirts of the circle; wanting to get close without disrupting the filming. "Once they see her, they'll probably want to sign her on the spot." I rode round and round hoping that a director or someone with influence would be as dazzled by her as I was. No one noticed. The cameras kept rolling.

Disappointed but undaunted, I brought her to the Arboretum, where the TV show "Fantasy Island" was filmed. We walked around the set. I proudly held her hand as though I was holding the hand of the next great child star. Again, no one noticed. "I have to rethink this. There must be another way. I just haven't thought of it yet."

Living with my brother was exactly like living with my dad, but Joey was a younger version. Instead of beer, it was marijuana. His mood swings controlled the house and everyone had to walk on eggshells. His wife, Patti, had had enough. She'd endured for a long time, was tired of being treated so badly, and mustered the courage to leave him. She met John, a wonderful man who befriended her, at work. He helped her find an apartment of her own. Their friendship flourished and I was happy for her.

Of course, Joey thought their failed marriage was my fault. He ordered us out of the house. I'd saved a little money from my welfare checks and bought a little red Fiat station wagon. For the next few days, it was home. We'd spend most of our days at the park and when the sun set, I'd tape newspapers to the windows, find a quite place behind a grocery store, and park for the night. I had some time, as I cradled Amber in my arms, to think about my next move before falling asleep.

"Altadena Baptist Church." I called Pastor George. That Sunday, he pleaded our case before the congregation. One of the elders and his family, agreed to take us in. We lived with them for a couple of months until the father and son made advances toward me. "Time to leave," I thought. Again, we were homeless.

I called my old friend, Jan. She and George had married and moved to Milford, Connecticut. Michael moved in with them shortly after Amber and I had left for California. "There's a place, right next door, that has apartments for rent. One has two rooms and a bathroom across the hall; it's only $50 a week." It was music to my ears. I planned a way to get "Back East" and to that two-room apartment.

Amtrak was having a special promotion: Your child could ride free if you collected so many cereal box tops. My church, as well as my friends, pitched in. "With the money I can save from welfare, plus the $700 Greyhound gave me for losing my box, I could leave in a month." In the meantime, Patti, Joey's ex-wife, let us stay with her in her new apartment.

In August, my brother Harry drove us to the Pasadena train station in my Fiat. I left it with him on the condition that he transfer the title, get insurance, and send me $250, the cost of the car. And we were off. Headed, once again, for the land of opportunity, this time, we were going in style. We had a "Sleepette:" A tiny room with a fold-down bed, a sink, a toilet, and a huge window with a fantastic view of the world as we sped by.

As always, I had my movie camera in hand recording our adventures for posterity. Amber was now a seasoned traveler and I was there to record it. I needed to document my life, her life, our life together. It wasn't a decision, it was a compulsion. I had no choice. I simply listened to my inner voice and obeyed.

Living with my parents in Hell again / Moved in with Pat, Joey, Loretta, and Kesslyn and found some peace / Our little red Fiat we called "home" / One of my art panels

Amber's first
modeling shots,
Whittier College,
CA

# Chapter 5

## A Good Man

*"Hope is definitely not the same thing as optimism. It is not the conviction that something will turn out well, but the certainty that something makes sense, regardless of how it turns out."* —Vaclav Havel

This cross-country trip was different from the others. We had gone by plane, car, bus, and now train. It was a relief to be gliding along with the conductor taking control of my life. I didn't have to worry, or think, or plan... just relax and enjoy the ride. The snacks we brought helped sustain us but food was completely unnecessary. The excitement of our trip, the joy of being together, and the new friends we were making, were much more important. The train took us places that had long ago been forgotten with the coming of the highways and advent of the car. This was a view of America few people have the privilege to see and I was filming it all.

We arrived at Grand Central Station in New York City at 5 pm. Rush Hour. The pace was frenzied. Thousands of people running in every direction. The porters were busy. After several trips back to the baggage platform, I finally collected our meager possessions into the middle of the immense lobby: One bike, two large boxes, three suitcases, our carry-ons, and a guitar. Here we sat on the wooden suitcase that my Uncle Gary had built, like an island in the middle of a river of people. We waited for the chaos to subside. At 6:30, we finally flagged down a porter with a cart to help us to the train that would take us to downtown Milford. Through another long journey, Amber was a trooper. I carried her, exhausted and sleeping, to the train. We were nearly there.

Our apartment was small, but it was *ours*. After nearly a year, we had our first home. We called it "Our Castle." It was on the second floor of a three-family house. Below us lived the Murray's—Ann, Danny, and their three kids, Andrea, Tara, and little Danny. Amber quickly became friends with all of them. Tara was like the sister she never had. It was wonderful to finally settle down, make a home, and be a family even if was only Amber and me.

I was on welfare for eight months and desperately wanted to get off... to find a way to use my skills, my dedication, and my willingness to work hard to make a better life for us. I took a bus to downtown Milford where I walked from one end of the Green to the other putting applications in wherever they would take them. I scoured the newspapers for a nearby job. Since Harry had not sent the money for my car, our only transportation was my bike. Winter was just around the corner and panic was beginning to set in. I needed to find a safe, warm, and secure means of transportation.

Finally, I landed a job at Waterbury Lock, a factory that manufactured locks and their various components. Jan paid for one month of Amber's daycare so I could get a start. Between my job, the $15 a week I made cleaning Jan and George's house, and the $25 a week in child support, I could afford to buy food, pay my rent, and have a little left over for fun. We would take the bus to the mall, or get an ice cream cone, or walk to the local pizza parlor and get one "to go." It was a minimal life on its face, but a grand, exciting, treasured life in my heart. I cherished the simple routine that became our life.

During the week, I'd drop her at Sarah's daycare, take the bus to work and home again, get on my bike and ride to get her by 5:30. We'd sing and weave our way through the streets filled with neighbors we waved to every day, but as the months passed and winter approached, the cold weather drove them indoors. The streets became silent and snow was beginning to cover the ground. I'd try my best to steer through it, but it was difficult and dangerous. As I rode past the little strip mall, I could see our reflection in the windows of the buildings: Amber bundled up, huddling behind my back to shield herself from the frozen wind, her big, blue eyes peeking out to see the view; me: Cold but determined and wishing I was home already. It was another scene from that movie I kept seeing in my mind; one that I was determined to change. "A car," I thought, "I have to get a car and get out of this weather." I needed the money that Harry had promised to buy my car. I'd rush home from work to check the mail, hoping to find his check and his promise fulfilled. I found nothing.

Home at last, I'd fill the bathtub across the hall, put Amber in with her toys, and start to prepare dinner. I'd leave both doors open so we could talk and she could tell me about her day. She was two and a half now, and life was so exciting! "Mom! Guess what? I made a new friend today! And we played in the sand box! And ate lunch together! And we got to paint! And..." I smiled. She gave me *so* much joy. "Tell me more." "Well, Miss Sarah pushed me on the swings and took us to the beach to feed the seagulls and..." I let her play in the tub for quite a while. When she was done, we'd eat our dinner, usually macaroni and cheese, or hot dogs, or soup. Cleaning the dishes together was a special treat. She'd drag the kitchen chair over to the sink to stand on. I'd wash, she'd rinse, we let them drip-dry. I had a collection of children's books and tapes, and we'd read or play house, or she would play with Tara, who lived downstairs. All the while, the camera was rolling. I needed to capture every moment.

Just before Christmas, my sister Kathy was awarded a settlement from an accident. She bought me a light blue Volkswagen station wagon. I was thrilled. She had recently separated from her husband and asked me if I wanted to move in with her and her two kids, Courtney and Raymond. I jumped at the chance to establish a loving, close, family relationship with my sister. There had always been tension between us. She seemed to constantly be watching me, judging me, and condemning me, without giving me a chance to defend myself. Perhaps I was wrong. I needed to try.

I packed our possessions into the station wagon and we were off to the condo she rented in Ansonia. Two days later, while I was unpacking, I passed by the upstairs window and saw the neighborhood kids teasing Courtney about her unkempt hair. She was crying. I could see myself, my own childhood and the taunting by my classmates, as I watched Courtney cry and look for someone to rescue her.

I brought her into the bathroom, cleaned her up, shampooed, then started to trim her hair. No matter what, Kathy did not cut her children's hair. I was halfway through when she walked in, shrieked at the sight of me cutting Courtney's hair, and went crazy. She threw all that we owned down the stairs and into the snow. "Get out!" she screamed, *"Get OUT!!!"* For three days, we slept in the car in the parking lot outside Kathy's apartment, with newspapers on the windows for privacy, wondering where to go and who to turn to.

I called my Aunt Anne and Uncle Bill. They lived near my parent's hometown of Paterson, New Jersey, and agreed to take us in. Once again, I packed up. I was getting quite good at packing. "How can I make a living doing this? I could work for a moving company." I tried to see the bright side. "It might be nice to live where my parents grew up. Maybe I can understand them better; maybe it will help me to resolve my childhood... to find some peace and forgiveness."

MY CHILDHOOD. It loomed in the background like a monster. I'd spent a good deal of time thinking about it, trying to explain, maybe justify it. I was so different from my parents or hoped I was at least. In my wildest imagination, I couldn't see myself treating Amber the way I was treated. From the beginning, I *wanted* her. I *really* enjoyed her company. My love for her was so intense it was almost too good to be true. It was love in its purest and most profound form. I tried to convince myself, "I *do* deserve to be happy... I *do* deserve to find love... to know its beauty, joy, and caress."

Each time the thought of leaving her... of dying, came into my mind, I shuddered, then pushed it out. It wouldn't go away. "I just *know* I'm going to die before she's six, but I'm scared to leave her, God. Who will take care of her?" There was no one in our life that I could count on to raise her with the same open-hearted love that we shared. Sometimes, when I was alone at night, the panic would nearly consume me. I dared not let it out. "If I tell anyone, it will happen."

I tried, but couldn't shake this feeling of doom… this vision of a day when we would part… when we would say, "Goodbye." As time went on, I would see flashes of our future, revelations of what was to come. I could leave my body at will and hover over my life, looking down. I'd note the time of day, the lighting, the expression on her face and mine, the remarkable things she would say. It was almost as though I was freezing time… like I was directing a movie or seeing the present as part of the future. "But how can I know?" I was scaring myself and had no one to turn to but God.

Months earlier, I'd met Alan, a friend of Nancy's, at a party. We were growing closer but I suspected our backgrounds would eventually come between us. I was a divorced, Catholic, single mother; he was a Jewish student earning his business degree. Family ties were strong—perhaps stronger than our love—and were hovering on the edge of our relationship, threatening to pull us apart.

He came down from Connecticut to visit. After dinner, we wanted to be alone. Aunt Anne agreed to watch Amber while we went out. We bought a bottle of wine, went into the woods, laid down a blanket, and started drinking and talking. The more I drank, the more my inhibitions—my walls—came down. And then "it" slipped out. At first it was a phrase, then a sentence, then a thought. I drank to drown "it." All to no avail. I was speaking and I couldn't control my words. I told him *everything.* I couldn't stop crying and I couldn't stop talking. Between the tears and sobs, I confessed my fear of my future with Amber. Shortly, it would end. "Will you take care of her when I die? Please, Alan." Of course he said, "Yes." He comforted me as best he could well into the morning. In spite of my drunkenness, I knew I'd let "it" out and I was afraid I'd tempted fate or exposed a secret so deep… so profound and real, that I set the wheels in motion to make it come true.

Living with Aunt Anne and Uncle Bill was good, even though it was a bit cramped. My job at Van Vlaanderen Machine Company, a printing press manufacturer, was going well. I started as a clerk, then worked my way up to middle management. Amber went to St. Joseph's Preschool. We were happily settling into a routine... into the normal life I'd craved for so many years. To an outsider, my life might have seemed dull; but to me it was calm, predictable, and there was no turmoil. Elevated by the absence of drama and turmoil, I wallowed in routine and simplicity. I spent my time working, enjoying my daughter, and puttering around the house helping with the chores.

Our entertainment was a drive into the country as we plotted our course on the map and sang along to Simon & Garfunkel, or a day in the park exploring and swinging for hours, or a trip into Paterson to see the sights that were part of our heritage. Each moment we spent together, I cherished as though it was our last, though I secretly hoped I was wrong.

In March of 1979, I noticed a small lump on her left cheek. It was warm and inflamed, with two black dots in the center. "Amber, what's this?" "What, Mom?" "Here, on your cheek. Did you fall in school or get hit or something?" "Gee, Mom, I don't know. I can't remember nothin'." I looked closer. Something was lodged inside. "A pencil lead maybe?" It was odd and I couldn't figure it out. I talked with her teacher then made an appointment with a doctor.

He brushed away my concern. "It seems as though *whatever* it is has been encapsulated. That's part of the healing process. It would be more of a risk to give her anesthesia and surgically remove it, than to let nature take its course and wait until her body absorbs it." I wanted to believe him. I *needed* to believe him. I didn't.

Over the next few weeks, there was no change in the lump, but she was having low-grade fevers and was constipated a lot. I took her back to the doctor. He reassured me that the lump was fine and recommended that I give her more bulk foods. I felt uneasy.

Uncle Bill was getting tired of Amber and I living in his home so he asked us to leave. I started looking for an apartment in Paterson. The rents were $500-700 a month. I went to work and asked for a raise so that I could afford to move. Although they liked my work, more money was out of the question. It was time to move on.

I called Alan and asked if we could stay with him. He was living in West Haven, Connecticut with Jan's sister, Nancy, and her boyfriend, Jimmy. He'd talk with them and call me back the next night.

No matter how hard I tried, I could not stay in one place long enough to establish myself. I knew that some of the choices I made were not good ones, but it seemed as if nobody wanted us or maybe they were too involved in their own lives and problems to care about us or maybe I was doing something—*everything*—wrong. Either way, I felt sorry for Amber. I wanted to give her the "Rainbow Room" she wanted for so long, a place to call her own... a sense of stability... friends down the street to play with... a home… an oasis. Through her, I could give them to me, too.

Michael still lived in Milford, but now with his girlfriend, Sharon, a beautiful and very supportive woman who loved Amber as her own. I asked him to take Amber for two weeks until I could find a job and save enough money to put her in preschool. "Two weeks! No way! Ten days. That's all I can do." He'd hardly been involved in her life up until now. I don't know why I kept expecting... kept hoping for more, but I did. Just looking at her and watching her live her life, she seemed like an angel. "How can anyone, especially her father, *not* want to spend as much time as possible with her?" I had no answers, only questions that hung in space, then disappeared into the edges to allow me the space to move on. "I *have* to find a way… a life for Amber." I was obsessed with finding happiness… with finding a way to provide Amber… to provide US, with a sense of contentment and peace.

Before long, Alan called to say it would be okay to stay with them, but only temporarily. I gave my two week notice at work and St. Joseph's. This time I couldn't fit all that we owned into my car, so I bought an enclosed car top carrier. I really didn't want to leave, but I didn't want to stay where we weren't wanted either.

Shortly after we got to Alan's, I sat myself down for a good talk. "O.K., Patti, enough is enough. You can't keep moving all over the country. You've got to do *something* to make enough money to get a place of your own and create a stable life for Amber. Waitress? No. Secretary? No, I can't type. Clean houses? Not enough money. I've got it! Construction! Those guys make great money! I can do *that!*" Realizing the work would be hard, physical, daunting, and challenging, I could only see possibilities, not problems.

Thinking back on my life, I reflected on all of the jobs I'd held: Dishwasher, waitress, short-order cook, fast food drive-in worker, electronics factory worker, Kirby vacuum sales person, glass blower, bookkeeper, in-home daycare, artist, lock-making factory worker, secretary, house cleaner. "What can I do to earn enough money to get our own place and start a new life?" I asked myself, then got right to work searching. I bought a local paper and searched the classified ads for construction jobs. I went through the Yellow Pages and called contractors, then drove around the area looking for buildings that were under construction, stopping to ask if they needed help. I got a lot of "cat calls" and whistles, but no job. "This is no time to let female pride stand in the way of finding a good paying job and supporting my daughter." I took their comments as a compliment and went on to the next job site.

Just off I-95 near New Haven, I saw a Denny's restaurant going up. "Well, hell, it's worth a try." I parked the car and walked to the construction office trailer. All the men stopped working to watch me. I found the superintendent. "Hi, my name is Patti Calistro. I was wondering if you need any help?" Of course he thought I was joking, but to test me, he said, "Sure. If you show up tomorrow morning at 7, you've got a job." "Great! I'll be here. What do I need?" "A hammer and a tool belt, that's all." I drove away, barely able to control my joy, and straight to Michael's house. "Amber, I got a job!" I told her all about it. I could see how proud she was. That night, Alan and I went shopping for the tools I needed.

"Brand new shiny hammer, leather tool belt, work boots." The reflection in the mirror spoke. "I definitely *look* the part. Yep, that's me: Patti the Construction Worker. God, I'm scared." I carefully studied myself. "Are you *nuts?* What are you thinking? They'll laugh you right off the site! You can't do this." I didn't listen. Early the next morning, I grabbed my purse, my lunch, walked down the stairs, got into my car, and drove away. The conflict continued. "You can turn around anytime, you know. No one but you will know the difference." My car was pulled to the construction site. "Do this," I heard, "You need to do this."

I was greeted with surprise, even shock, as I arrived on site at 7 am. Nobody expected to see me again. If they knew how desperate I was, it might have been different, maybe even easy. Regardless, they gave me a run for my money. "I want you to get up on that roof and help the roofers." I obeyed without question. For the next eight hours, I worked. I mean, *I really worked.* As a woman in man's world, I had to do more—and do it better—than the men. By the end of the day, I had blisters on my right hand, a battered and bloodied thumb on my left hand from the missed hammer strikes, and various cuts and bruises from head to toe. But I was proud. My sense of accomplishment eased the pain. "I did it! Despite a world of doubt, I did it!!!"

I went to work the next day, and the next, all to the delight of some, the indignation of others. "Women aren't *supposed* to do this kind of work. You should be *home* taking care of your kid." "That's why I'm doing this. I'm taking care of my kid. I need the money." I *wanted* to be living My Dream: Husband, home, taking care of the kids, but knew it wouldn't be possible any time soon. In the meantime, I had to work. I hoped that the men on the job would at least tolerate me, if not completely accept me. No other job could've paid me $5 an hour to start and I actually liked the work.

The situation at home with Nancy and Jimmy was unsettling. They were having their problems at the same time that Alan and I were breaking up. He was moving in with his parents. Amber and I were asked to leave. I called Social Services in Milford and explained my circumstances. I had a job but needed a place to live. "We really can't find a place for you. I'll ask around but I can't guarantee anything. Give me a call in a week." In despair, I wrote a Letter to the Editor of *the Milford Citizen*:

*June 8, 1979*

*"I came to Milford from California in 1978 and have been trying to establish myself and my daughter in this area ever since. First, I had to find day care for my daughter so that I could find a job. There are two in*

59

Milford, both are full. I found a private home at $50 a week. Next I had to find a job that paid enough to support us. I found a construction job in West Haven. Now I am looking for a room so that we will have somewhere to stay while I save money for an apartment (first, plus last, plus security).

The alternatives to this are to give up or go on welfare. What are the single parents without relatives and friends doing to survive out there?

I'll have to return to California if I cannot find a room. I'd rather be in Milford. Please let us stay.

From that letter, I received a call from a reporter at *The New Haven Journal-Courier.* She asked if she could write a story about us.

### "Woman Struggling to Win Her Battle with Hard Luck

*Patti Calistro is a 25 year old, upwardly mobile, commercial artist. She is also the parent of a 3 year old, is struggling to stay off welfare, and shortly will be faced with no place to live. The hard luck part of her story is, at the moment, winning.*

*'Most people I know that are divorced, have parents and relatives to help them out,' Ms. Calistro said, 'What is a single parent supposed to do if they're on their own?'*

*Ms. Calistro does have family but, with few exceptions, they are in California. She had returned there after she and her husband separated in Connecticut in 1977, but decided she 'couldn't get ahead' and moved to Milford.*

*Here, she had a two-room apartment and a bicycle for transportation, but what stymied her was the lack of day care. 'If you want to work, you have to put your child in a day care center,' she said. 'This is the crux of the whole problem.'*

*They lived on welfare until a friend offered to pay for a babysitter for a month and, during that time, Ms. Calistro found a job with a local manufacturer. But she gave it up to move in with her sister, an arrangement that lasted two days, and since then, she has bounced back and forth between coasts.*

60

*'My post office box here is the only constant thing in my life,'* she said.

*Currently, she and her daughter are living with friends in West Haven, and an arrangement was made a month ago, that they would move out this weekend. But Ms. Calistro, who would like to settle in Milford simply because she likes the town, has been unable to find a place to live within her means.*

*Her means right now are $25 a week child support and the money she has earned from her week-old job with a construction company. Welfare is out of the question until she establishes residency, and she would rather keep off it, anyway.*

*But in spite of these concerns, Ms. Calistro seems almost cheerful. 'Oh, I get down,' she said. 'But I'm young, healthy... I know we can always live in my car, or pack up and move back to California, or do something.'*

*And she is full of ideas of what she can do, once she gets back on her feet. She has rebuilt her portfolio, after the original was lost en route to California, and has become interested in calligraphy and interior design."*

I was living in my car in Nancy's garage. Michael and Sharon agreed to keep Amber until I found a place to live and I was eager to find one. Social Services called and gave me the name of a woman who had a room for rent in Milford. I called her and went to see the room right away. The house was hidden by overgrown trees and shrubs. Through the brush, I found the front door. The entry was white at one time but gray and dirty now. It hadn't been cleaned or swept in a very long time and reminded me of my parent's house, the misery inside, and the childhood I had escaped. I hesitated, then knocked nervously. A woman, aged beyond her years, opened the door just a crack. I recognized that look, the smell that hit me instantly, and the hovel she called home. She led me through the house, to the room in the back. A man with an alcoholic look about him sat in an old chair, tucked into a dark corner, drinking a beer and watching TV. He mumbled "hello" and followed me with his eyes. I had a very bad feeling about this.

The room was behind the kitchen. It was about 8'x14' with one small window that was obscured by the ivy growing outside. A twin bed and a dresser were the furnishings. At one end was a dinette table with two chairs, a hot plate, and a tiny refrigerator. The bathroom was off to the side. The place reeked of mildew and urine. I thought, "I can scrub it from head to toe... paint the dresser and the bathroom... put a rug down next to the bed... get a pretty tablecloth... some nice pictures, clean sheets. I could make this 'home'." "The rent is $50 a week. I don't like no noise or comin' in at all hours of the night. Well, you want it?" It was *this* or my car. I thought to myself, "Michael said he'll only keep Amber one more week," but out loud, "Oh yes. When can I move in?" "Today if you want." I drove back to Nancy's to get my things.

I tried to cover the mattress with as many blankets as I could, then put one on the floor to step on until I could mop it. That first night, I lay in bed listening to a rerun from my past: Yelling, cursing, slurred speech, unknown banging noises. It was the same scene, different actors. I was terrified that they would come through the door... grateful that Amber was at Michael's... sorry that I had failed so miserably. "God, why is my life so hard? I'm *really* trying my best. I just can't seem to get ahead. Amber deserves so much more than this. Are You listening? Are You even *here???*" Silence. I cried myself to sleep with no hope of tomorrow.

Three days later, I checked my post office. To my surprise, there were a lot of letters in response to my "Letter to the Editor." Sue Kelly, a widow with children grown and gone, invited Amber and I to live in her home. She lived in a big house in the country, surrounded by woods. We would have our own room, but could share the rest of the house. She was so sweet and generous in that letter, but even more so in person. "Most people call me Bambi." She made me feel as if I was already home. I moved in that night.

The next day, I brought Amber home. She was thrilled to be there; especially since Bambi had two miniature white poodles, Jill and Snipples. Loving Bambi, her dogs, and her home was just what we needed: A family. We easily fell into a routine. I'd get up, make Amber's favorite breakfast of oatmeal and applesauce, kiss her awake, dress her, comb her hair, and sit her at the table to eat and watch cartoons while I got ready for work. Then, I'd drive her to Marlene's house; she had a preschool in her basement. As I was leaving, we'd go through our ritual: I'd hug her and kiss her, then say, "Okay, I'm off to work now. Have fun, but not too much fun. Don't laugh or play or anything. I want you to cry all day long." I knew she saw the twinkle in my eye because she had to hold her hand over her mouth to contain her giggles. All of the other kids gathered around to watch this "play" we'd go through. "Yeah, let's not have *any* fun today, okay?" "Hey, Mom, I'm laughing... see?... I'm having fun!" Their laughter followed me up the stairs and out the door. My heart stayed with her but my body left for work.

Another twist of fate came from that letter and the newspaper article that followed: A new job. One day while I was at work on the Denny's site, a man came up and told me that he was head of the Laborer's Union. "We need women in the union. Most jobs have a quota to fill and no one to fill it. I have an opening right now that pays $8.15 an hour." "$8.15? Are you sure? Where is it? What do I have to do?" "It's in New Haven, near the harbor. They're building "Teletrack," an off-track betting theater. You'd be helping the tradesmen—carpenters, plumbers, electricians—getting their supplies, running errands, setting up scaffolding. It's a huge job... should last four or five months. Let me talk with the superintendent and get back with you tomorrow."

The next day he came back. "Yeah... the 'super' asked me about you... if you were a hard worker. I told him 'Yes.' You'd be the only woman among 300 or so guys. Can you handle it? You want the job?" I was skeptical. It seemed too good to be true and I wasn't ready to risk leaving a sure thing for a possible dream. "I think so. Can I let you know tomorrow?" "Yeah, I'll stop by tomorrow. Let me know then."

I "slept on it" then decided to take the risk. I finished out the week at Denny's and started Teletrack on Monday. I was told to be on the site and to report to the office at 8 am. I arrived at 7:30. A few guys were milling around half asleep, but woke up at the sight of me. By then, I'd become a "seasoned construction worker" and looked the part: Overalls, t-shirt, scarf, work boots, tool belt with my hammer hanging on it, and tape measure in my pocket. I didn't know what to expect, but was quickly filled in on the chain of command, status of the job, and the local gossip. They felt a bit uncomfortable having a woman on the job site and kept apologizing for their cuss words. I began to cuss, too. They were friendly, but not too friendly. More and more workers showed up. I felt like I was on stage, but tried my best to blend into the crowd; it wasn't easy. Out of the corner of my eye, I could see them laughing and pointing and checking me out. The boss walked up and settled things down. Gruff and in command, he said, "Follow me."

He assigned a partner to me who gave me a tour of the job site and taught me the ropes. It was a huge, round, cement building, five stories high, with ramps that wound around the interior walls. It was open in the center and the floor sloped down to the front wall where, eventually, a giant floor-to-ceiling screen would telecast the horse races around the country as they happened and people could place their bets instantaneously. To install the ceiling over interior, scaffolding filled the center of the room and a plywood floor, known as "the dance floor," sat on top. Around the outside of the building, various piles of building supplies waited to be brought inside for installation. I was impressed but not daunted. "I can do this. I *can."* For Amber, I could do anything.

I thoroughly enjoyed working that job. Physically, it was hard, but it paid well and the days went by quickly. For the first two weeks, a few of the men tried their best to break me, hoping that I would quit and leave their "man's world." But once they realized I was there to stay and why, most of the men accepted me; some were very protective. They went out of their way to show me that I *was* a part of their world, even to the point of writing a big "WO" in front of the word "men" that was written on the door of one of the many "Porta Potties" that circled the outside of the huge building. I felt honored to have gained admittance, but I knew where to draw the line. I would joke, swear, and talk about sex just as they did, but I made a vow to myself: Never go out with anyone on the job. Keeping this job, making good money, and improving my life with Amber came first and I kept my focus on that, not them.

For over a month, Alfie, one of the carpenters on site, kept trying to get me to meet a friend of his. "No way, I don't date anyone I work with." "C'mon. You guys have so much in common. He has a son who's just a little older than Amber and he's a carpenter. He works for Wil Armster, an architect up in Branford. He's a *really nice guy.*" I held my ground. After a couple of weeks, I gave in. "On one condition: I don't want anyone at work to know or I'll never hear the end of it."

The next Saturday, Amber and I drove down to Brown's Boatyard in Stratford. I got there a little early, hoping to see him first and from a distance. I wanted to leave "running room" just in case I had doubts. We sat in the car, playing my Joni Mitchell tapes, watching the docks for this man. In the distance a good looking man with a pony tail came striding down the dock, swinging a blonde-haired boy over his shoulder. My first impression was "Hmmm... nice looking... fun... healthy... strong... good father... confident. Yeah, I'd like to get to know him." I got out of my car. "Gary? Are you Gary?" "Yeah," he acknowledged with a smile. He invited us down to his boat.

"Sea Wing" was a pretty sight. Sitting at the dock like a young filly, bobbing up and down as boats on the Housatonic River passed by, straining to break free. She was a 34' white 1946 Alden sloop, with mahogany trim. Sleek and graceful, she seemed almost alive. I fell in love instantly.

Gary came to greet us. He was kind, caring, helpful, and sincere; all of the qualities I hoped a man could be. "He's a good man," I thought. We hit it off instantly. So did Amber and his son, Todd. That evening, he invited us to dinner at Blake and Sharon's house where he lived. Of course I accepted.

The house was a large white summer home not far from the beach of the Long Island Sound. Blake and Sharon were a nice couple in their late twenties who had built a marriage, a future, and a life. They welcomed us into it. We sat around their big dining table sharing a meal and getting to know each other. I could see that Gary had a special relationship with them, one that would carry on and deepen. I loved the normal... the peaceful... the hopeful life they lived and I longed to have a marriage like that, too.

After our visit, Amber and I drove home to Bambi's chattering like a couple of squirrels. "So, Amber, whadyathink? Gary and Todd are nice, aren't they?" "Oh yeah, Mom. Todd's fun. He shared his toys with me and likes to play and..." She was glowing, but tired. It was a long and happy day. Both of us were satisfied, contented, and ready to fall into bed. As I lay next to Amber, the hope and excitement of what was possible, kept me awake. "Should I even hope? Or should I let everything go? Is he different? Will he love Amber? What about Todd? How will he accept her?" The questions kept coming; the answers would take more time.

Alfie was right. We had a lot in common. Though our upbringing was different, our values, interests, morals, and goals —the four corner posts of a solid relationship—were very much alike. Fathering Todd was top priority, just as my mothering Amber was. We shared a real sense of adventure and both longed to travel. Gary's dream was to outfit "Sea Wing" and sail to the Caribbean to live, maybe even sail around the world.

Our relationship flourished. It had been a long time since I'd been in love and I needed to share my life with a man again. It felt so right to enjoy our kids, to give to someone who cared for me and for Amber, and to dream our dreams together. I had forgotten what being in love and building a future felt like: "Butterflies" at the thought of him, anticipation to connect, longing to be close. Our lives had changed direction and we were moving down a positive path. I couldn't imagine my life without him.

During the day, I worked construction and tended to Amber. But every night and on weekends, I thought about Gary, talked with him, or spent time with him. Life was good—*really good*. I was young, healthy, had a nice place to live, a good job, a beautiful daughter, and now a man who loved me. Life was perfect...

... until that August evening.

Yes, *that* evening. The one I want to eliminate from my history, from Amber's history, from the history of the world. I want to type the words "IT DIDN'T HAPPEN" and have it be so. I want to be *normal,* not *"chosen."* I want to be *reading* this book, not *writing* it. I want to know that *both* of my children, not *one* of them, are healthy, happy, and alive. I want my life back. *"FIND*

*SOMEONE ELSE TO DO THIS, GOD... NOT ME! I CAN'T DO THIS! GIVE ME ANOTHER TASK. CHOOSE SOMEONE ELSE, DAMMIT!!!"*

Despite my desire to change the course of fate, I find myself going on. I can't seem to stop, no matter how hard I try. I continue to type the next letter... word... paragraph... page... chapter. "On to the next chapter," I hear. I'm startled.

On command, I reach back into my past to relive that time— moment to moment. Even though I feel my fingertips dancing on the computer keys and see the words on the screen as I write, my present gives way to my past. I feel the pain and shock and disbelief and anger. I see Amber lying there on the bed, so peaceful... so innocent. She's unaware of the story about to unfold... the message she is destined to deliver... the Life Task I am still living.

The street light illuminates her body as a halo surrounds an angel. She seems almost saintly. And then I remember THE LUMP. It's hidden by her beautiful curls. Obliterated... gone... an illusion. Nobody will know it's there. "But *I* know. And I know it's cancer... and I know she will die. But I can't just sit back and watch You take her from me! Oh, God... *I have to save her life!"*

Living in CT again /
Meeting Gary /
Michael's girlfriend,
Sharon

Living on the Housatonic River aboard Sea Wing with Amber and Todd

# Chapter 6

# *Dream Life...*

*"Truth will always be truth, regardless of lack of understanding, disbelief, or ignorance."* —W. Clement Stone

With Amber asleep, I left the bedroom and called Michael. "I found a lump behind Amber's ear... it's hard... about the size of a nut." There was panic in my voice and I knew it. "Oh, Patti, it's probably nothing. Don't get so upset. You always expect the worse. She probably fell down and bumped it or something." "Michael, I'm taking her to the doctor tomorrow. What if it's cancer?!" "Cancer," he laughed, "Oh, quit exaggerating, will you? You don't *need* to take her to the doctor tomorrow. Just wait; it'll go down in a couple of days." "It's *not* a bruise, Michael. It's not black and blue at all. I'm going to take her to the doctor tomorrow!" "Don't take her yet. I'll come over tomorrow after work and take a look at it. I'm not paying half of a doctor bill for something I haven't even seen."

I spent the night tossing and turning, afraid of the truth, avoiding the demons. My eyes would open, I'd reach over to Amber to search out The Lump and—DAMMIT—find it still there. "Why won't it go away... just disappear?" I wanted to exist in this wonderful world we just discovered with Gary and Todd, not the anguish of losing my daughter. I wanted to rush the night to know what it was. Morning couldn't come soon enough.

At 9 am sharp, I called a naturopath, Dr. Soda. He had an office just off the Milford Green. "Yes, I'll see her without an appointment." I called Michael at work to see if he wanted to go with us. By 10am, we were walking up the driveway to his office. I knocked. He seemed kind and comforting and knowledgeable. He led us through the Waiting Room and into the Examining

Room. I pulled back her hair to show him The Lump. Neither my body language nor my expression betrayed the alarm I felt inside. I knew that Amber was studying my face and I didn't want to frighten her.

He felt it, tried to move it, pushed on it, looked perplexed. "It's probably a calcium deposit." "Are you sure? Could it be cancer? Do kids even *get* cancer?" He seemed to be amused at this. "No, it's not cancer." He exchanged looks with Michael and then looked at me. He, too, thought I was overreacting.

He explained "body salts" as he handed me a bottle of homeopathic "CALC-FLOR 6x, The Schuessler Cell Salts." He instructed me to place three tablets under her tongue three times a day. "Come back in seven or eight months and we'll check it again." I left, feeling uneasy deep in my heart, but in my mind I tried to see things logically. *"He's the doctor, not me. How do I know what it is? They're right, I'm just overreacting. I'll just give her the salts and it'll be gone in no time."*

I was in the middle of a juggling act; three balls were in the air at once: Amber's health, my job, and my relationship with Gary. It was now September and I could feel the chill of winter in the air. The Teletrack job was coming to an end; the building was nearly finished. The thought of working construction outside, struggling to stay warm, and trudging building materials through the snow was not appealing at all.

"I'll open up that art studio I've always wanted." I found a couple of rooms on the second floor of a building on the Green in downtown Milford. The landlord would give me two free months rent if I cleaned, painted, and fixed them up. Oh, how I wanted to have my own business; a legacy for Amber that would carry on if anything should happen to me. I signed the lease and got to work.

I was busy—*very busy*—so busy in fact that I hardly had time to think. And certainly no time to let my mind wander. I worked full time, took care of Amber, and began to renovate the studio. Since the address was 15 River Street #3, I named it "Studio 3."

A month went by as I faithfully gave Amber her salts and kept a wary eye on The Lump for any changes. Call it "mother's intuition," "nagging doubt—" whatever—but for some reason, I couldn't stop thinking about the possibility that they were wrong and I was right. "This is *cancer.*" It was still on her head and it seemed to be *growing.* "Or is it? Am I getting carried away with this? Nobody else is concerned. She doesn't have any symptoms and it isn't bothering *her.*" I tried to accept it, make it part of her anatomy, even part of our life. Amber even gave it a name; she called it her "Bump."

I tried to stay involved, wrapped up, some would say. I didn't want to have any idle time to dwell on my anguish that lingered just below the surface. The studio was a good diversion; work was, too. I needed to become physically exhausted every day before I could fall asleep at night. No matter what I did, The Lump was becoming the center of my life. It dominated *everything.* I washed her hair and touched it; feeling myself silently gasp. She'd laugh and toss her head; it flashed at me like some obscene gesture. I couldn't will it away, pray that it would disappear, or even expect a miracle. No doubt in my mind, *it wasn't getting smaller.* It was growing—slowly, slightly—but *growing.* And with it, so was my fear. Nobody would believe me. There was nothing to worry about. I was overreacting.

It didn't seem to bother Amber at all. Of course, in *front* of her, it didn't bother me either. Learning how to hide my true feelings, pretending to the point of convincing myself, and maintaining a facade were skills from my childhood that I mastered. They proved to be useful, even vital, as I did my best to protect Amber from anything or anyone that would hurt her and that included my growing fear.

Just like a typical three year old, she'd go to school everyday and play with her friends. She was typical, until they noticed. "What's *that?*" "Oh, just my Bump," she'd explain. "How did you get it?" "I don't know. I just *got* it, that's all. Hey, you wanna play on the swings?" She diverted their attention—and hers—to more important things.

We were both doing the same thing, trying to forget. Our life up to this point had been a struggle. Although we overcame each one and emerged stronger and still smiling, we were tired. Finally, our life had taken a turn for the better. Aside from The Lump, our life was perfect. We had moved aboard Sea Wing with

Gary and Todd. We finally found a family, a loving home, and hope for the future.

Docked at Brown's Boatyard, the boat became our refuge. Each morning, we'd pop our heads out of the companionway and watch the oyster men comb the river bottom collecting their gourmet treasures. At night, we'd gently rock to sleep, listening to the sounds of the water lapping against the hull. On weekends, we'd go sailing across the Long Island Sound to Port Jefferson, a quaint little harbor with huge sand dunes for climbing. Spending time together, being away from the pressures of land, spinnaker flying, taking the dinghy up the creeks to explore, cooking a meal while at anchor, watching the sunset from the forward deck, cuddling up in the cockpit to read the kids a story, these were the simple pleasures I relished. And I didn't want my fairy tale to end.

Winter was fast approaching and so was the cold weather. Living on Sea Wing, would be difficult at best. She was not insulated, we were living on the river, and the only source of heat was a very small coal stove. Though Gary and I did not want to live apart, we knew it would be hard on the kids, especially Amber who would be there full-time. It might even be dangerous as the docks would be covered with snow and ice. One slip, and she would be in the water and under the frozen surface. Even with a life jacket on, it would take only moments before she would die from hypothermia or drowning or both. Gary moved in with his parents; we moved back with Bambi. She was one of the few people in my life that always accepted me without question and supported me in my decisions. "You're always welcome in my home, Patti." We settled back into our room and some semblance of our old routine.

As a builder and craftsman, Gary was one of the best. He was putting the finishing touches on a house that Wil Armster, the architect/owner of Wood, Steel, and Glass, was building for the Winograd's. Jeff Winograd was a radiologist who worked at St. Mary's Hospital in Waterbury; his wife, Harriet, an artist. Gary told him about The Lump. "If Amber was my daughter, I'd find out *exactly* what it is." He recommended his friend, Richard Abraham, an internist. His office was in Canton, just over the mountain from the Bristol's and our old house. It'd been only a couple of years since Michael, Amber, and I had lived there, but it seemed like a lifetime away. So much had happened since those carefree days of striking off into the woods with Amber on my back and Tara at my side. Now, I was constantly on the move, never catching my breath, never stopping to reflect.

Before we drove to Richard Abraham's office, Gary and I decided to see our old house. As we came around the bend and passed it, I felt cold and empty. A ghostly presence—part of my past—was in the car with us. Remembering the pain of our life, our hope, and our dreams turned into nightmares, was simply too much to bear. I quickly suppressed any feelings of wistful longing. I didn't ask him to stop. I didn't want to linger. I didn't want to remember. That pain was in my past and I wanted to keep it there for as long as I could. The pain in my present was nearly more than I could endure and I needed to be strong for Amber.

Every so often, I'd turn around and watch Amber as she slept peacefully in her car seat. "Look how beautiful and innocent she is, Gary, almost like an angel. God! How that lump scares me! What if it *is* cancer?" I whispered. "Don't worry, Patti, it's nothing serious." "But what if it *is???*" His desire to make it good... to make it right, dominated any doubt he might have had. "It's not." Oh, how I wanted to believe him, but didn't.

We walked into Richard Abraham's office and then into the Examining Room. After introductions and explanations, he sat her on the table, pulled back her hair, and eyed The Lump. I studied his face. He was nervous... perplexed... anxious. He took out an instrument and measured it. "Three centimeters... no need to worry." His eyes were filled with doubt and betrayed his words. "I think you should bring her to George McGowan. He's head of Pediatric Surgery at Hartford Hospital." I thanked him for seeing us and told him I'd call McGowan.

I walked out of the office numb with worry and followed Gary and Amber to the car. I was drained of all hope. On the outside I was normal; inside, I could feel the twinges of panic about to break loose. My thoughts went out of control and I wanted to run away into the woods that I knew so well. The same woods where Amber, Tara, and I would hike and play and be with God. Beyond the din of my own thoughts, I heard that voice again. "I am here... you are not alone... I will guide you through this." I dismissed it as quickly as it came. "I must be going crazy." I continued to worry.

My appointment with George McGowan was two weeks away. In the meantime, I moved through my life in a daze. Robotic movements replaced genuine feelings and expressions. I distanced myself from the world around me instead of being connected and involved. A wall went up to keep my true fears and emotions *in* and everyone else *out*. Time was not measured. I'd find myself sitting at a traffic light wondering how I got there and where I was going. I'd hang up the phone and forget who I just talked to. Food had no taste; it was merely a means to survive. Every child I saw was healthy —*every single one of them.* I was a machine, not a person. I had to function, not live.

Death was something I had no experience with before now. No one I knew died: No relatives, no friends, no one. Though I believed in life after death, reincarnation, and God, I'd never been faced with death. My growing fear gave way to the possibility of death... of Amber's death. For the first time, I allowed myself to envision it. I caught a glimpse of what was to come, in a barn in New Haven.

Gary and I took the kids to look at a building that an architect friend was considering for renovation. It was a large, three-story, abandoned barn near the downtown area. For days before our visit, it had rained and rained, and as we climbed the ladder that led to the hay loft, I could smell the musky odor of wet wood and straw. When we reached the top, we scattered in different directions. Gary and Stewart went to the far end to inspect the beams, Amber and Todd were holding hands and exploring the eaves, and I stood in the middle of the room, scanning the scene.

It was a huge room filled with bits of wood and straw and little else. A large hole in the roof was open to the sky; all the rain from the past few days had soaked the floor beneath it. I turned to look at the architect's plans when, without warning, Amber screamed, *"Mom...!!"* The word instantly faded away. I spun around to see the shocked faces of Amber and Todd as they disappeared through the floor. *"Dead... they're dead!"* It was more than a thought, it was real. For a split second, I hesitated. I didn't want to face it; I didn't want to know. In two giant leaps, I was at the ladder and sliding down the steps. I expected the worse.

They were laying on the pile of wet wood, the floor they were standing on just seconds before. My eyes begged for signs of life and then I heard a moan. Gary ran over to Todd. I ran over to Amber. I saw her body move. *"She's ALIVE!"* I glanced over at Todd. He was sitting up—too stunned to cry—clutching his wrist. "Amber are you O.K.? Does anything hurt???" I strained to suppress my panic. "Stewart, call an ambulance!" She just laid there and moaned. Her eyes opened. "Amber, I'm here... I'm here... I love you... You'll be okay. The ambulance is on it's way. Just hang on." I was sure she had internal injuries. "Oh, God, please don't take her from me. *Please...*" I could hear the sirens getting louder. Within minutes, we were in the back of the ambulance and on our way to the hospital. I felt like I was standing on the edge of a cliff, grasping Amber's hand, trying to help her up. I could feel her slipping. I was losing my grip.

After x-rays and tests, Todd walked away with a sprained wrist. Amber was sore and shaken but had no other injuries. "A reprieve... a little more time." I wondered, "How will I ever go on if I lose her? I'm not sure I can endure the agony... the grief... the emptiness. God, I don't think I can." "You will."

Until our appointment with McGowan, I worked hard at surviving the day. Our routine was the same: Get myself up, fix a cup of coffee, wash, and get dressed. Afterwards, I'd go into our room and lay on our bed next to Amber, stroke her hair until she woke up, get her on the toilet, and start breakfast. She would sometimes watch cartoons while she ate and I fixed her lunch. Then, we'd pour ourselves and our belongings into the car, head to daycare to drop her off, then on to the construction site to work. The Teletrack job was finished but the Laborer's Union had another job for me. A wing was being added to Yale-New Haven Hospital and they were at the beginning stage of construction: The concrete footings.

I arrived at the new job site at 7 am dressed in thermal underwear, overalls, flannel shirt, sweatshirt, wool socks, work boots, and hat. I kept a scarf around my neck to keep out the dust and fumes. It was a frigid, windy, wet October day. I parked my car and walked to the edge of an immense pit. The foundation wasn't poured yet. My job was to carry the concrete forms to the workers so they could put them in place and ready for the concrete pour. I stood there, transfixed. A few heads began to turn in my direction, and then a few more. "Hey, lady, you need any help?" "Uh... yeah. Where's the job superintendent?" "Over there!"

Among the bulldozers, cranes, backhoes, and dump trucks, men marched around; some with loads; some empty-handed. Each one had a definite purpose to his movements; a job to do as part of a collective. They were so deep in the pit, they looked like ants and moved like them, too. I followed his finger. "Over *there* next to that trailer!" The wind carried his words away. "Thanks!" Undeterred and grateful, I aimed for the trailer and pushed my body through the steady wall of cold wind.

By the time I reached it, nearly all the men on the site knew I was there. A woman in a "man's world." What a sight to behold! And they did. It was 1979 and we were in the midst of the "Women's Liberation Movement." Women were just beginning to gain the same God-given power as men even though the "Equal Rights Amendment" had not yet been passed into law. Discrimination based on gender was still rampant. There was a war in the workplace between men and women and I was at the forefront... in the trenches—literally.

The "super" saw me. "Can I help you?" he said in a polite tone. "Hi, I'm Patti Calistro," as I shook his hand with a strong, confident grip. "The Laborer's Union sent me over." His eyes said, "Oh shit! Not a *woman!*" But I heard, "Oh, yeah. They called and told me about you. Well, what do think? Think you can do this kind of work? You have to carry those concrete forms up and down those hills and set them in place. Each one weighs seventy pounds, ya know." "Oh, sure, I can do that." As if saying it made it so. He held back a smile. "Well, you try it for a day and see how you do. Go over and talk to the foreman." I was grateful he was willing to give me a chance. I needed to support Amber... I needed to build a better life for us as much as they needed to build this wing of the hospital.

Down, down, down into the pit. I made my way past the obstacles to the foreman. *"What? Are you kidding? You can't lift those forms!"* I walked over to one, collected my strength, and lifted it. "See... no problem." Despite my small, 110 pound frame, I was stubborn (desperate) and it showed. I joined the "ants" who were lugging the forms from one place to the next. I was sweating and straining and trying my best not to let it show. "I *need* this job. I *can't* give up now." My body kept moving... moving by sheer determination, not strength. After a few hours, I began to feel weak, nearly defeated. "Not yet. If only I can make it to the end of the day." Another hour went by. 'Lunch." I grabbed a sandwich and a hot coffee off the lunch truck, hoping food would rekindle my spirits and give me strength.

Oh, how I wanted to walk back to my car, not back into the pit. I felt the warm tears on my cold face. I pulled up the hood of my sweatshirt, wiped them away with my scarf, and returned to work. But the tears continued to flow. Soon, I couldn't stop them. I kept my head down and kept walking so they couldn't see my tears... they couldn't see me fail. I thought about Amber. "I'm strong... I can do this... I *have* to do this." And I did...

...until 2:00. At break time, I found the superintendent and admitted defeat. I was surprised that he didn't taunt me; he praised me instead. "Not many women would've done what you did. You should be proud of yourself." He was right. I was. But pride was not enough. I still had bills to pay and a daughter to support. I applied for a job working as a waitress in the clubhouse at Teletrack.

On November 1st, Amber and I drove up to Hartford Hospital to see George McGowan. Our favorite tape—the soundtrack to *The Muppet Movie*—was playing in the cassette player of my Volkswagen Square-back. We knew all of the words to all of the songs and happily sang along. When Gonzo started to sing *I'm Going to Go Back There Someday,* my eyes kept drifting from the road to Amber. She was sitting on her pillow so that she could see out the window; her hair was pulled into a ponytail. Sweet and innocent, she sat there with anticipation of another road adventure; her pudgy cheeks, button nose, and dimples on the tops of her hands. She was singing her heart out.

*"This looks familiar... vaguely familiar*
*Almost unreal, yet, it's too soon to feel yet.*
*Close to my soul, and yet so far away.*
*I'm going to go back there someday.*

*Sun rises, night falls; sometimes the sky calls.*
*Is that a song there, and do I belong there?*
*I've never been there, but I know the way.*
*I'm going to go back there someday.*

*Come and go with me; it's more fun to share.*
*We'll both be completely at home in mid-air.*
*We're flyin', not walkin', on featherless wings.*
*We can hold on to love like invisible strings.*

*There's not a word yet, for old friends who've just met.*
*Part heaven, part space, or have I found my place?*
*You can just visit, but I plan to stay.*
*I'm going to go back there someday.*
*I'm going to go back there someday."*

"Is she singing along to the song or singing to me?" I silently wondered. It was as if she was singing the future to me. Tears came to my eyes and I hoped she didn't see. Unlike me, Amber seemed to have a purpose... a meaning in her life. I got the sense that she knew who she was and why she was here on earth. "How can she *possibly* know? *Is* she truly sent from God? And if she *is*... WHY?" I tried to be rational. "No... this can't be. I'm too ordinary... too human... to fallible to be the mother of a *messenger from God!* No... no... not *me!*" I couldn't see myself but I *could* see Amber in that role.

Once again, I was living a divided life: I was two separate people. Publicly, I was happy, optimistic, and hopeful. Privately, I was bewildered, frustrated, and scared to death. Only God could see inside me as He had throughout my life. Only He could help me now. I surrendered my life to Him. "God, make me your instrument. I can't do this on my own."

McGowan's Waiting Room was small and crowded; it had the same smell as all of the other doctor's Waiting Rooms. True to its name, we waited and waited and waited. He finally examined her. Though he couldn't explain what it was, he saw no need to look further. "Let's wait a month and see if it grows." "But it *has* grown." He dismissed my expression of concern with, "Don't worry, Mrs. Calistro, lots of kids get lots of lumps and bumps. Look at her, she looks *perfectly healthy.*" I wasted no time to reply. "What do you mean *'perfectly healthy?'* I could look 'perfectly healthy' and be *dying* inside. You can't diagnose her by the way she *looks.*" I left his office feeling humiliated, angry, and confused. In a state of doubt and disbelief, I thought to myself, "What the hell is going on here? How can he dismiss me... dismiss my concerns without looking further???"

I called Jeff Winograd, who worked as a radiologist at St. Mary's Hospital, and told him what happened. He reached out to comfort me and offered to keep looking. Just like me, he wouldn't... he *couldn't* give up. "Bring her here, to St. Mary's. I'll take some x-rays and hopefully, they'll give us some answers."

The following day, I drove to St. Mary's with Amber. Jeff took a series of x-rays and then brought me into his office. "There is a slight thinning of the skull bone... possibly cartilaginous tissue." POSSIBLY. That word stuck in my mind. *"Possibly... you mean you don't know?"* I knew that he wanted to give me a definite answer, but with the information before him, he couldn't. He looked helpless. And sorry. "Take her back to Rich, let him examine... measure it again. Let me know what he says."

On December 4th, we were in Rich's Canton office again. Nervously, he measured The Lump. "It grew. Last month it measured 3 centimeters and now it's 4." My heart stopped; my stomach plunged. I kept my composure for Amber's sake. He urged me to see McGowan again and tell him it was growing.

A week went by and somehow, I lived through it. We were back in McGowan's office. This time, I brought the x-rays that Jeff had taken with me. He measured The Lump. "There's no change." *"What??? What do you mean 'no change'???"* He was unmoved. "It measured 3 centimeters last month and 3 centimeters this month." "But Richard Abraham measured it and found a 1 centimeter difference... and *I know* it's been growing. What about a biopsy? I want a biopsy. I want to know *exactly* what it is." "I don't feel it's necessary. The risk from the anesthesia would be too great." "But you don't even know what it is... you're *guessing!*" I could see he was insulted and getting angry. "You're a *mother,* not a *doctor.* You don't have any formal training." I was beginning to see things clearly: It was a power struggle. *He* knew; *I* didn't. To pacify me and get me out of his office, he said, "If it will make you feel better, I'll show her x-rays to a neurosurgeon and the Radiology Department."

Indignant and desperate, I called Jeff. "No change," I said, "McGowan found no change." "Bring her up to St. Mary's again. We'll take another set of x-rays. *This* time, we'll tape a metal disc to the outside of the lump. Metal shows up solid on an x-ray. We'll compare these with the ones we took last month."

I drove up to Hartford Hospital to pick up the Radiology Department's consensus and Amber's first set of x-rays. I hurried out into the hall and tore open the envelope. "After examining the x-rays, our conclusion is that it is a normal variation of bone growth..." *"NORMAL???"* By now The Lump was the size of a ping pong ball and was visible through her hair. "We see no reason to biopsy or remove it at this time." "I can't believe they think this is *normal!*" Although I was not a doctor, I knew it was definitely *not* "normal."

One part of me wanted to believe them. After all, they were the authorities... *they* were the doctors; I was just a mother... a mother who knew her child. "Maybe it will dissolve... go away in a couple of months. They are *doctors* after all. They *must* know what they're talking about." I tried to persuade myself to surrender to their studied opinion. "I'm sure I'm just looking at the negative side. Besides, God knows she's the only family I have. He wouldn't take her from me... I know He wouldn't." I didn't believe myself.

Somewhere deep inside there was an unspeakable terror; the knowledge that no matter how much I didn't *want* this to happen, it would all take place without my consent. As hard as I tried, I just could not find a *reason...* a justification for it. *"Why???"* I kept asking God. Nothing but silence. It would be much later before

He would answer that question. In the meantime, as her mother, my job was to do my best to save her life, help her cope with the pain to come, and live each day together as though it was our last. I wanted to savor each moment and make it last forever.

I compiled some of Amber's photographs into a portfolio. Come hell or high water, I was determined that she was going to be a model. I started the search for a modeling agency to represent her. In the Yellow Pages there were only three listed; one was in Greenwich, the other two in New Haven. Two had agreed to meet us.

I dressed to impress, then primped Amber to the point that they *couldn't* say no. Hiding The Lump behind her ear took skill and I prayed they wouldn't see it. We drove to the agency in Greenwich first. They liked Amber, but tried to caution me about a model's life, especially a *child* model. "You'll have to go back and forth into The City... one assignment after another... rejection... long hours... a lot of 'dues' to pay." After what we'd already been through, it sounded pretty easy, even fun.

Our appointment with the Montage Agency in New Haven was next. On a cold January day, we parked the car in Macy's garage in downtown New Haven. I fussed over Amber. "Hair combed... ribbon just right... no, you can't see The Lump... dress ironed... patent leather shoes shined... white stockings... hmmm, they're a bit too big... maybe this safety pin will hold them up. Oh... let me wipe off breakfast. Com'ere, Amber, stick out your tongue." I took a tissue and dabbed some spit from her tongue, then gently wiped the milk off her cheek. Inventory completed, I grabbed her portfolio and we emerged onto the street. The brisk wind caught us and drove us along at a fast pace.

My feet carried us forward. With each step, the cold concrete grounded me, but I was hovering above watching another scene from "Amber's Movie." I was noticing all the details: The gray streets, wind whipping at the hats and coats and scarves of the people who were scurrying along, cars stuck in their downtown traffic jams, buildings towering above us, blocking out the sun and the sky; me, clutching her hand; her, nearly airborne trying to keep up; us, racing to this meeting, hoping to carve out a different future for us and yet knowing what's in store. I was holding on to her for dear life. I was determined, powerful, accomplished, in control... vulnerable, weak, a failure, a victim.

The meeting went well. "There's hope!" They wanted to represent her. We spoke about layouts and deadlines and contracts. As Amber played in the office, I prayed her hair would continue to hide The Lump. "Oh, please don't spoil this now, God." Our lives had been resurrected. We returned to Milford triumphant.

Down the street from Studio 3, two photographers had set up a photography studio called Quality Images. They were photographing models for ads and creating portfolios for them. I asked them to take some photos of Amber. I brought her in with three different outfits... three different "looks." Todd and Gary came as well. The sessions started out with Amber and Todd together. You could see that although they were a lot alike, their differences were striking: Amber had dark, curly hair, blue eyes, and a sweet demeanor, while Todd had straight, blonde hair, green eyes, and was rambunctious. They were like two bookends. Within the hour, Todd had definitely had enough. Gary took him back to the studio while Amber finished the photo session.

I was quite surprised at how well she adapted to modeling. We treated it like a game and had lots of fun playing. She took direction well. "Smile... look over here... now into the camera... sit up here and wave... hold your head up." She was a natural. As I sat on the sidelines watching her with pride, I thought, "Yes, this is meant to be. Someday she'll be famous. She was born to do this... go before the camera, make people feel good, and enjoy doing it. *This* is the reason she was put on earth. I *know* it is." Any thoughts of cancer or dying or Amber's message or Life Tasks, were locked away in another world. I wanted to linger in this one.

When she was finished, she ran over to me and squeezed my neck just as the camera clicked. "Ooo... Mommy, I *love* you!" "Mmm... I love you, too, Amber." This moment was suspended in time. This memory of our happiest times, would never be forgotten.

A week later, Amber got her first assignment: Model a stick-on thermometer. I laughed as she filled out the contract and signed her name. "Thirty-five dollars an hour! Gee, Amber, you make more money than *I* do!" She beamed with pride, *"Really, Mom? I do?"* She changed into the pajamas I brought to the set. She did have a slight cold, so it wasn't a stretch for her to look sick. Off to the side and beyond the cameras and lights, I watched. "God, she's so remarkable... so amazing. I feel like more of a spectator... a guardian, than her mother. If they only knew that behind her ear and under her hair, there is The Lump." I shook off the thought and returned to the scene. She was finished and eager to go eat some lunch. "How'd I do, Mom?" "Perfect, Amber, just perfect."

After tasting this other world, I didn't want to give it up. It was fun! We were actually enjoying this. But I needed to stop the nagging doubts once and for all. I needed to *know.* I called Jeff. "I want a biopsy, Jeff. Do you know a surgeon who will do it?" He told me about Dr. Quigley. His office was in Waterbury.

A few days later we drove up to Waterbury stopping at St. Mary's to see Jeff and compare both sets of x-rays he'd taken. Amber knew the nurses by name and enchanted them in the outer office while I went over to the light table to examine the x-rays with Jeff. He overlaid the x-ray with the metal marker and the one without.

The small, almost inaudible gasp from Jeff was in perfect time with my heart skipping a beat, then landing in my stomach. "Yes, it *has* grown." He turned to me. Our eyes met. Then he turned back to the films and tried to be clinical. "You see..." he pointed with his pencil, "The marker clearly shows that the lump has grown." I could see the difference. It was bigger, noticeably bigger. "Oh, God, another step closer to the truth," I thought.

We drove to Quigley's office. He examined Amber and agreed to do the biopsy. We set a date: Tuesday, the 29th of January. Nearly five months had gone by since that evening in August... five months of pure hell abbreviated by periods of ignorant bliss. Finally, I would *know.*

The only thing I *did* know about cancer was how to spell it, that's all, nothing more. I'd never experienced cancer in my life— no family, no friends, and certainly no children. "Kids don't get cancer," my logical mind told me. I didn't know exactly what it was, or what caused it, or how you cure it. Why would I? Cancer happened to *other* people, not me. And certainly not to my little girl.

As the biopsy date neared, Amber came down with a cold and a fever. I called Dr. Quigley. "We'll have to wait until she recovers. Her lungs have to be clear for the anesthesia." We rescheduled the surgery for the middle of February. My life was on hold again, stuck in this quicksand of doubt, fear, and dread.

Then *I* began to feel sick... very sick. I felt like I was going to die. Gary took me to the Emergency Room. "Pneumonia... you've got pneumonia." The doctor gave me a shot of penicillin and sent me home to rest. I could barely get up out of bed, except to use the bathroom. Amber nursed me. "Don't worry, Mom. I'll take care of ya. I'll fix dinner, rub your head, and then you'll feel better, O.K?" This was her nature; she was a giver. Always concerned for everyone else, her happiness came last.

I slowly recovered, but Amber just couldn't shake her cold. Until she did, surgery was out of the question. We waited.

Her fourth birthday was coming: February 28th. I knew that this would be her last. Dread was a feeling more common than joy and I was all too familiar with it. Like a rabid dog nipping at my heels, I was constantly running to avoid being devoured... to fend off any harm and to protect my daughter. The urge to give her life and now sustain it was as strong as the urge to stop her from dying, even stronger. Now that I held her... had her in my life for all these years, I wasn't going to give her up—not willingly, not ever!

Amber had never had a birthday party before and I wanted to make this one special. We invited all her friends from school, planned games and goodies, and bought her a dress for the big day. The festive mood lifted me. I played the doting mother. I spoiled her completely. "Whatever you want, Amber." As always, I had my movie camera in hand to record the event... the last moments of her life here on earth.

After the party, as we were getting ready for bed, a song came over the radio: *You and Me Against the World.* Amber was in the bathroom brushing her teeth. I began to cry. Just as she walked into the room, I turned away and pretended to hang up some clothes. "Hey, Mom, how 'bout we listen to *Thumbelina* tonight... wanna listen to *Thumbelina* with me?" I scooped her up in my arms, held her close to me, and danced to the music. Our bodies moved as one. I clung to her; she relaxed into me, tired from her jubilant day. In the background, the music played on. *"... and when all is said and done, I'll be alone and carry on... it's you and me against the world."* At the end of the song, a voice that sounded like Amber's sang out, *"I love you, Mommy."* I had a vision of my life without her and this was her voice, reassuring me, from the "other world." At that moment, my heart broke in two.

Pulling myself together, I set her down and reached for her *Thumbelina* book and tape. We lay on our bed and listened—*really listened*—to the words of Hans Christian Andersen's fairy tale. It was her favorite and she loved to read along in character. We imagined her as Thumbelina; we could see the pictures that were painted with words and in detail. We loved to escape... to live this fairy tale often. We lay together: Me holding the book; she tucked into the curve of my arm. She drifted off to sleep as the story ended. Within minutes, I joined her.

Over the next two weeks, we both regained our health. I re-scheduled with Quigley for the biopsy. In the meantime, I did my best to live a normal life... to shield Amber from pain... to keep as much of a routine as possible. But this fairy tale we'd just begun to live, would soon come to a crashing end.

After the photo shoot, Amber
ran over, threw her arms
around me, and said, "Ooo... Mommy,
I love you!" / Her only modeling
assignment:
A stick-on thermometer.

Modeling photos /
Three months later, the photos
on the right were taken. It
was the night before her
surgery: March 23, 1980, the
night the doctor told me, "It
can't possibly be cancer."

# Chapter 7

## ... To Nightmare

*"Great men, great nations, have not been boasters and buffoons,
but perceivers of the terror of life, and have manned themselves
to face it."* —Ralph Waldo Emerson

Protected from the cold winter, we spent a cozy, quiet evening at home. Bambi sat in her chair in the living room next to the window reading the paper, I prepared lunches for the next day, while Amber was in her "jammies" playing with the poodles. Off the dogs went with Amber close behind. She'd chase them, catch them, cuddle them, then set them free and start all over again. Her giggling and romping was music to my ears. Though I knew she wasn't, I could pretend she was normal. I was good at pretending by now, *real good.*

The fireplace was unremarkable: Brick, with a raised hearth about knee-high and very sharp edges. We spent many evenings in front of it, enjoying the fire, absorbing its warmth. This was not one of those nights.

I called from the kitchen, "Amber, be careful. Don't run near the fireplace." Involved in her game, she didn't hear me and she didn't see the pile of newspapers on the floor in front of the fireplace. A second later, it happened. I turned the corner, to warn her again. Instead I saw—in slow motion as if to remember every detail—Amber trip on the papers and fall *full force* on The Lump. I heard it crack on the edge of the hearth. She fell to the floor in a heap.

In one movement, I rushed to her side, took her in my arms, and felt the depths of my despair rise to the surface. She was crying. I tried to soothe her. Inside my head, I screamed at God,

*"WHY??? Why Amber??? Why me???"* My feeble attempts to calm her were working. She stopped crying and I forced myself to look at The Lump. It was bleeding. I pressed it with a cold cloth and rushed her to the Emergency Room at Yale-New Haven Hospital.

They examined her and she seemed to be okay. The bleeding had stopped and she had no other symptoms. They gave me the name of the Chief Pediatric Resident, Tom Dewitt. We went home.

In the morning, I called for an appointment. He examined The Lump. By now, it was the size of a lemon. A small bruise formed where she had fallen on it. He looked bewildered as he pushed and probed it with his fingers. "Hmmm..." *He* couldn't explain it either. "It's not a tumor... it's hard and bony... it's immobile... it's benign. If it was soft and mobile, then we'd worry." He tested her for tuberculosis, gave me the name of the Chief of Pediatric Surgery, Dr. Touloukian, then asked me to collect all of the test results and x-rays that were taken over the last six months and drop them off at his office. I drove up to St. Mary's and then to Yale. For months, I'd meticulously collected every bit of information that would give me any answers... any shred of hope. I reluctantly handed them to Dewitt, never to be seen again.

The earliest appointment I could get with Touloukian was two weeks away. In the meantime, I watched her forearm for a reaction to the TB test. "At least TB is *curable,*" I lamented. Three days later, there was still no reaction. "Thank God."

At 2:30 pm on March 20th, we walked into Touloukian's Examining Room. He was a kind man in his forties with a very gentle bedside manner. He did his best to put us at ease, chatting with Amber as he lifted her onto the table. Her back to him, she busied herself with a book. She faced me, so I had to be careful how I reacted as I studied his face for clues. "Now... let's see what we have here," he said matter-of-factly. He gently pulled her hair aside exposing The Lump. It was HUGE by now.

THE LOOK. *THAT* LOOK. I will never forget the look on his face as he confronted it. And I saw it before: At Rich's office and on Jeff's face when he compared her x-rays. It was the same look... the same gasping terror as I felt that night in August when I first discovered it. *"CANCER!!!"* I swear I could read his mind. It *was* cancer. My suspicions were confirmed. At that moment, I wanted to die. I wanted to die and take Amber with me. I wanted to leave this world for the one beyond where there was no pain, no suffering, and no cancer.

He tried to cover his fear with rationality and professionalism, but he knew I saw "the look" and there was no turning back. Our eyes met. I knew he was a human first and a doctor second. I could feel him pulling away, distancing himself from what he knew to be true. He got down to business but with an urgency. "I want to take a look at this right away. I'll make arrangements to have her admitted Sunday afternoon. We'll operate Monday morning."

Amber, sweet Amber. She was absorbed in her book and reading the words out loud, then louder as he said those words. "Does she know?" I wondered. Quickly—almost frantically—she kept reading. She didn't look up but stayed glued to her book as if she could block out the world that spun around her.

My racing thoughts began to swirl. I felt dizzy, whirling, like we were being sucked down a drain and into a vacuum. "Here we go! Hold on!" I had no control over the spinning world around me... around her... around us. It was happening. I could only exist and allow myself to be swept along. I was an object, not a person. I had no feelings, no needs, no life as I felt Amber's slipping away.

Again I heard God's voice. Peaceful and soothing, He said, "I'm here. You are not alone, but in Me. This *must* happen. It is meant to be. Her death will come soon and I will help you through it." Every part of my being wanted to deny this. My motherly instinct to protect my child was replaced with a hesitant, knowing, acceptance. I looked at Amber differently now—almost reverently — as though she truly *was* a messenger from God... an angel sent to me. Her life, and now her impending death, had meaning and a purpose not yet revealed.

No matter the destiny or outcome, I was put on this path to save her life first, if I could. Whatever it might take, I was willing to try... to sacrifice... to beg if I had to. *I wanted my daughter to live!* I *needed* her to live a full and happy life. I longed for My Dream to come true and to share it with Amber, Gary, and Todd. This family and the bond that we formed could not be abandoned.

I explained it all to Gary. He knew the truth now, but still refused to say it out loud. We didn't talk about reality. We continued to know but pretend that everything was okay. Still, our actions betrayed this. He helped me pack her suitcase for the hospital.

It was a Sunday afternoon like any Sunday afternoon. Spring was in the air. After a long and dreary winter, the world had renewed its hope. We stopped at the local hamburger stand for some lunch, hoping to delay the inevitable. Neither one of us had much of an appetite, but the kids were ravenous. We fed most of our food to the pigeons as we watched Amber and Todd playing on the picnic tables. This was the last glimpse of our fairy tale life together and we knew it without words. We said volumes with our eyes. He reached for my hand and squeezed it. We were in this together.

Somehow, word by word, step by step, we got through Admissions. Our private room on the third floor was in the "Experimental Wing" of Yale-New Haven Hospital. Small, but bright and cheerful, we set about making it home for the next several days. My cot was placed next to Amber's bed. We put the toys she brought on the table, some drawings on the walls, and her stuffed animals in bed. It was late afternoon. We got acquainted with the staff then set out to explore our new world—the playroom, other patient's rooms, the laundry room, the halls. Since it was Sunday, things were pretty quiet. Amber was the only patient on the floor.

Later in the afternoon some students came by to examine Amber. At that point, my daughter became a "patient," not a person... not a human being with an illness. They talked about her as though she wasn't even there. Probing, squeezing, studying The Lump all the while forgetting who was attached to it. I heard various expressions of perplexity and clinical analyses exchanged between them as they discussed the ramifications of surgery. Then they left, barely acknowledging Amber, a little girl who was facing cancer, and a mother who was at her side.

That night, another series of x-rays were taken. We wheeled her on a stretcher down to the basement where the x-ray department was located. The technicians were taken aback by the enormity of The Lump. It was now the size of a tennis ball. I shifted uneasily from one foot to the other as I watched them prep her. I laughed and joked. I made it a game so that she could live through it... so that WE could live through it. I acted like this happened every day. Yes, I *acted* to keep her from sensing my underlying panic. I knew how to act by now.

While Amber was in the x-ray room, I asked Dewitt, "Are you *sure* this isn't cancer? I mean, it's so *big!*" In two weeks, it had doubled in size. "No, Mrs. Calistro, it's not cancer; it can't possibly be cancer." "Can't possibly be cancer... it can't *possibly* be cancer." Those words went round and round in my mind as I waited for her to come out of that room. I wanted to, but couldn't, believe him.

Back in our room, Amber and I read a book about kids and hospitals that the staff had given us. "Mom, are they gonna take my Bump off? Will it hurt? Are you gonna be with me?" I answered her questions as casually as I could. "Yes, they are going to take it off tomorrow morning, Amber. It'll hurt a little bit but the doctor will give you some medicine to make you feel better. I'll be here the whole time. I'll never leave you, Amber, *never.*" After our discussion we went on to more important things like coloring and playing with her Barbie doll.

Gary came by to see us and find out what we needed... what he could do. He picked up the pieces of my life—paying my bills, cleaning our clothes, making sure our loose ends were secure. Knowing he was at my side and Amber's, was the "rock" I leaned on for strength and courage. Nothing obligated him to be here, but his love for me *and* for Amber, compelled him to stay. He was the one person I could count on... the one person who cared.

Michael visited for an hour or so. He hadn't been involved much and I didn't have the inclination or energy to find out why. I needed to focus on Amber. I asked him to bring his camera, since I didn't have one, so I could take a "before" photo of The Lump. Although I wanted to document this, I didn't know why. The reasons were about to unfold.

Surgery was scheduled for 8 am on Monday morning. The nurses came to wake us at 6:30. I woke up but was sure I was still dreaming as I looked around the room through pre-dawn eyes. "A hospital room. *Where am I???"* I looked around. "Amber... oh, God... The Lump." I heard the nurse moving in the room. "C'mon, sleepyheads. Today's the day. Time to wake up," she said cheerily. I rolled out of bed and walked over to Amber. I bent down to her face. "C'mon, babe, time to get up," I whispered. As usual, I kissed her awake; first her arm, then her shoulder, then her face. She stirred, moaned, then opened her eyes. "Hi, Mom," she smiled. It could've been any other morning. I only wished it was.

The nurse gave her a shot to keep her calm and then prepared her for surgery. She was transferred to a stretcher. It seemed like the middle of the night as we wheeled her down the halls toward the operating room. Very groggy now, she reached out for my hand. "Mom, are you gonna come?" "I can't go in, Amber. It's a special room. No germs are allowed and I have *a lot* of germs. I'll be here when you wake up, I promise. I love you..." I heard myself as the words trailed off and followed her past the double swinging doors, leaving me behind. I bid goodbye to her innocence, her health, and any hope of a normal life. "Finally I'll know the truth."

Nervously, I paced the floor of the Waiting Room like a sort of zombie. The hours went by—*I know they did*—but it seemed as if time stood still. People came and went, nurses asked if they could get me anything, I sat, then walked, then sat down again. I could hear hospital sounds off in the distance, but my whole being was focused on those swinging doors. Each time they moved, I stopped breathing and waited to see who appeared. "No... not for me." My breathing resumed.

I thought about how vulnerable she looked as she lay on the stretcher earlier that morning. Even though she was now a little girl, she was still my baby. I had done my best to protect her, even in the most dire circumstances. She was well fed, clothed, and cared for. I loved her more than life itself and I just couldn't accept the fact that something was hurting—maybe even *killing*—my daughter. "How can I fight this thing? I don't even know what it *is."*

Alone in the Waiting Room, my thoughts turned to Michael. All of the anger I felt for him but had buried, came to the surface. "He's not even here! I can't believe this! His daughter is having major surgery and he's not here!" I left the room and went to the nurse's station. "Can I make a call?" "Sure." She handed me the phone and I called his house. Sharon answered. "He went to the health club, Patti." I called the club and left a message. I was furious, but again, I buried it. I couldn't take time to feel it now. Amber was due out of surgery.

Back in the Waiting Room, my fury turned to fear. The doors opened. Dr. Touloukian stood before me. As I searched his face for a clue to Amber's fate, he spoke. "I removed a large mass... I got all I could see... I scraped the bone... there's no apparent damage... she came through just fine... she's in the Recovery Room." "Was it cancer?" "I sent tissue samples off to Pathology. We won't have the results back until Wednesday. She'll be back in her room in an hour or so. Why don't you take a break and get yourself something to eat? The cafeteria is on the fourth floor." Nothing more could be said. "Thank you, doctor." I was grateful for his skill and his willingness to care.

I slowly walked down the busy corridor. Alone now, my only comfort was God. As I begged and pleaded and prayed, He began to direct my thoughts, my feelings, my steps, my breath. I couldn't carry this burden alone; I needed His help to live on. "I am guiding you through each step. I will make the decisions. Listen... just listen... then follow what you hear."

When Amber came back to our room, she was sleeping. Her head was covered with bandages—like a turban—and a plastic tube to drain the fluid, came out where The Lump used to be. She looked old, tired, and weak. Dark circles were under her eyes. I sat next to her and held her hand—the same hand that caressed her books and her baby dolls, the same hand that would never wear a wedding ring, the same hand I would hold as she died. The nurse came in and told me she'd be asleep for hours. I wasn't about to leave her now.

Michael came in. A few minutes later, I asked to see him outside. We walked down to the end of the hall, out of everyone's ear shot, especially Amber's. "I can't believe you weren't here!"

"What do you mean? *I* had surgery when *I* was seven and it was no big deal." *"NO BIG DEAL!!! ARE YOU CRAZY???"* I screamed in a whisper, "Your daughter is having major surgery while you're at the health club and that's *no big deal???*" My anger turned to disgust. There was nothing more I could say and I didn't want to hear anything *he* had to say. Besides, Amber needed me. I walked back in the room. Michael left.

We would get the results back from Pathology on Wednesday. It was three days away though it seemed like forever. In the meantime, we concentrated on getting well and distracting ourselves by coloring, watching TV, reading, sleeping, and playing in the playroom. Gary was there most of the time. He brought Amber gifts and goodies and stayed with us until she fell asleep. Then he and I would sit on the couch, talking in low whispers well into the night. *He* was Amber's father, if not by blood, then certainly by intention and spirit.

She was weak and getting weaker. To help her recover, the hospital fed her Jello, ice cream, and ginger ale; no real, healthy food. She needed nourishment. She needed good, clean, unprocessed food. I spoke with Dewitt about this. "Can't we give her some vitamins? She's not getting any nutrition from what you're feeding her. Isn't it true that 'you are what you eat'? Can't we feed her some real food or at least give her some vitamins?" He didn't think they would do any good, but ordered some to appease me. My doubts about the "Medical Establishment" began to the surface. "What are they teaching these people in medical school? Anything at all about nutrition?"

Tuesday evening, Gary stayed late. After he left, I lay on the cot next to Amber's bed studying her and letting my imagination run wild. I saw her whole and healthy with no gash in her head and me, picking her up in my arms and walking out of that place. I wanted this dream to come true. I just wanted her to be healthy, that's all. I didn't care about money, or houses, or whether I had a job. I just didn't want to hear the verdict from Pathology. I desperately wanted to be WRONG.

Before I opened my eyes, I could smell that antiseptic "hospital smell." I looked over at Amber. "Still sleeping." In my mind, I followed the pattern of days. "Monday... Tuesday... oh,

God, Wednesday... today is the day I will know." I grabbed my clothes and tip-toed down the hall and into the bathroom, got dressed, and walked over to the window that overlooked the streets below. It was a long drop.

The new wing of the hospital rose up to greet me. It was only a short time ago I remembered. "I was *under* that building, carrying those forms, struggling to make a better life for us. It's only been four months, but it seems like four years." A world away, it reminded me that life does go on. We are all unique, but replaceable. Man will act as a whole to achieve whatever goals we set, picking up the slack of those who leave us. "How can I be *here* when I was just *there????*"

Standing alone in the bathroom, looking out at the world, gave me a sense of rhythm... of nature... of the perfect order of things. I watched as New Haven woke up. It was a simple act... just watching. I shook my head at the dichotomy: "To the rest of the world, today is just another day. How can they go on with their lives? Don't they know about Amber?" But to me, that day was a profound turning point that would dictate the rest of my life. The knowledge, and what I did with it, would become my Life Task.

I finished getting dressed and was now prepared to know the truth... to hear it spoken out loud.

Gary came early and stayed in the room with Amber while Michael and I were led to an empty room at the other end of the hall. Dr. Touloukian came in. His eyes were cast down. I didn't wait. I assaulted him with my questions. "Well???" I asked nervously, *"What is it????"* He hesitated, then dove right in. "It's rhabdomyosarcoma... it's in the third stage." I could feel the sting as his words hit me like rounds from a firing squad. "It's *malignant????"*

Painfully... deliberately, he spoke. He tried to choose them carefully, but the words slipped out. "Yes, it's malignant." Instantly, the world as I knew it before this moment, fell away and *this* world took its place. I was now living in "CancerWorld." It was a closed in, set apart, horrific world that no one would ever enter willingly; they had to be pushed to the door. The only "key" that got you in were the words: "It's cancer."

## Note:

I don't have any photographs of the time between Amber's surgery to remove the first tumor on March 24, 1980, and Gary, Amber, and I leaving for the Immunology Researching Centre on Grand Bahama Island on May 7, 1980 (Chapters 7-10).
I do have movies which are on our website.

# Chapter 8

# *Welcome to "CancerWorld"*

*"Obstacles cannot crush me. Every obstacle yields to stern resolve. He who is fixed to a star does not change his mind."* —Leonardo da Vinci

At last, my anger was released and with it, a flood of tears. I turned to Michael with a vengeance. *"I knew it!!! I KNEW IT!!! WHY DIDN'T YOU BELIEVE ME???"* His silence was deafening as he sat in the chair dumbfounded. I thought of ME and nobody else. I pressed Dr. Touloukian for answers. *"Why didn't they diagnose this sooner??? Why wouldn't they biopsy it?!?! They said, 'It can't POSSIBLY be cancer.' Why..."* He fumbled through the answers trying, but unable, to ease my pain and anguish. As much as he wanted to, he could not commute the sentence. Our eyes connected in some awful space—his full of pity, mine full of rage. He apologized again and again, then quickly backed out of the room.

I lost it. Crying uncontrollably, I screamed at Michael. *"No big deal, huh. Why didn't you believe me??? How can you NOT care about her??? You don't care about anyone but yourself, you selfish bastard!!!"* I didn't want to hear his defense; I was sure he'd scramble to find one. I left the room. I needed to find a safe place to explode... to release all of the pent up outrage at the "Medical Establishment," the animosity toward Michael, the anguish at what was, and at what was to come. My escape was in sight.

"The Laundry Room." I aimed myself in that direction. Hoping it was empty, I burst through the door and collapsed in the corner to cry until my tears ran out. I needed to calm down and empty myself so that I could make room to absorb this blinding reality.

When I was drained, I began to fill myself up with "pep talk." "O.K., Patti, Amber is *still alive. She isn't DEAD. You can fight for her.* Don't give up. You are all she has and she needs you *NOW!"* I snapped out of my daze, lifted myself up, and splashed cold water from the sink on my face again and again. With each jolt of the cold, clear water, I strengthened myself... I restored the energy and power that had just been stolen from me. I took a long, deep breath then braced myself and grabbed the handle of the door. Slowly and deliberately, I opened it and walked through. I turned in the direction of Amber's room. I knew she and Gary were waiting. Pushing myself forward, I took the first step and then many until I got closer. Picking up the pace as I neared the door, I switched back to my "outside" self—the Patti that was strong, capable, confident, and calm.

Without hesitation, I pushed open the door to our room. Gary was playing *Chutes and Ladders* with Amber. Michael had gone. I looked at Gary. Instantly, he, too, knew the truth. "C'mon, Gar, it's your turn. Oh hi, Mom. We're playin' 'Chutes and Ladders' and *I'm winnin'!* Wanna play?" "Oh... that's okay. You guys go for it. I'll just watch." I was now an active observer and dug deep into my soul to find the joy in the game... to ease Amber's painful experience and celebrate their fun.

Later in the day, I met with Diane Komp, Chief of Pediatric Oncology. She explained what rhabdomyosarcoma was and gave me a book to read, *Cancer in Children: Reason for Hope.* I turned to the index and looked for Amber's cancer. *"Rhabdomyosarcoma of the head and neck, in children, is usually a relentless, progressive tumor, which results in the death of a child in a relatively short time. Origin of the primary tumor in the head and neck, is much more common in children than adults."* Amber was napping. I went out into the hall and cried. "My God... *this* is 'reason for hope'? Did Komp or Dewitt actually *read* this book?"

Our "Prognosis/Protocol Meeting" was scheduled for the next day. Dr. Chen, a radiologist, Komp, Dewitt, Michael, Gary, and I sat around a table in the middle of a very small room. As they spoke, the room began to shrink. Amber's prognosis: She had very little chance of surviving this cancer and only if we caught it early on. We didn't. It had grown substantially through the months.

They explained. "There are four stages of cancer... the first stage is the beginning, the fourth stage is near death... Amber's in the third stage. Rhabdomyosarcoma of the head and neck in children is *extremely* rare... only two cases have been reported in the last two years." On and on and on they went. When one dropped the ball, the other picked it up. They rattled off figures and data and ratios. "Is this supposed to make me feel better?" I thought above the chatter, "Are these people *real or robotic*? Amber is a *person*, not a *number*. If they're so right, why didn't they know it was cancer *before* they opened her up? Why did they refuse to biopsy even when I pleaded with them to do it?"

Next came the protocol: What they intended to do about it. "Radiation to the head and spinal cord... chemotherapy..." "What will happen to Amber because of this treatment?" "She'll probably get nauseated from the chemotherapy and over a period of years, her trunk will be stunted three or four inches from irradiating her spine." Sarcastically, I thought, "Oh is that *all?*" They planned to do more testing to see if the cancer had spread: A spinal tap, radioactive liver-spleen, bone scan, miscellaneous blood tests, x-rays, and a CT scan. After they learned the results, they'd have a better idea of exactly where we stood. We'd have to stay in the hospital for a few more days.

In the afternoon, some students came into our room. A resident was explaining Amber's case. Cold and clinical as if Amber was an object... a thing, he grasped the drain to show it to the others. He told me he was going to remove it. "Doesn't she need an anesthetic?" "Oh, no, it won't hurt." He ripped it out. Amber screamed, "Ow... ow... Mommy, it hurts!" She started to cry. "How would you like it if I did that to *you???*" I glared. He was insulted. I pushed my way past the students and took her in my arms to comfort her. "Why don't you all just leave." I wanted them and the cancer to go away and never come back.

The next few days were spent going from one floor to another. Tests, tests, and more tests. Another room, another machine, another technician. More pain. I stayed at her side always. Although she seemed to radiate confidence, I knew she was scared and tired of the pain. "Mom, can't we just leave now? I don't want to get another test. *Please!*" she begged. "Soon it will be over, Amber. I promise. Soon."

As we waited for Amber to get a spinal tap, I looked around the Waiting Room. Since we were rather isolated on the third floor, I hadn't noticed that there were a lot of sick children; some were bald, others were pale and weak. "God, this is bigger than I thought." I wondered how many more children were going through the same thing. Like cold water on my face, I heard her name. "Amber Calistro?" I snapped back to reality. It was her turn for torture.

We walked into a small, sterile room that was filled with stainless steel instruments of pain. Amber squeezed my hand. The doctor and a nurse came in. He advised me to leave the room. "I want to be here for her." "It will be worse for her to see you standing here unable to help. It should take about thirty minutes." Amber begged, "Mommy, please don't leave... *PLEASE!!!*" She was on the table now, groping for my hand. The nurse was holding her down. I felt physically bound to her and painfully pulled away. "I'll be back, honey... I *promise*. I'll go get some presents for you. I love you, Amber. *I love you.*" I backed out of the door. "Mommy... Mommy... *PLEASE!!!*" My heart was breaking as the door closed behind me. I turned around and ran.

All the way to the end of the hall, I could hear her begging me to come back. I ran to the gift shop without stopping. It was in a new wing that was built on the same footings that, only a few months earlier, I worked on as a laborer... I worked to make our life better. The irony did not slip past me but I didn't have time to indulge my thoughts. I needed to focus on now.

Just a shell, not a person, I frantically searched the shelves for trinkets to ease her pain and my guilt for leaving her. I felt empty inside. The real me was still in that room with Amber, suffering right along with her. Tears poured down my face and I didn't try to stop them. People saw me and wondered, wanted to ask, but left me alone to grieve. I was glad for the isolation as the pain was so great that any words would be like salt on a wound.

I raced back to the room and got there just as the spinal tap was over. Her eyes were puffy, her face was red, her voice was raspy. She looked like she had been through hell. I swept her into my arms. "I'm sorry, Amber, so sorry. I wish I could protect you from this." Whatever happened in that room, was more than she could endure and I knew it. I wished I'd held my ground and insisted on staying by her side throughout. I would never leave her again. Never.

Friday, the results from the tests were back. "No other metastases... the cancer bore an eighth inch hole in her skull... there were a few suspicious cells in her spinal fluid." The Lump—the *cancer*—was gone, or at least this was my hope. "How did she get it in the first place?" I wondered, *"How? She's just a child."* I combed through our history together and made a mental list.

· "From the beginning of my labor, the doctor who delivered her seemed to be in a hurry. He used forceps to literally yank her out of me. I could feel the pressure of him pulling... pulling *hard.*" I remembered her baby picture, the one they took just after birth, and how her right hand seemed to be holding the exact place on her head where the tumor was... where the forceps grabbed hold of her head. "Could the pressure of the forceps create such trauma that her 'embryonic cells' would develop into cancer?"

· Stress is known to have incredibly negative effects on the body, including the release of cortisol, which triggers our "fight or flight'"response. "Did Amber internalize my and Michael's destructive relationship? How did Michael's apparent rejection of her affect her health?" Although she never mentioned it, I began to wonder.

· "Maybe it was that foreign object that got lodged in her cheek at St. Joseph's nursery school while we were living in New Jersey." I asked her about it. "Amber, what's this in your cheek?" She couldn't tell me and I never did find out what it was. Shortly afterwards, she began to have low-grade fevers and was constipated. The doctor said that her body would just absorb *whatever* it was; it never did.

· "Is it possible that all of the asbestos I breathed in while working at Glass Instruments had a hand in her cancer? After all, I *did* conceive her while I was working there." My mind was searching for a clue.

- "Maybe the fact that I continued to smoke throughout my pregnancy actually *gave Amber cancer!*" I shuttered to think it was *me*. I remembered bringing her to my meetings of the "Five Day Plan" when I quit smoking. She was just a newborn, in her car seat asleep at my feet when I saw that movie of a mother dying of cancer and the little girl wondering why.
- "Could Michael's punch to my stomach, while we were living in Long Beach, have damaged Amber or 'set the stage' for her cancer to develop?" I shuttered to think that her *father* may have caused her cancer.
- The area we lived in northern New Jersey with Aunt Anne and Uncle Bill had a huge number of cancer deaths. "Could she have gotten cancer from the water? Or food? Or their home?"

I wanted... I *needed* to find someone or something to blame, to hate as much as I hated this cancer and what it had done to my little girl who was innocent and pure.

We left the hospital that afternoon. God, it felt so good to breathe the fresh air. She was very weak and couldn't walk, but she was alive! My first job was to build up her strength with *real* food, not the dead food full of chemicals and preservatives they fed her in the hospital. Gary went to the health food store and got all her favorite goodies.

We settled her into our room at Bambi's. Everything she needed was brought to her side. This was Amber's "control room." I was grateful that she slept a lot of the time; sleep kept her from feeling any pain. When she woke up, she complained, "Mom, my head hurts." My heart went to my stomach. I gave her some baby aspirin and lay down next to her, rubbing her back and singing. I catered to her every need, gave in to her every wish and command, and spent every waking moment trying to erase her trauma and pain. I felt so helpless, despite all of my efforts. There was very little I could do and yet I was the only one who could save her. "God, please point me in the right direction. Please show me the way."

I was determined to deal with this monster and dedicated to saving my daughter's life, but I didn't know anything about cancer. I didn't even know kids *got* cancer. I was ignorant, afraid, and alone, except for Gary. Arming myself for the battle ahead was something I could do. First step: To know my enemy. I went to the library and checked out every book on the subject of cancer I could find.

Dewitt called. He wanted to know about the protocol. "We don't want to take a chance on a reoccurrence. We need to start chemotherapy and radiation as soon as possible. Can you bring Amber in tomorrow?" "I'm not sure... I'm just not sure about bombarding her body with poisons." He sensed my skepticism. "Why don't I set up a meeting with Dr. Komp?" "Okay."

In the meantime, I needed to learn. I felt as though I had no power because I had no knowledge about what was happening to my little girl. I stayed up all night reading my library books, as the personal computer and internet weren't even invented then. My resources were the library, friends, TV, and newspapers.

Gary and I drove to Yale-New Haven with Amber. We walked into the room. Komp, Dewitt, and Chen were ready with their arsenal of facts and figures and documents. We were not a team. It was a dictatorship and I was to do as I was told. They were convinced; *they're* way was the *right way*—the *only* way to save her. They tried their best to convince us, too.

After they finished their speeches on radiation and chemotherapy, I asked them, "Is this all there is?" Diane Komp answered. "Yes, Mrs. Calistro, this is all there is." "You mean, they can put a man on the moon, but they can't cure cancer? There's *got* to be more than *this!*" I simply could not believe there was no other way and found it impossible to trust them. As they fumbled to make a feeble attempt to sell me, my thoughts echoed my "Mother's Instinct." "If they fed her junk food to help her regain her strength, wanted to use poisons to kill cancer and *normal* cells, and wouldn't believe me when I told them it was cancer FOR SIX MONTHS, how can I just blindly follow their advice *now???*" I pacified them. "I need to think about this."

I left the hospital convinced that there *had* to be more and dove head first into researching other cancer therapies. Knowing that those suspicious cells might be growing... spreading, I agreed to let them give her radiation to her skull. I had to do *something* and decided on the lesser of two evils presented to me: Radiation and chemotherapy. The race was on to save her life. Quick decisions had to be made and they had to be intelligent ones. There was no room for error.

"Chad Green." I remembered the story about the little boy who had leukemia. It was all over the news a few months earlier. His parents, Jerry and Diana, had refused to give their son chemotherapy. Instead of blindly consenting, they did their own research and decided to give Chad a less poisonous, more natural treatment. Massachusetts General Hospital took them to court, they were declared "unfit," and a guardian was appointed by the court. The police came and took Chad away, placing him in the guardian's custody so that they could give him chemotherapy. To pursue the treatment *they* thought was best for Chad, his parents kidnapped him and secretly traveled to Mexico, where the cancer therapy was allowed. In the end, Chad died, but *not from cancer.* As Diana tells it: "Chad became increasingly depressed because he was away from his home and his family. His cancer was in remission. He died of a broken heart."

Frightened, I thought, "Can this happen to me... to Amber? If I don't do as they say, will they come and take her away and label me 'unfit...' a bad mother? I *know* I'm a good mother, but do *they?*" I called the *New Haven Register* and pleaded my case. "There *has* to be other cancer therapies out there besides surgery, radiation, and chemotherapy. I just don't know where to begin looking and I don't have much time. Can I make a public plea asking for information?" The City Editor set up an appointment with a reporter.

With Amber in tow, Gary and I drove to the newspaper office in downtown New Haven. After three hours of discussion, the *New Haven Register* agreed to run our story. Needing advice and support, I asked, "Do you know how I can get in touch with Jerry and Diana Green?" She directed me to *The Associated Press* office down the hall.

The AP reporter listened then gave me the phone number of a reporter in Hastings, Nebraska. "She just did a story on them and may have a current phone number." As soon as we got home, I called her. She agreed to get in touch with the Green's and give them my phone number. That night, they called and we talked for a very long time. Though we were connected by a circumstance too horrible to imagine—a child with cancer—it was reassuring to hear their voices.

They warned me: "Patti, don't let Yale-New Haven know that you're searching for other therapies. You just don't know what they'll do." They spoke from experience. Considering what had happened to Chad, I took their advice seriously. Outraged, I asked, "You mean, if you don't do what *they* say is right, they call you 'unfit' and take your child away?" "Yes," they answered sadly, "They will." "I can't believe this is happening and happening in America!" More than ever, I was determined to go public. "I'll make Amber everybody's child. The 'people' won't let Yale-New Haven secretly take her away from me, not if everything is out in the open... not if they know I am a good mother who wants my daughter to LIVE."

As a mother, I wanted to do my best to save Amber's life, no matter what the cost. I had little to go on except what Yale-New Haven was telling me, what I'd heard and seen in the media, and what made sense—common sense—to me. Decisions had to be made quickly, they had to be made with conviction, and they had to be made factoring in ALL of the available information. The "Medical Establishment" had misdiagnosed her cancer again and again, dismissed my concerns, answered my pleas with disdain, and fed her processed foods filled with preservatives and chemicals to build up her strength.

The few doctors who did their best along the way—Jeff Winograd, Rich Abraham, and Robert Touloukian—softened my inclination to group them all together and declare them "Guilty." But I needed to make decisions based on knowledge, love, past results, "Mother's Instinct," the odds, and common sense. Loyalty to one school... one American school of medicine played no part. "It's a big world and the answer to cancer should have nothing to do with borders, politics, or profits," I lamented. I was naive.

Meanwhile, Michael was beginning to involve himself in Amber's life. I was grateful and glad that he finally saw her need for a father and made an effort to fulfill it. He found out about Dr. Harold Manner, professor of Biology and Chairman of the Biology Department at Loyola University. He'd studied the link between diet, vitamin supplements, laetrile, and cancer. He documented the improvement in his cancer patients. His book, *The Death of Cancer,* contained the results of his research. I was ready to find out more, to try this therapy *if it did her no harm,* while I gave her radiation and continued to search the world for the answer to cancer... the lifeline to help her live.

The nearest doctor that practiced Manner's therapy was just over the border in Massachusetts. I couldn't talk to the doctors at Yale-New Haven about him for fear that they would start legal action to take Amber away from me and force her to get chemotherapy. I was beginning to feel like a spy or a criminal when all I wanted to do was save my daughter's life and do it without harming or killing her in the process. The danger involved with chemotherapy seemed too risky. If she didn't die from cancer, she would most certainly die from the "cure."

On April 4th, we secretly drove up to Dr. Giustini's office. It was 8pm or so. His nurse took Amber into her office to keep her occupied, while Michael, Gary and I spoke with the doctor. He explained the therapy in detail: "Metabolic diet... all natural foods... juices... spring water... vitamin and enzyme supplements... coffee enemas... laetrile. You'll receive the laetrile by mail in a few days." I asked him some questions to help clarify things, we thanked him, and left his office with a copy of Manner's book and the supplements.

For the first time in months, I felt a twinge of hope. It made sense to me: remove toxins from her body, then stimulate her immune system to heal the cancer instead of bombarding it with poisons. Neither Manner or Giustini made a claim to "cure" Amber's cancer, they simply stated what their research and data had concluded.

Every two days, we went to Yale-New Haven for radiation treatments. We'd sit in the Waiting Room reading the books we brought, playing a game, or drawing. All of the other cancer patients were adults; she was the only child. They'd watch her and say with their eyes, "Oh my God, *she's got cancer? She's just a baby. Why?"* Our eyes met. "I don't know," as if they could read my mind, "I just don't know." Amber was oblivious to it all. She was in her own little make-believe world, just like a typical four-year-old. She'd dance around the room singing to herself, animating each and every word, and just pretending.

The technicians painted purple lines on the right side of her face, head, and neck to mark the boundaries of the area that would get irradiated with each visit. They were semi-permanent; which meant that she had to wear them in public—to school, on the street, in the stores. It looked as though she had been mischievous and scribbled herself with a purple marker. People would stare; some would gather up the courage to ask. In my best nonchalant voice, I'd say, "Oh they mark the area for radiation." I couldn't yet say, "She has cancer," out loud; somehow the words might make it real... might carve it in stone, never to be erased or forgotten.

The radiation treatments seemed harmless; silent except for a slight buzzing sound as the machine emitted its deadly rays. She suffered no obvious side effects, at least not *yet;* she still had her hair to mask the incision where the initial tumor was removed. The stitches were gone and the site was nearly healed. If it wasn't for the purple marks, I'd swear she was *perfectly healthy.*

On Easter Sunday, the day of resurrection, we started on the "detoxification phase" of Manner's therapy. I was anxious to build up her strength and give her back the energy that seemed to be slipping away ever since we returned from the hospital. Although this therapy was intensive, I wanted to give it a try. "But does *Amber?"* I read the instructions for the therapy—the fasting, the huge number of pills she had to take each day, the enemas, the dietary restrictions, and wondered, "How on earth will I get her through this? I don't even think that *I* could get through it and I'm an *adult."*

## *Manner's Detoxification*

Two day juice fast:
> *You must purchase a juice extractor*
> *No solid food during the juice fast*
> *You may drink bottled water*
> *You may drink as much juice as you wish*

*Start with juice consisting of 50% carrot and 50% apple. Gradually add celery, beets, potatoes, etc. Juice the whole food—skin, seeds, etc. Juices should be "chewed."*

<u>Bowels:</u>
*The bowels must move two times a day. If the juice fast does not normalize the bowels, LAXADYN is advised. Colonics may be necessary.*

<u>Coffee enema:</u>
> *Brew one cup of real coffee*
> *Allow coffee to cool to room temperature*
> *Lie down on your right side*
> *Introduce 1 c. of coffee with a rectal syringe*
> *Retain for 15 minutes*
> *You should take 1 cup a day for 21 days*

<u>Diet for 21 days:</u>
*NO...*
> *Meat or fish*
> *White sugar*
> *White flour products*
> *Additives*
> *Canned goods (including home-canned)*
> *Dairy products*
> *Caffeine*

Unbelievably, she had to take 40-50 supplements—pills of all sizes and shapes—a day! I divided them into portions; one hour before meals, during meals, and one hour after meals, three times a day. *Nine times a day,* I had to persuade Amber to swallow those pills. I played a game to make it easier, but even that was wearing thin. I called Dr. Manner. "How do you get a four year old child to swallow 50 pills *every day?* Some of them are the size of horse pills!" He admitted that his therapy was designed with an adult in mind. He felt sorry for us, especially Amber, and suggested that I buy a mortar and a pestle, grind the tablets, then add something like honey. I tried it. To my surprise, she actually *liked* it.

Bambi's kitchen turned into a sort of "headquarters." Bottles of pills lined the counter, along with a juicer, mortar and pestle, books, and special foods. I, alone, was fighting "The War Against Cancer" and this was my ammunition. I was grateful that my daughter was only wounded in this grotesque battle. I was determined to heal her and return to our somewhat chaotic normal life.

Amazed at her resilience, I couldn't believe she was following the therapy without putting up much of a fuss. Already I could see a tremendous improvement: The color was back in her cheeks, the dark circles under her eyes were gone, and she laughed and giggled again. "Maybe this nightmare is over after all."

Michael took her for the weekend. Sharon, his girlfriend, really loved Amber and took great care of her whenever she stayed with them. She treated my daughter as her own and helped us with the therapy, including the coffee enemas, the restrictions, and the numerous supplements. I called to see how she was doing on her juice fast and recorded the call.

- *Me: Amber??*
- *Amber: Hi, Mamma.*
- *Me: Hi sweet thing, I love you.*
- *Amber: Guess what?*
- *Me: What?*
- *Amber: They're gonna take my blood... you know how?*
- *Me: How?*
- *Amber: Like when we go to Angela and Troy's. You know, I'm not gonna be too upset... but just... they're gonna take my blood out in a little bottle. Remember the little bottle?*
- *Me: Yeah.*
- *Amber: They're just gonna do that... no wires or anything... no plugs... or no things I had in my hand.*
- *Me: You mean the IV?*
- *Amber: Yeah... not the IV's.*
- *Me: So... how's your diet coming? How's your juice diet?*
- *Amber: Good.*
- *Me: You like it?*
- *Amber: I'm just gonna have to keep poopin' and I'll be*

*gettin' better.*

- **Me:** *Is that right? How do you feel?*
- **Amber:** *Good.*
- **Me:** *How does your body feel?*
- **Amber:** *My stomach hurts and everything.*
- **Me:** *It hurts?*
- **Amber:** *Yup. I had a enemen (sic).*
- **Me:** *Did you have an enema?*
- **Amber:** *Uh huh... and guess what?*
- **Me:** *What?*
- **Amber:** *They put a little... um... Vaseline on it... and guess what? They put a little stuff on it and they squirt it and it goes into my body and takes all the bad stuff out.*
- **Me:** *And did it?*
- **Amber:** *Yup! My blood stayed in.*
- **Me:** *Good! You're doing SO well!*
- **Amber:** *Guess what? I have a Christmas song on. Are you gonna come over and hug me? I forgotta hug you, Mom.*

Yale-New Haven kept calling; trying to put pressure on me to start chemotherapy and resume more frequent radiation treatments. I'd slacked off, wanting to give Amber some breathing space. I could hardly keep up with all of the information I was getting, so to keep things straight, I decided to tape most of my phone calls. I informed Chen, the radiologist that was treating Amber, when he called.

I wanted to bring him up-to-date and recounted the events of the past couple of weeks: The contradictory information from Yale-New Haven, Harold Manner's metabolic therapy Amber was now on, and my visit to the *New Haven Register* to make a public appeal for other cancer therapies. He made an effort to be open-minded, but I could see from the way the conversation was going that he was truly indoctrinated by the traditional medical establishment and their way of thinking. I broached the subject of nutrition. "In the past two weeks, since Amber's had this tumor surgically removed, there has been virtually nothing done by Yale-New Haven as far as nutrition goes." "Well... we really... basically, we don't... we don't believe in it." "Yes, I know."

Chen began to push, then shove me, to increase Amber's radiation treatments. He was becoming aggressive, almost threatening. I got nervous and felt very afraid... afraid they would take her from me. I thought about my conversation with the Green's. "Be careful... don't let Yale-New Haven know you're searching for other therapies." I tried to pacify him. "O.K... I see... uh huh..." I didn't want to provoke him into filing charges against me.

After I hung up, my feelings came to the surface. My daughter not only had cancer, but I was perched on the edge of an enormous political controversy in the cancer world. How extensive it was, I could only guess. I knew very little about cancer, but everywhere I turned there seemed to be more disagreement and contradiction. "What... who is behind the information that's given to me by the hospital, doctors, newspapers, radio, and TV?" I knew there was more but I didn't know where to look for it.

Under the circumstances, I tried to keep Amber's daily life as normal as possible. She went back to nursery school and brought along all of her pills and special foods. She played with her friends as though nothing had happened and she looked just like any other child. The only visible difference was the purple radiation marks on her face. Sometimes the children would tease her, but we pretended it was face paint and she was an Indian. Treating this deadly disease as a game was the vehicle we used to ride this out... to cope with the crushing, consuming, day-to-day intensity.

Laetrile was a critical part of Manner's therapy but since it was illegal in the US, I had to find an "illegal" source. To get it, I had to fill out an affidavit, signed by the patient and a physician. Cyto-Metabolics in Linden, New Jersey, was one of only a few places that made it available. It sold for $13 a vial (20cc), $9 an ampule (10cc), or tablets for $.85 each (500 mg). We couldn't do this alone.

I contacted Dr. Cole, the physician that Dr. Manner recommended. He agreed to help, but needed the protocol from Yale-New Haven. After getting the paperwork in order, we made the two hour drive to his office in Floral Park, Long Island, New

York. "Hey Amber, wanna go on an adventure?" "Sure, Mom," she said but not with enthusiasm.

The office seemed like any other, but the patients inside were different. *They* seemed to be in control of their lives, rather than handing themselves over to their doctor and expecting *them* to do the healing. They were well educated, successful, average people, except that they had cancer, that's all; a physical setback that *could* be overcome. It was the first time I'd seen real hope and optimism in the face of this dreaded disease. Their attitude was refreshing and unexpected; they were certainly nothing like the people in the Waiting Rooms at Yale-New Haven.

Cole explained the therapy to me: A "cocktail" (small amounts of chemotherapy, DMSO, vitamin C, and laetrile) was put into a bag and given intravenously to the cancer patient. I felt that much too familiar undercurrent of fear in his voice. He was reluctant to treat her. "She's a minor, and the use of laetrile is *very* controversial." He was treating people with cancer differently than the traditional doctors and wanted to avoid persecution or prosecution. I begged him. He could see I was desperate. We set an appointment to start the "cocktails" the following week.

Amber started to balk at the pills, despite my efforts to disguise them... hide them... make them palatable. I'd grind them up with the mortar and pestle and put the powder in special pill packs: Small containers that had divided sections and labeled with the days of the week. When the time came, I'd pour the powder into a cup, add honey, and make a sort of sickening paste. At first, it was novel. Now, it made her gag. I increased the measure of honey.

Putting myself in her shoes, I asked myself, "Could *I* do this? Coffee enemas every day, a very restricted diet, eating that disgusting "vitamin paste" nine times a day, people staring at me trying to figure out what those purple marks are, needles, tests, surgery, and pain... a lot of pain. My life was not my own. It was forever controlled by CancerWorld. I knew I couldn't do it and continued to be astounded at how *she could*.

Amber's lesson—to endure pain and uncertainty with strength, patience, and grace—was one that I would continue to learn. The roles were now switched. Instead of *me* teaching *her*, she was now teaching *me.* I prayed to be open to all of her wisdom and to be true to my daughter, myself, and to God. I asked for His help again.

"God, please help me keep my heart open, my mind clear, and my intentions true. I need to *live* the truth, not just speak it." As always, my prayers would be answered, but not in the way *I* wanted; the answers would be what I needed to know… what I needed to keep me from being completely overwhelmed by the life I was living. "The CancerWorld will not corrupt or consume me," I vowed. I hoped that those words would stay true, but feared my being human would force me to deviate from my course… from my purpose here on earth.

# Chapter 9

## Underground Escape

*"Hope is both the earliest and most indispensable virtue inherent in the state of being alive. If life is to be sustained hope must remain, even where confidence is wounded, trust impaired."* —Erik H. Erikson

I wanted to stop bombarding her... to leave her alone and let her live her life the way it used to be—no pills, no radiation, no doctors, no pain—but that would mean watching her die. I simply could not do that. As her mother, I gave life to this child and I refused to let it slip away without a fight. Besides, I'd noticed a remarkable change in the past two weeks. She went from crawling to running, whining to laughing, and sickly to... well... as healthy as she could be and still have cancer. "Maybe the alternative treatment is working," I prayed.

Along with her renewed strength, she began to assert herself... to take control. After all, it *was* her life even at four. She knew how important it was to go for radiation treatments, follow the diet, and take the pills, but *she* had the power to live or die, not me. If she didn't want to do any of it, she wouldn't. "How can I blame her? How can I force her? Why would I want to if the outcome was the same?"

In my quest for cancer information, I combed the bookstores and libraries. I came across *"Choices,"* a book about cancer, therapies, and the choices that are available. I was hungry for information and would not be satisfied until I devoured every last bite. Since Amber was asleep for the night in our room and Bambi was in hers, I went into the living room, made myself comfortable, and began to read. I quickly looked up "rhabdomyosarcoma."

*Chapter 20, Childhood Cancer, Tests for Childhood Cancer:*
*X-rays*
*Angiogram*
*Intravenous pyelogram*
*Cytoscopy*
*Brain scan*
*Biopsy*


"Biopsy!" The word shouted from the page. I was shocked. The preface was written by Joseph Bertino, MD, Chief of the Section of Medical Oncology and the American Cancer Society, Professor of Medicine and Pharmacology at... *what?... YALE SCHOOL OF MEDICINE!* "Yale had this information and they didn't do any of these tests on Amber? Even the night before surgery, when the tumor was huge, they told me, 'It can't possibly be cancer.' What *do* the doctors actually *know?*" I had no idea where to look or where I could turn to find the truth. The medical world I grew up trusting, came crashing down around me. I calmed myself down and read on.

*TYPE: Rhabdomyosarcoma*
*AGE: 2-6*
*SYMPTOMS: Swelling, bleeding, unusual mass ("What?!?!") found in the head, neck, eyes, genitourinary system, extremities, chest, and abdomen.*
*TREATMENT: Surgery, followed by chemotherapy and radiotherapy. High cure rate in the early stages.* ("EARLY STAGES... why didn't they believe me?")
*WHAT IS RHABDOMYOSARCOMA? This is the most common* ("Most common?") *soft tissue cancer among children... it occurs most frequently between the ages of 2 and 6. Symptoms depend on where the tumor is located.*
*HOW IS RHABDOMYOSARCOMA TREATED? Treatment depends upon where the tumor is located and the cell type. Since this cancer is highly malignant,* ("She's going to die.") *the stage at which it's found is an important factor. Metastases occur early, and often spread to distant organs, generally, the lung. Biopsy is usually performed to establish diagnosis.*

I stared at the book through my tears and couldn't blink them away. It was a blur. I could not go on. My world was shattered. For the first time in my life, I couldn't bend down and pick up the pieces... turn this thing around... make it whole again. Perseverance and persistence were the driving forces that always helped me transform pain into power. But *this* was something I had never experienced: Utter helplessness and despair not only for me, but for my daughter

Words were sloshing around in my head: "Incompetence... liars... power-hungry... uncaring... selfish..." I could not make sense out of this at all. They *had* the information "in house" the entire time before and after Amber's diagnosis and surgery. They could also have gone to the bookstore, like I did, and bought *Choices* along with other books on cancer therapies, to get up-to-date on rhabdomyosarcoma and all of the treatments that might help. If they weren't sure, couldn't they look it up in a book... the same book that Diane Komp handed to me just hours after the first tumor was removed? All the answers, the tests and the hope, were there for the asking, yet no one bothered to do it. It was up to me, not them. I took their ignorance to heart and continued on my quest for a cure.

Anger was bubbling up and I couldn't deny it. I was right all along but I didn't want to be. The memories came back: All the times I had tried to convince the doctors and the dismissive words they gave me in return. "How can I change the past *now?*" I thought. I cried for a long time. And then I was enraged. "Dammit, God! Why have You done this to me... to Amber? I've been good... I *am* good and so is Amber! Why didn't You choose somebody else? I WANT OUT! *I WANT MY LIFE BACK!* I don't want to go through this anymore!!!" I was furious at God... the doctors... Michael... at anyone, at *everyone* who had ever treated us badly. I broke down, sobbing out of control, hoping my plea would provoke a miracle... hoping I wouldn't wake Amber and Bambi.

On April 14th, nearly three weeks after the surgery, we drove to Long Island for her first "cocktail" with Dr. Cole. After a brief wait, the nurse led us to a back room—the Treatment Room. It was small, about 10'x14', and lined with brown reclining chairs on both sides of the walls. There was a row of windows at one end with a door at the other. It had white walls with nothing on them. It was unremarkable except for the people. *It was filled with people.* Each one was hooked up to an IV bag, which hung on a hook next to their chairs. Some had the needle in the top of their hand, others had it in their arms. All of them chatted like long lost friends.

The moment we walked in the room, they stopped talking. At once, all of their eyes looked up at me, then down at Amber. *"A child!"* their collective thoughts said. They were surprised, saddened, touched. She quickly scampered over to the empty seat and sat down with her little stuffed dog. She brought him along to get a "cocktail," too. I greeted everyone, introduced myself and Amber, then sat down, lifting her onto my lap.

The nurse explained that she would be given an IV; it would take about 45 minutes to empty the bag. I could feel Amber starting to squirm and tried to distract her with the cassette tape and book of *Pete's Dragon* we brought. We were reading along in the book when the nurse wheeled over the IV. "Now, honey, you'll feel a pinch right here," as she pointed to the top of her hand, "but it'll be over in a second." She took out the swab and cleaned her hand. I held her arm. Ever so slowly, the needle poked through her skin. "OW! MOMMY! OW!!!" No vein. The nurse pulled it out and tried again, despite her shaking hand. She tried to steady it as the needle pierced Amber's skin again. Nothing.

Near hysterics now, her body jerked with each stab. She begged and pleaded, "Mommy, mommy, PLEASE don't let them do this! Mom??? *PLEASE???"* I was powerless. I could feel her pain throughout my body, but could not take it from her. She couldn't see me crying, as her back was toward me, but she *could* hear my voice trying to calm her, soothe her, get her to accept this agony. "I'm here, Amber... she's almost done... it'll be okay... it will, I promise." I was trying to convince everyone, including myself. Tears were falling down my cheeks and I didn't dare wipe them. I had to hold her... comfort her... pretend that everything was alright. I had to be strong for Amber.

The nurse left to get someone else to try and find her tiny veins. Everyone in the room was visibly shaken; they all had tears in their eyes. They knew exactly what she was going through, but they were *adults*. They understood that they had cancer and they chose this form of therapy. It was heartbreaking for them to see a child be victimized like this. I wanted to protect her, heal her, save her, but couldn't. Helpless... we all felt helpless.

Another nurse came in and, thankfully, found her vein quickly. We dried her tears and sat back to listen to the tape and read along with the book. The time went by quickly. By now, time was surreal; it would fly or it would crawl. It no longer had the steady rhythm that it did before the cancer. Tick... tick... tick. Each second, minute, hour was the same. Days turned into weeks, into months, into seasons. Everything was different now, even time. Depending on the activity, our life was either a dream or a nightmare. Reality was only a concept, a memory that existed in my head, not in the world we were living each day.

By the time we got to the car, she was exhausted and slept the entire way home. It was difficult to drive; I just wanted to stop, relax, and watch her sleep. I carried her limp and weary body into our room, laid her on the bed, carefully undressed her, and tucked her in for the night. I stood back and watched her. "She looks so innocent. Why? Why is this happening to *her*, God? She's been through Hell. How much more can she take? Give her a break, God, will You?" If He was in the room, I would have slugged Him—even *HIM*—to release my rage and protect my daughter.

The Green's sent me a letter to let me know they cared and would be there for me. They also sent some valuable research information and a $50 bill. "How did they know I needed this money?" I asked myself. I was grateful for their gift. They told me that homeopathic doctors were having good success with cancer patients. I looked up "homeopathy" in the dictionary. *"Homeopathy: A system of medical treatment based on the use of small quantities of drugs, that in massive doses, produce symptoms similar to the disease under treatment."*

A few days later, Amber refused to take the "pill powder." "I don't want to take pills anymore! I'm gonna go where they won't give me pills!" I couldn't really blame her, but I couldn't let her know that. I didn't want her to get discouraged and give up. I cut back on the dose and tried to reason with her. "Amber, *please*, this will make you well. *Please.*" It was no use. After all, it was *her* life not mine. *She* would choose how to live, how to die, and when. "She's just four years old. She can't make those decisions." I heard this again and again. I began to see how much prejudice there was against children, especially children with a life-threatening disease like cancer.

As we approached the circular on-ramp to I-95 heading towards New York, Amber asked with suspicion, "Mom??? Are we going to get another cocktail?" I toyed with the idea of lying to, of tricking her, but decided against it. "Yes, Amber, we are." She had had enough. "No! I don't want another cocktail!!! I'm done getting cocktails!" The words were at the tip of my tongue, "But you'll die if you don't!" Instead, I searched for the words that would not scare, but convince her. "Amber, we need to get you better and this is the way to do that. You want to go back to school, play with your friends, and not have so many pills, right?" Quietly, she relented. "Yeah." "Okay. What tape should we listen to: *The Muppet Movie, Thumbelina,* or *The Little Engine that Could?"* With subdued resignation, she mumbled, *"The Muppet Movie."*

Several people recommended that we see Dr. Joseph Kaplowe, a homeopath practicing in New Haven. When I saw his name on the list that the Green's sent, I called for an appointment. His assistant, Rosemary, told me to come at 7:30 that evening. Gary drove us. The office was located on a residential street lined with very large houses, dating back to the 1940's. We felt welcomed immediately. "This office is not typical," I thought, "It seems so warm and comfortable, more like a home than a doctor's office." Rosemary met us, gave us a brief tour, then talked with us for a while. I brought her up to date: "Cocktails" in Long Island four times a week, radiation to her skull every other day, the supplements, and her special diet. It was a lot for such a little girl.

She led us into Dr. Kaplowe's office: A large room filled with lots of books, magazines, photos, and certificates. "This man is well-read," I thought. There were plants everywhere. A distinguished elderly gentleman greeted us. He was slight with a full head of white, curly hair and a quiet, gentle manner. His eyes were kind and knowing. He spoke with us at length about Amber

—her diet, habits, personality, tolerance to medicines. During our conversation, Rosemary came in with the latest copy of the *New Haven Register* and held it up for us to see.

*"Mother Ponders Cancer Therapy for Child."* There it was, right on the front page, along with our photo and a story. It explained Amber's journey with cancer, her experience with the doctors, and our predicament now: "How do we find a therapy that will cure, not *kill*, her?" It ended with a quote from me: "We were afraid that they (doctors) might think *their* way was best, even though they can't prove it."

Dr. Kaplowe had a twinkle in his eye and a smile on his face. I could tell he'd been through this "underground therapy" scene many times before. He wasn't deterred form his purpose: Do the best you can for Amber, regardless of the cost. He continued with our visit and described our options.

Dr. Lawrence Burton, who practiced immunotherapy in Freeport, Grand Bahamas, was his choice for therapy. He explained. "From good, healthy, donated blood, five protein fractions are extracted. Many protein fractions make up the immune system; Burton has isolated five. Then, blood is drawn from the cancer patient, analyzed, and the levels of these protein fractions are measured. Whatever levels are low, are then raised by injecting the cancer patient with the protein fractions that were isolated from the 'good' blood. This maintains the immune system at the optimum level to fight the cancer on its own." No poisons; it worked naturally with the body. Rosemary would contact Dr. George Beatty, Dr. Burton's liaison here in the states. It sounded good, but I needed to sort through it. "Can I call you tomorrow?" "Sure. You think about it and call if you have any questions."

As a result of the newspaper articles, we were flooded with letters, calls, and telegrams from around the world. I was unprepared. Since *The Associated Press* put it over the wire service, people around the world knew Amber, and all of them cared. "No one will let them take Amber from me. No one." I prayed that I was right.

"Have you heard of Dr. Burton... Kelly... Contreras...?" The list went on and on. Hundreds of scientists all over the world—not just in the US—were working on a cure for cancer and many were seeing success. I was astonished at the number of people who were aware of other ways of treating cancer. "Why isn't everyone working *together* to cure... to *prevent* cancer?" I simply could not see the reasoning behind the apparent "close-mindedness" of the American medical establishment. "What is more important than this? Why isn't this information available to everyone?" I couldn't understand why I had to dig... why I had to go to the newspapers and publicly beg for information about cancer.

During our "Prognosis/Protocol Meeting" at Yale-New Haven just a few weeks earlier, they said there were only three cancer therapies available: Chemotherapy, surgery, and radiation. "Why didn't Yale tell me about *all* of the cancer therapies when I asked them, 'Is this was all there is'?" With certainty in her voice, Komp said, "Yes, Mrs. Calistro. This is all there is." I was incredulous! "What is going on???"

Though I needed to know the story behind the story, I didn't have time to dig further. My focus needed to be on Amber... on saving her life. I did my best to navigate through the maze of cancer therapies and ignored the politics behind them. I couldn't care less about the politics, not now. It was my first glimpse into the "cancer culture," or subculture, I'd suspected all along. In a matter of days, I was thrust into the underworld. I felt like I was a criminal living with other criminals and outcasts: People who had cancer and wanted another, less toxic way of healing themselves. I was now a member of "The Cancer Club," a private club in "CancerWorld" where you or a loved one searched for treatments and a cure. You had to have cancer to be admitted. I didn't want to belong.

I called Rosemary and asked her to set an appointment with Beatty. A few days later, we drove to Greenwich to see him. I opened the door to his office, but wasn't sure I was in the right place. The people inside were talking, laughing, sharing pictures. It looked like a family gathering. "Is this Dr. Beatty's office?" "It sure is! Come on in... Hi, I'm..." They went around the room introducing themselves and their cancer. "No way!" I thought, "These people can't have cancer! They look healthy and happy!" Instead of the dread, fear, and hopelessness I saw in the Waiting

Rooms at Yale-New Haven, I saw laughter and optimism. We sat down to join them and all talked openly about cancer. It was refreshing.

They had great respect for Burton, believed in his therapy, and eagerly told me of their experiences. Many had exhausted the traditional cancer therapies, been sentenced to die, and gone down to Freeport, Grand Bahamas, only as the last hope. Their healthy bodies before me were a testament to the effectiveness of Burton's treatment. My thoughts began to soar. "I walked into heaven and this is a miracle! Maybe Amber will live after all!"

"Amber? Come right this way." We walked into Beatty's Examining Room. He warmly introduced himself, then bent down to Amber's level to talk with her and put her at ease. He turned to me. "I've just gotten off the phone with an 'Angel.' She's donated $3000, a thousand dollars a month, for living expenses. Burton will treat Amber at no charge." Those words came straight from God. I was stunned. I had to sit down. "You mean, we are going to Freeport and Dr. Burton will treat Amber for free? And we don't have to worry about money while we're there???" "Yes." He woke me up. It was true; it wasn't a dream.

He explained that we would have to find an apartment to live in once we got there, but the other patients would help us. He handed me a piece of paper with all the information on it; written across the top was "Arla Amara." "Ask for her as soon as you get to the clinic; she'll know what to do." He gave us a timer and a thermos. "You'll need to keep the syringes cold and time them an hour apart." I wasn't sure exactly what he meant, but at that point I didn't care. Amber was going to live, that's all I wanted to know.

Somehow, I drifted out of his office holding the supplies and Amber's hand, got into our car, and drove to I-95. This time, we were headed north to go home, not south to get more "cocktails." The traffic swept me up. We were moving along at a nice pace and, for the first time in months, I was truly happy. Then it hit me: "God's wrong. She's *not* going to die, she's going to *live!!!*" My joy had no limit. I felt as if I had given birth to her all over again. I pulled off the highway and hugged and kissed her. "Mom, what are you doin'? Is everything okay? How come you're so happy?"

"Oh, Amber, I'm happy 'cuz I have more days to be with you... lots more days to do whatever we want."

I couldn't tell anyone in the media or at the hospital about our plans until we were safely out of the country. I placated the doctors as best I could. It was like walking on a tightrope. All I wanted to do was heal Amber without harming her. I didn't want to take the chance that they might declare me "unfit" and take her away, just like they did with Chad Green. The time we would spend in court fighting a useless battle, was time we just didn't have to waste. Time was *not* a luxury we could afford; it was merely a container for our actions, and the container was getting smaller every day.

I continued driving to Long Island for her "cocktails." The four hour round trip gave us a chance to talk. Her growing resistance to the pain of inserting the IV was justified but the treatments were necessary. We'd drive down the road, heading for the highway, and just as we got to the ramp, Amber would say with suspicion, "Mom... where are we goin'?" She already knew the answer but hoped it would be different. I looked over at her as we made the loop and merged onto I-95. "Mom, I don't want another 'cocktail'... I *don't!!"* "I know, Amber, I'm sorry. Soon it will all be over."

Dr. Kaplowe revised her supplements:
- 2 Livatrophin
- 2 Cyroplex
- 3 Thymus
- 3 Pancreatrophin
- 4 Hepatrophin
- 6 ACP
- 2 B15
- 3 Neurotrophin
- 1 K zyme
- 3 dismuzyme
- 1 calcium
- 1 tsp liquid B complex
- 14 apricot seeds (laetrile)
- Homeopathic

- 3 tsp tupelo honey
- 3 Retenzyme
- 1 1/2 Intenzyme
- 4 vitamin A complex
- 2 packets of Emergen-C

Forty-one pills plus various powders, liquids, etc.! I tried to grind them all up ahead of time, so Amber didn't have to watch. Still, I was running out of games to play to help her cope with all of this. I was tempted to stop... to stop the pills, the "cocktails," the constant game-playing instead of the truth, but I couldn't. I just couldn't let her slip away from me. Not now, not ever.

The events of the past few months were so overwhelming I had to write them down. I started a journal. Since I couldn't share my deepest, most intimate thoughts with anyone, I held a lot inside. This was my release; my shoulder to cry on. I could let it all come out and didn't have to worry about being judged for my feelings. What I really wanted to do was take a giant eraser and rub this whole mess out of our lives. Instead, I wrote.

### *April 28, 1980*
### *One month after surgery and my first journal entry*

*Amber's had enough. "I'm sick of those vitamins, pinpricks, and no milk!" I wonder if she senses that her body is dying. What does she feel like inside? How do you reassure a four year old child that's going through hell, that everything will be okay? Does she really understand any of this? Is she mad at me because I can't take away her pain? What does SHE want to do? I'm afraid to ask her because I know what she'll say. "I don't want to do this, Mom. I just want to play with my friends, eat regular food, and not have any more 'cocktails'!" If I stop now she will surely die.*

*Although I'm trying my best to save her, there's a feeling... a knowing... that we don't have much time left. I want to make these few months we have together as fulfilling as possible. I want to linger, not rush. I want to experience joy with Amber; use my tape recorder and camera to capture her reactions, ideas, messages, songs, stories, and insights. I want her to write a book about herself, life, the world, me, nature, and fill it with tidbits of knowledge.*

After the newspaper articles were published and the story spread, hundreds of people offered their help. The *Milford Citizen* and the *New Haven Register* were following the story closely, printing updates as they happened. The letters and phone calls kept coming. Because my pain was shared with the public, it lessened the agony somewhat. Amber was not just *my* child; now she belonged to everyone. Through her, we were linked forever. Nothing could break the chain—not time, distance, or adversity. We all had cancer in common and Amber was the symbol that united us.

Coffee cans, with a photo of Amber on the front, were placed in stores around Milford. People helped with donations to supplement any other medication or blood tests she would need. A raffle and a car wash were held. Since I was taking care of Amber full time and unable to work, the money helped tremendously. I thought about feeling ashamed, but my own petty feelings had no place in our life now. My goal was to save her life and I would've done anything to do that, including begging for money. Pride was an indulgence for people who had choices. We did not.

I planned a "Celebration of Life" for Wednesday, April 30th, at the studio. Both newspapers printed an open invitation for people to come, meet Amber, and celebrate her life. I also wanted to thank everyone for their love and support. Hundreds of cards and letters of encouragement were sent to us; many of the senders came. It was truly a miraculous time, shared with people who loved Amber and wanted her to live, too. Late into the night, after Amber had fallen asleep on a comforter in the corner, people stayed to talk about their own experiences with cancer. Their journeys paralleled our own. Each one of us had to fight for more information about cancer therapies. To be forced to do this while you are weak, vulnerable, and fighting for your life, seemed to be a crime. "Why isn't this information easily available?" I couldn't stop wondering but had no time to find an answer.

As I lay in bed reflecting on what had happened that night, I heard that voice again; it had been a long time since I heard it last. I dared to believe that the voice belonged to God. A part of me still doubted His existence. "I still haven't *seen* God. How do I know He is real?" I was sure He had abandoned me; gone on to create a miracle in someone else's life. "Each person is put on earth to learn a Life Lesson and to complete a Life Task. Until you do this, you will return to earth in a different body... a different life... each time coming closer to realization and fulfillment. Your lesson is PATIENCE. Your task is to WRITE AMBER'S BOOK and then share her message with the world. You will open the eyes of the world to cancer. Amber will teach through healing. Listen closely. Listen with your heart and I will tell you how." I fell asleep and dreamt of angels.

When she first had The Lump, it was small and could be hidden by her hair. As it grew, it was impossible to hide and glared at me without end. It couldn't—it *wouldn't*—be ignored. After surgery, when it was removed, her hair would cover the incision and, for a brief time, I could pretend she was healthy. Eventually, even this illusion was taken from me.

The radiation Amber received was beginning to reveal its deadly side effects. Her beautiful, dark, curly hair was falling out in clumps. Each morning, as I brushed it, I saw more and more on the brush. Her pillow was covered with it, as well as her clothes and toys. It was everywhere. Within a few days, she was nearly bald. Now there was no pretending. Her bald head exposed the incision and I would never see her as "normal" again, even in my dreams. This was the first of very visible, very drastic changes that would *show* me what cancer was all about. My dream was becoming a nightmare and now I could no longer deny it. "This is too obvious to ignore. Every time I look at her I'm reminded: CANCER... AMBER HAS CANCER."

I asked Chen about this. "It's nothing. That's the least of her problems. Don't worry about it. It'll grow back eventually." I was exasperated. He refused to see Amber as a *child... a person* with cancer and me as her mother... as a woman who wanted her child to live. My anger stifled my reason. I quickly got off the phone. Even though I couldn't express it, I could feel rage simmering inside. I knew they were trained to be clinical, not human, not emotional, and not connected. But I couldn't stop wondering, "Haven't those doctors ever loved someone, lived with them, then watched them go *bald because of cancer?"* Realizing they needed to sustain some degree of separation... of impartiality, to keep a level head and maintain a clinical outlook. It was painful to the point of being inhumane. I wanted them to be professional, caring, and proficient *people,* not "Robotons" and not human machines.

We treated her hair loss the way most people treat tooth loss. We started collecting her hair and saving it in a plastic bag to give to the "Hair Fairy." When the last strands fell out, we put the bag of hair under her pillow before she went to sleep. "The 'Hair Fairy' is coming tonight, Amber." "Mom, are you *sure* there's a 'Hair Fairy'? I never heard of her *before.* Can I stay up and wait for her? Will she bring my hair back?" I answered all of her questions but lied. It was the only thing I could do.

Although the three inch incision from her initial surgery had healed, a small lump began to grow underneath the scar; it looked like a slash through a written mistake... a hurried attempt to obliterate what was not meant to be. Red, glaring, and glossy, this mistake could not be denied or erased. It fed my desperate sense of urgency and forced me to face what I feared. I couldn't pretend anymore.

Our plans to go to Freeport were taking shape. I had one last meeting with Linda Bouvier from the *Milford Citizen* and Judy Doherty from the *New Haven Register.* I filled them in on Amber's condition, Burton's therapy, and our plans. I reminded them of Chad Green and the legal turmoil that his family went through. I didn't want to take any chances. I didn't want to lose Amber to the court system. "Please don't publish your story until after May 8th. By then, we'll be safely out of the country." Thankfully, they both agreed.

The cancer was bad enough, but the fact that I had to be deceptive, feel like a criminal, and sneak out of the country, only made matters worse. I never realized what went on behind the headlines in "CancerWorld." I never had a reason to care. Now, it was different. Cancer had reared its ugly head and invaded our lives, just like it had for millions of others. "If this is happening to *us,* what is happening to everyone else? Why is it so difficult to get the information you need to make an informed decision? Why do they make it so hard to save my daughter's life?"

For years, Amber wanted to go to Disney World. I knew that this would be her only chance. We'd stop for a couple of days before flying to the Bahamas. Gary called the main office and explained our situation. "We'd love to grant her wish. Come to the Main Gate, give them your name, and there will be three passes waiting for you." The Disney folks restored my faith in "big business" with their very generous gift. "Amber! We're going to Disney World!" She was thrilled. At last, I saw pure joy lighting her world of pain. She was radiant, glowing, and wriggled with anticipation of our upcoming trip. It would be the respite we needed before the long and arduous course of immunotherapy, another attempt at saving her life.

Gary, Amber, and I packed up our belongings, closed the studio, and said goodbye to our friends. On May 6th, we left JFK and flew to Orlando, Florida. I knew we'd be in this for the long haul, so I was prepared for anything. We brought thirteen boxes full of household goods and clothing, a rebounder for Amber's exercises, three bikes for transportation, plus our carry-ons.

Our stay in Florida was the "time out" we all longed for, a sorely needed break from the ugly reality of cancer. For a couple of days, we could live in Fantasyland or take a peek into Tomorrowland. No piles of pills or pain, only fun in the sun. Amber had gotten her wish to "run away from it all" and now she could do nothing but play. "Oh God, two whole days without cancer. I wish we could stay forever." I knew I was taking a risk to be off all therapies… to wallow in "normal" one last time. It was a risk I was willing to take but only for a couple of days, not forever.

I bought Amber a sun hat for three reasons: One, so that her newly bald head wouldn't get sunburned; two, so that she could look normal. Whenever we went in public, I ached for her. Out of the corner of my eye, I could see heads turning to look... to stare. "What happened to her? Why is she bald? She looks funny." Sometimes kids would laugh and then their parents would reprimand them for being rude. They were only being kids:

Curious, outspoken, innocent, and unpolluted. I hoped they would never know cancer themselves.

The third reason was that I was embarrassed and ashamed to admit it, even to myself. I didn't want the attention and I didn't want Amber to get it either; at least not for *this.* "What happened to My Dream? I hoped that someday she would be famous... a famous model. Everyone would know her... look at her when we were in public. 'Oh, isn't that Amber, the famous model?' they would exclaim. I want My Dream, God, not this nightmare."

Although the incision was completely healed, the scar was quite obvious and so was the new small lump, about the size of a grape, that was beginning to grow underneath it. Without her hair hiding it now, I was forced to see the new tumor that appeared to replace the old one, every time I looked at her. I gently insisted that she wear her hat, but I didn't tell her *all* of the reasons, only the first. Besides, I could delude myself a little longer if I couldn't see it.

### *May 7, 11 pm*

*We're at the Howard Johnson's just outside the main gate at Disney World. Amber's at the desk writing in her workbook and listening to "Thumbelina," Gary's on the other bed writing postcards. Today we went to Disney World and had loads of fun! It feels so good to slow down, unwind, and feel the sunshine. I am taking the time to savor each moment and cherish this time together.*

*Amber's head is down; she's beginning to nod out. She must be exhausted by now. The cancer is taking its toll. When it's time for her pills, I hear, "I'm gonna go away and find somebody who doesn't know me and tell them not to give me any vitamins!!!" Her words stab me just as her cries of pain tear through my heart.*

*In The Haunted House and Snow White's Scary Adventures, she was anxious. "Is anybody gonna give me any needles?" Her nerves are raw and no wonder. How many adults go through what she has in their lifetime? She fluctuates between happy and cranky, with no in-between.*

*I've decided to give her a break from the pills. She suspects all of the food and drink I give her. I'm taking a chance, I know. But what other choice do I have?*

Our two days living a fantasy life at Disney World came quickly to an end. Though all of us wanted to linger, we knew our journey to save Amber's life was not over; it was only just beginning. We were off to the Miami airport and our "adventure of a lifetime." Our hopeful, healthy future was waiting for us just across the Caribbean Sea and I longed to live—to *truly* live it.

# Chapter 10

# *Cancer in Paradise*

*"There are only two ways to live your life. One is as though nothing is a miracle. The other is as though everything is a miracle."* —Albert Einstein

The flight to Freeport was like entering a time warp. It was almost science fiction-like as we moved from one world to the next. The United States disappeared over the horizon; before us, only turquoise blue ocean. This was our first trip to the Caribbean and we were thrilled to be on our way. Both Amber and I clung to the edge of the small plane window, straining to see what lay ahead. We were hypnotized. "Mom, look! You can see through the water! Is that a big fish there? Hey! There's a big boat over there!" In the distance, our last hope came into view: Grand Bahama Island. A cruise ship was just entering the harbor. "Oh… to be living *that* life," I thought. Every part of me ached to be on that ship with Amber and Gary and Todd, enjoying life without a care in the world.

Before we left the mainland, we'd booked two nights at the Atlantik Beach Hotel to give us a chance to get our bearings and find a home for our indefinite stay. It was quite a distance from the clinic but the price was right. Since we were on a limited budget, we needed to find a place to live and *fast*. Gary went down to the lobby and bought a couple of local newspapers. We scanned the ads; two looked promising. We called and set appointments to see the apartments, then went down to the pool for some much needed "R&R."

The cool ocean breeze greeted me as we stepped onto the beach. My toes sank into the soft sand. "Ahhh," I sighed with contentment. All I could see were pastel colors: Cream-colored sand, light blue ocean that deepened as it neared the horizon and met the orange and blue sky, peach-colored buildings near the pool, tanned bodies laying around it. They were on vacation, I could tell. Their pace was slow and graceful. Most of them were laying on chairs that were scattered about haphazardly; drinks in hand or a book finally read. Many of them just lay there with their eyes closed—face to the sun—absorbing it all. A faint smile of pure pleasure would appear now and then. Our worlds were separated by a million miles, but I was in this one for now.

A few children played in the pool. Amber headed in that direction. "Mom, Gar, wanna go swimmin' with me?" She threw her towel on the chair, kicked off her flip-flops, and took her hat off. "Oh... No!" I thought. Nobody noticed. She scurried over to the edge of the pool. "Come on you guys!" In a splash, she disappeared beneath the water. I lay down to vegetate. Gary was delighted to oblige and quickly joined her. "Ahhh... now *this* is living!" I closed my eyes and snuggled into the chair. I could feel a faint smile on my face and gave in to the pleasure as well.

The next day, we set off on an expedition to explore our new world and learn our way around. We took a cab to downtown Freeport. The Immunology Researching Centre was located directly across the street from one of two shopping centers on the island. It was a simple, modern, yellow building trimmed in white. Adjacent to it stood Rand Hospital, undersized by our standards, but the only hospital on the island.

I reached into my pocket, found the piece of paper that Dr. Beatty had given me, and walked up to the receptionist. "Hi, I'm Patti Calistro. Dr. Beatty told me to ask for Arla Amara. Is she here?" "Sure. Have a seat. I'll get her for you." We found our seats in the Waiting Room and studied our surroundings. Tastefully decorated and although nearly empty now, it could seat about twenty people. It was clean, modern, pleasant, and accommodating. Magazines and books were on the tables between chairs that lined the walls. It gave me the confidence to continue.

Within moments, a young woman bounced in. She was all smiles and brimming with life. I was amazed at her beauty. She was tall and thin with dark hair that came to her shoulders and brown eyes that took you into her soul. "Hi!" She shook my hand; her eyes were smiling. "I'm Arla." She looked down. "And *this* must be Amber!" Bending down to meet her, she shook Amber's hand. "Hi, Amber. I'm Arla. Welcome to the clinic. Want me to give you a tour?" Amber nodded and took Arla's outstretched hand. We finished introducing ourselves then followed right behind them.

"Well, this is the Waiting Room." We went on. "This is the Blood Pull Room." Off to the left was a small, white room with two large chairs at either end, both with wide extended arms. A refrigerator stood in the corner; cabinets and drawers ran the length of the room. A door, which led to the laboratory was closed, but the window next to it had its curtains slightly drawn. Curious, I glanced through the opening.

Inside the laboratory, people were working the rows of modern machines and equipment. Beyond the lab and through another door, a kindly, somewhat middle-aged gentleman sat at his desk. He was sporting a pipe; glasses were perched at the end of his nose. "He looks like Santa Claus," I thought. He looked up from his computer screen to meet my gaze. "Is that Dr. Burton?" I asked Arla. "Yes, it is," she smiled. The tour continued. "Bathroom... Examining Room... Dr. Clement's office... Conference Room... Mrs. Burton's office." I wasn't sure what to expect when I'd decided to bring Amber to the Bahamas for immunotherapy. I was pleasantly surprised and somewhat relieved when I saw the clinic's modern facilities.

Arla told us that she lived at the Sea Sun Apartments with her family: Gary, her husband, and their three kids, Macey, Paul, and G.P. Her father was on Burton's therapy for a brain tumor he had. "He nearly died, but since we've been down here, he's doing a lot better. C'mon over and meet the kids. They'll be thrilled to have someone else to play with." She told us about the orientation at the clinic on Monday. "You need to be there. The therapy will be explained in detail and any questions you have will be answered." I was pleasantly overwhelmed, but confident that we were where we should be.

After arranging to store our possessions on the front lawn of the clinic until we found an apartment, we walked across the street to the Town Centre. This was the "happenin' " place; all the local Bahamians shopped here; the tourists shopped at The International Bazaar. It had a few miscellaneous stores, a post office, a couple of banks, and a Winn Dixie supermarket that served as the hub of the complex. It was a bustling place where conch was sold fresh from the back of a pickup truck, school children would meet for a soda, and local business people met for the latest gossip. Anyone who was anyone came here to meet, talk, and be noticed.

Freeport was much more sparse than my image of a tropical island. It was completely flat, with scrub-brush here and there, palm trees, and man-made landscaping. The island seemed to be neatly laid out, with some sort of master plan in mind. Lush flowers and trees lined the highways. The houses were modern and well kept. There was an intricate system of public transportation: Small, privately owned vans that cruised the roads at regular intervals. If you wanted a ride, you stood on the side of the road and waved them down. For fifty cents, you could travel anywhere.

We went back to our hotel room for one more night. I relished this time to forget. The rest of the world just dropped away as we played "tourist" not "cancer victim." The three of us went for a long walk on the beach, played in the waves, and buried Gary in the sand. Then, we returned for a swim, a shower, a nap, and a nice, long, tasty dinner. We went to bed early and slept right through 'til morning. No worries, no nightmares, no dreams disturbed my sleep. I gave myself up to the Bahamas and to Dr. Burton's therapy.

The next morning, we checked out of the hotel and hailed a cab. With only faith and no home, we loaded all of the luggage, rebounder, and thirteen boxes, in and on it. "Thank God it's a Cadillac." We headed into town, stopping at the clinic to unload our stuff on the lawn. We were sure we'd find a place to live that day. We had a couple of prospects.

After lunch at Winn Dixie, we took the bus to Kwan Yin Apartments to meet Sandy Kaiser. She had placed one of the ads that caught our eye: "Studio apartment, fully furnished, $300 a month." It was located across the street from the Princess Hotel and Casino and down the road from The International Bazaar. It was an impressive building, four stories high, yellow with white trim, and shaped in a "U" with a large pool in the center. We took the stairs to the second floor. Sandy stopped at the third door down the hall and opened it.

The apartment was bright and cheerful with yellow and white decor. As you walked in, there was a small kitchen on the right, a full bath with tub and shower on the left, and beyond, a large room with two studio couches at one end and a dining room table at the other. A sliding glass door opened onto the balcony that overlooked the pool area. We loved it! "Sandy, when can we move in?" "As soon as you'd like." We finally found a home; one that would be our refuge as we navigated this life-threatening storm.

With new energy and joy, we went back to the clinic to collect our things. One of the patients had rented a compact car and offered to help us move in. It took several trips, but by evening we were home. We spent the weekend unpacking, food shopping, swimming, and enjoying "the good life." Sunday afternoon, we picked up our bikes at the airport and rode straight to the ocean. It felt so good to be independently mobile again... so good to be free from cancer and enjoying life to the fullest.

As we rode along the back streets, we marveled at the sights and sounds of the Bahamas. Strange new plants and animals were a feast for our eyes. Amber sat on the back of my bike—the same $13 bike I bought in Whittier two years earlier—babbling on and on. "Mom, let's take that road there. No, not *that one*, *that* one. Can we stop and explore those ruins? How far away is the beach? Can we go swimmin' in that canal? Oh, Mom, isn't this fun? Hey, Gar, I'll race ya! Come on, Mom, go faster!" I'd strain to peddle as fast as I could; Amber just laughing with delight; Gary pretending to lose the race; all of us surrendering to the wind, the sun, and the feeling that we had escaped from the world. We were happy, truly happy.

Unable to hold off reality, we arrived at the clinic at 8 am sharp. We were back... back to the reason we were here... back to the CancerWorld again. I tried not to show my disappointment but a sinking feeling clouded my thoughts, if not my words and actions. "I need to stay strong... to stay upbeat and optimistic for Amber."

Before the orientation meeting, Amber needed to have her blood pulled. It was a new term to replace the old one: Blood drawn. We were led through the Waiting Room and into the Blood Pull Room. Because of what she'd already been through, she was terrified. But as she looked around the room and saw the other patients treating the needles so "matter-of-factly," her fear began to subside. Hand in hand, we stood in the doorway watching, just letting her fears float away and finally disappear.

The scene was unusual: People simply sat down in the chair, chatting all the while as if they were visiting with their best friend. Lee, the technician, put the tourniquet on their arm, swabbed the injection site, put the needle in, drew blood out, released the tourniquet, removed the needle, and put pressure in the area to stop any bleeding. All of this was done in a couple of minutes with no crying and no screaming; they didn't even flinch. Amber studied their faces. The patients continued to talk and laugh through the whole process.

From this scene, she collected her courage. "Okay. You can take my blood now... but it better not hurt too much." She hopped up into the chair as I stood by her side. "Here, Amber, squeeze my hand if it hurts." At the beginning she did, and then I felt her hand relax. She felt proud as she held the cotton swab on her arm to keep it from bleeding. Now she was a "pro" like the rest of them.

Dr. John Clement was the medical doctor who did the actual examination. Since Burton was ostracized in the States and could not practice his immunotherapy there, he came to the Bahamas to continue his practice and research. According to his agreement with the Bahamian government, Burton was allowed to practice his therapy as long as he didn't treat any Bahamians (they didn't want them to be used as "guinea pigs") so he had a MD on staff. Since Burton was a Ph.D., he couldn't work directly with the patients.

Dr. Clement was a tall, lean, very good looking man with an English accent. I could've fallen in love with him instantly, had the circumstances been different. I buried my thoughts. "Well, hello Amber. I'm Dr. Clement and I'll be taking care of you. Now, tell me about this." He pointed to her scar and the small metastasis underneath. "Well, I used to have a *big* bump there and then the doctor cut it off, and I got a lot of pin pricks and needles and..." He looked at me and then at her. "I don't wanna get any more needles or 'cocktails' okay?" He smiled. I had to explain. "I was taking her to Dr. Cole in Long Island, New York, for an intravenous combination of small amounts of chemotherapy, DMSO, laetrile, and vitamin C. He calls them 'cocktails'." "Oh... I see. Let's just take a look at this." I could tell he was enchanted by her as he studied and probed the tumor site. "Does this hurt?" He moved the tiny lump that grew under the scar. "Nope." He weighed her, measured her, and took her temperature. With the examination over, I thanked him, took Amber's hand, and walked to the Conference Room.

The meeting for new patients was just getting started. Gary took Amber across the street for pancakes, while I attended. As I looked around the conference table at the other potential patients I realized, "For most of us, this is the opportunity to save our loved ones' life. I can see my own desperation in their faces," I silently rambled, "I wonder what kind of cancer *she* has. I don't see any evidence... any tumors. And *him,* I can't see his cancer either. How did all these people find out about Burton?" It was as if we were all thrown together in this room for our last hope for a cure... for our last chance at life.

The door opened and Mrs. Esther Burton, almost comical with her "beehive" hairdo, walked to the head of the table and sat down. She seemed stern and serious; a stark contrast to my clinic experience so far. As she looked up from the pile of papers before her and cleared her throat, the expression on her face told me she was not amused at our attempts at light conversation. The whole mood of the room changed. Like a soldier to her troops, she explained the therapy to us. "First thing in the morning, 3cc's of blood is drawn. Then you leave and return at 10:00 to pick up the patient's syringes, usually four of them. They must be kept cold and injected one hour apart. You have to eat plenty of protein, especially chicken." She went on to explain a few facts about island living and where we could go food shopping, send a telex, make phone calls, etc. I stayed to fill out some forms, then slowly rode my bike back to Kwan Yin. I needed more time to digest the information. There was a lot to think about and I needed to wrap myself around it… to find a way through it to get to the other, the living side.

<u>*May 13, 1980*</u>

*We started Burton's "serum treatment" today. They pulled her blood at 8am. At 2, we went back to pick up her shots. They were in a plastic bag in the refrigerator with "Calistro" written on it. Four small, slim 1cc syringes filled with various amounts of a cloudy white liquid were inside. The first one needed to be given at 2:45. Lynn, the registered nurse, gave Amber the shot in her bum. Her reaction? Fear, intense anxiety, begging, "Please… don't do this! Please!" Then just as the needle penetrated the skin, a high-pitched scream. Helplessly, I watched. "Oh, my God, I don't think I can do this. I can't… I know I can't." Thankfully, no one could read my mind. Gary took Amber outside while Lynn instructed me on the procedure of giving injections. She tried to boost my confidence, but I could feel it sagging. I was certain I could not do it.*

*We rode home, jumped in the pool, and concentrated on enjoying the day and each other. My split personality that I'd spent a lifetime developing, began to emerge. I needed it to emerge and take control now. I was splashing and playing and joking and watching the clock. The alarm went off and inside my head I jumped. "Damn! 3:45… time for another shot." I scooped Amber up out of the pool. "Come on, sweet thing, let's go get a snack."*

*We went up to our apartment. Amber knew what was happening and tried to distract me. "Mom… I wanna tell you somethin', okay?" I didn't want to do this either, but pretended for her sake. "Amber, we'll do this real quick and then we'll go back down to the pool." I numbed the area on her butt with an ice cube, rubbed the spot with an alcohol pad, stuck the needle in, pushed in the plunger, removed it quickly, dabbed the spot with a pad, and told her to put pressure on it. She cried and pleaded the whole time. Though it seemed like an hour, I'm sure it only took a few minutes. I made three mistakes: I didn't pinch the skin, I put the needle in crooked, and I didn't cover the spot with the alcohol pad before I took the needle out. We returned to the pool and Gary.*

*For the next injection I asked, "Amber, where do you want it?" She played the game "Stalling for Time" and wanted it everywhere except her arm or her butt. She finally chose her arm. I closed the windows so she could scream and the neighbors wouldn't hear. Things went a little more smoothly, but I'm still not sure about this.*

*At 5:45 we were making tuna sandwiches. I pushed the tuna aside, put her up on the counter, and prepared. I gave her the shot and her reaction was quite mild. "Is she becoming accustomed to this so soon?" After we were done she said, "Hey, Mom, maybe, just as the needle goes in, I can bite on a piece of Energy Bar, okay?"*

*I wanted Amber to become familiar with the pulls and shots, so I got an orange and some grape juice and let her practice. I called the grape juice "Good Guys" (serum) and watched as she gleefully shot them into the orange. "Mom, can I give my animals 'Good Guys', too?" "Sure. Let's switch the grape juice with water and I'll stand them in line for their shots." We agreed that Gary and I will get shots (sterile water) tomorrow, and Amber will give them to us. God, I'm scared.*

To an outsider, this therapy may have seemed bizarre; but to those of us who lived this way every day, it was normal. We were the rule, not the exception. People had come from all over the world to receive Burton's therapy. I saw the faith they had in him and it wasn't "blind." They'd already been through most of the traditional therapies and had, after extensive research, decided on this one. At least it was available, even if it *was* in the Bahamas, but I wondered, "Why are people forced to leave their homes and their loved ones to get the therapy they wanted? Why can't this be done *within* the United States, especially since chemotherapy and radiation are still experimental as well?" It was a question I just couldn't stop asking. It seemed so absurd, ridiculous, and unspeakably cruel to those who were already suffering and their loved ones who watched from a distance in paralyzed anguish.

<u>*May 19, 4:30 pm*</u>

*Well... tomorrow, another day at the clinic: 8:00 blood pull, 10:00 pick up shots. This goes on Monday through Friday, five days a week and sometimes Saturday, too. I don't know how long I can do this. I only know that if Amber has the courage to go through it, I have the courage to face tomorrow.*

*After setting a routine, things are a bit easier. Gary is giving her the shots while she straddles me and holds on tight. Sometimes she bites on her stuffed lion's ear just as the needle goes in. It's her way of "biting the bullet." I see that she, too, is groping for ways to cope.*

*Unbelievable! She pulled Gary's blood today! I know that it helped her to accept her own pain. I was so impressed that I just had to take photographs as I'm certain that no one will believe me. She did it perfectly! I would not have thought it possible that a four year old child could draw blood. When it came to the water injections, both Gary and I chickened out. I didn't even have the courage to let her give me ONE injection, much less 4 or 8 a day! I admire Amber so much! I doubt that I could be as strong as she is.*

<u>*10:50 pm*</u>

*Amber is sleeping soundly. I'm so grateful that she has no symptoms and I hope she never will. Dr. Clement says she is responding to the therapy and doing well. In the two weeks since we've been here, the 1 cm metastasis under the scar is beginning to flatten and shrink! I can't believe it and neither will anyone else! I took some pictures for proof.*

Shortly after Amber began the treatment, I learned how to pull her blood myself. This way, I could take it down to the clinic and she could stay and play with Gary. We started to incorporate the routine into our daily lives, *almost* like brushing our teeth. I could pull her blood quickly and relatively painlessly; so much so, that she wouldn't even flinch. "All done." She'd hop off the counter and go wake up Gary. She would bug him until he got up and promised to wrestle with her, or make breakfast, or take off on

146

an expedition into the surrounding area on our bikes. I'd put the blood in a glass vial, put a rubber plug in the end, write her name on the label, strap it into the blood rack on the back of my bicycle, and ride the mile or so to the clinic.

Within a couple of weeks after we arrived on the island, Dr. Burton was on *60 Minutes.* The program explored his history, the immunotherapy he discovered, why he left the United States, some of the cover up and politics of the "Cancer Industry," and his battle with the medical establishment. He came across as abrasive, feisty, fed up with the obstacles that were put in his way, a rebel in his own right, and with good reason. Regardless of his personality, Burton's therapy *was working* and not just for Amber. Hundreds, perhaps thousands of people were maintained on his therapy here in the United States, as well as around the world. They came to the clinic every so often for "tune ups" and left with enough serum to last until their next trip to Freeport.

The FDA and the United States government had been harassing him for years. Their argument was that Burton's documentation techniques did not meet the standards set by government agencies. Yet, the standards kept changing and as they did, he got tired of the fight. He wanted to concentrate on cancer research, improving his therapy, and saving lives; not filling out reams of paperwork, adjusting to standards, and pleasing the bureaucrats. Stubborn as hell and disgusted with the battle, he appealed to the Bahamian government. They agreed to let him set up his clinic and practice there, but set conditions; ones that he could live with.

After watching *60 Minutes,* I began to question the legitimacy of the three accepted treatments for cancer: Surgery, chemotherapy, and radiation. "What makes them 'acceptable'?" According to the medical establishment, every other therapy except these three, was "unconventional," "radical," "unacceptable," "unproven quackery." I tried, but could not understand their arrogant behavior. "Couldn't these words describe surgery, chemotherapy, and radiation, too? Aren't they still experimenting with these therapies and using the American public to collect statistics... to voluntarily participate in 'clinical trials' so that these therapies can be 'proven'?" No cancer therapy has been proven to *cure* cancer, only keep it under control. Having an open mind—whether you are a scientist, lay person, or doctor—is the *only* way to conquer cancer.

I remembered when we were at Yale-New Haven and the doctors told me about the central data bank—The National Tumor Registry—that receives all the information about all the cancer patients in the United States: Their type of cancer, location, age, weight, sex, etc. The doctors determine the patient's protocol based on this information and what was effective for other patients with similar statistics. Then, it's a kind of "guessing game." The patient's treatment would depend on these factors. It seemed to me that instead of using *MICE* in experimental research like Burton was, the American doctors were using *PEOPLE!* The cancer epidemic was just beginning to emerge and *everyone* was experimenting with ways to fight it. *NO* therapy was proven yet, whether it was inside or outside US borders.

I found myself caught in the middle of a war, not the "War on Cancer" that Nixon had declared in 1971, but among those who were *fighting the battle against it.* I could see the casualties—the people who had cancer and their loved ones—but I couldn't understand *why* this war was happening. "How can they keep fighting amongst themselves while so many people are *dying?*" I wanted to help, but I didn't know what I could *do* about it, especially since I was isolated on an island that had very little communication with the outside world. Before computers, cell phones, and satellites, my only links were landlines and Telex, and they were too expensive to use. I decided to focus my attention and effort where it would do the most good: Where I was, my daughter, the other cancer patients at the clinic, and how I could help them.

### *May 25, 9:30 pm*

*I've been spending time organizing my art and office supplies. I'll print a newsletter to help the patients and their companions and hold meetings once a week to bring us all together. It might help us cope if we know we're not alone. I'll put up an open invitation at the clinic tomorrow.*

*The new metastasis under the scar continues to shrink! If I didn't see it with my own eyes, I would not believe it! Amber has so much strength and energy. (Does she really have cancer?) She has accepted the blood pulls and needles now. Lately I've been pulling her blood twice a day and giving her 6 to 8 injections. Dr. Clement says her "numbers" look good. Her immune system is fighting the cancer. Everything seems to be fine.*

The morning after *60 Minutes* aired, the clinic was inundated with reporters, camera operators, and producers. Cancer patients on stretchers, in wheelchairs, and on crutches, got there anyway they could: Plane, boat, air ambulance, taxi. They limped... walked... nearly crawled to the clinic. They came from all over the world hoping to be accepted into Burton's immunotherapy program. Some came prepared, others just came. As I rounded the corner on my bike, the line was out the door, down the street, and growing.

Several patients had moved into the Kwan Yin Apartments where we lived. I got quite good at pulling Amber's blood and some of the patients asked me if I would pull theirs, too. Each morning, after I pulled Amber's blood at 6:30, I'd go down the hall to pull blood from the people too sick to get out of bed, then head down to the pool area. Ten to fifteen people would be waiting. I'd pull their blood, label each vial, then put it in the blood rack on the back of my bike. On the way to the clinic, I'd stop at a couple of other apartment complexes and do the same.

Once at the clinic, I'd give the blood to the lab technicians and help with the new patients. An assembly line of sorts was set up. Two of us worked together. Like a drum on a battlefield, my thoughts kept time to the rhythm: "Tourniquet... swab... 'Make a fist, please'... release... needle in... pull blood... needle out... 'Put pressure on it'... release tourniquet... on your way... 'Next?'" At least I felt useful; I was doing *something* to fight the battle against cancer, ease my feelings of helplessness, and take my mind off my own private agony.

The weekly meetings with the patients and their companions were going well. I rotated the location between three different apartment complexes so that those who were too sick to travel could attend. They became a therapy group, a source of information, an informal "gripe session," a political debate, a sense of belonging to alleviate the desperate loneliness that all of us felt. The island we were on was a symbol for the cancer in our lives. In both cases, we were isolated from society.

## *May 29, 10 pm*

*I've decided to document my experience here. I taped my first interview with a patient, Marian DuBerrier. Originally from Lafayette, Indiana, she now lives in Monte Carlo, Monaco. She's an English professor and editor; she has cancer of the eye. For three years now, she's been maintained on Burton's therapy and is here for a "tune up." She absolutely knows she is alive because of it. I asked, "What do you think about making Burton's treatment readily available?" "Oh... I'm all for it. I'd love to do something to help his therapy become available and, not just for cancer patients; everyone needs immunity boosts. I think it's far greater than just a cancer remedy. I'm thoroughly sold on Burton's program. I think it's far reaching and very, very important in the world of healing and extending life."*

Amber continued to make progress. We were beginning to relax and find our place in the world again. Thanks to our "Angel" in Greenwich, Connecticut, we were able to take care of Amber, pay our bills, buy groceries, and not have to worry about trivial matters like making money and surviving. We could also spend time helping the other patients and making their time easier, too. Each day we lived was like another gift from God, and we knew it.

Apart from the daily regimen, we found time to explore the island. We'd pack a lunch, hop on our bikes, choose a direction, and go. Usually, we'd head for our "Naked Beach" in Lucaya. It was near the jetty at the entrance to the canal. No tourists had discovered it and so it was isolated; it belonged to us alone. To swim naked was the most extraordinary feeling; the warm clear ocean on my bare skin; no restrictions, no resistance, nothing to get in the way of my freedom. I had returned to the womb and could return to the bliss: That state of perfection we leave at birth. Here in the ocean, I could wallow and rest, but only for brief interludes. Comfort, serenity, pleasure, satisfaction. "The womb is the 'way station' in our journey from heaven to earth," I mused. Our "Naked Beach" was that and more, much more.

We bought snorkels and masks and brought them on our next trip to the beach. "Wow! There's a whole other world under the water! Amber, check out these fish!" I could hear her scream with delight through her snorkel. We'd bring our leftover peanut butter sandwiches into the water with us and feed them to the fish. Thousands of them would slither by in their quest for grub. The three of us would be dancing and screaming and singing and having so much fun. Days like this made cancer seem *almost* insignificant, as though it never existed at all.

### *May 30, 2 pm*

*I'm sitting on our beach. As I look out on the horizon, I see clouds hovering over an iridescent blue ocean. Amber's in the foreground singing and dancing. Her body is tan all over; no tan lines. Her hair is beginning to sprout and I can see a "five o'clock shadow" covering her head. She pirouettes over to me. "Hey, Mom, want me to make you some lunch? I'll make you a mud pie!" She's giggling... probably thinking, "Hee, hee, I'm so funny." She brings me a glob of sand. "O.K., Mom, open up and I'll feed ya." Her eyes twinkle with mischief as the spoon of sand nears my mouth, both of us wondering who will give in first. I do.*

*Earlier in the day, we dug a sand chair. Using our hands, we scooped out a large hole, shaped like a chaise lounge. I put a towel down and sank into it. She plopped on top of me and we became one, just like she had when I grew her. We sat together and just looked out on the water, saying nothing. Within minutes, she turned to snuggle into me and give me a long, luxurious, loving hug. Soon, I began to feel her body go limp and heard the slow, heaving breathing of her sleeping. She must've slept for an hour at least. Again, she was a part of me; her heart beat next to mine; the smell of her sweet breath; her silky skin so warm and soft. I left us and looked down. Like a director looking through the lens of a camera, I captured the scene in my mind and held it forever.*

*From elation to the depths of despair, my emotions rocked me. I didn't want to wake her but I couldn't hold back my tears. I tried to cry without moving my chest. No use. The harder I tried to stop them, the faster they came. She woke up but didn't open her eyes. "Mom, what's the matter?" "Nothing, Amber, I just got a piece of sand in my eye and I can't get it out. Darn it. Hey, girl, wanna go back in the water?"*

*June 7, 10 pm*

*After being on the therapy for a month now, her general health is excellent. There seems to be a glow about her. She has no loss of appetite, no fever, no lack of energy. She's up at 6 in the morning, down at 9 at night. As McGowan would say, "She looks perfectly healthy." Indeed, she LOOKS perfectly healthy. The metastasis is hardly visible beneath the scar, nearly flat and gone. I hope it stays that way.*

*I am very busy these days. The other patients and their families really touch me. On my way to the clinic, I stop to pull Pat Curtain's blood, a pretty girl from Huntington Beach, California. She is only twenty-one and has cancer of the liver. She describes her cancer for me: "I feel like my insides exploded... like there's a lot of fluid." Then she described the biopsy: "Without anesthesia, they stuck a large, steel probe into my side, between my ribs, and into my liver. Then they snipped off a piece of my liver and pulled it out. I nearly went crazy with the pain!" She looks anorexic, but I know she isn't. Before this, she planned to become a flight attendant. Unable to leave her apartment and confined to her bed, she eagerly awaits my visits, even if I am just pulling her blood.*

*The stories I've heard from these people, convince me that this "war" I've suspected does exist. If it hadn't been for Amber's cancer, I would never have known. When I think of what other children are going through at this very moment, I want to shout to the world: "Please... stop bickering and fighting among yourselves! Can't you hear the cries of the children? Just get together, pool your energy and resources and information and end their suffering... PLEASE." I am on my knees and not ashamed to say so.*

When I forced myself to really look at the situation we were in, I was shocked. There we were on an island, away from family and friends, faced with the fear of Amber suffering and dying, pulling her blood, giving her shots, hoping and praying this would save her life, watching those around me go through their *own* version of my Hell. It took tremendous willpower to keep myself from giving in to the overwhelming situation we were in. At times, I couldn't help it. I would wallow in my anguish and realize the ordeal was so incredibly horrible, I felt I would die myself. It was like a plague. To survive it, I had to shut down my feelings or at least try to control them.

I could see that my earlier life with my parents was the training ground for my life now with Amber. It had the same characteristics of my childhood... of "The War." As I grew up with the feeling that I was being prepared for *something*, now it was clear what it was: Fighting in the War on Cancer. I would spend the rest of my life fighting to save the people who were too weak to fight for themselves: The children... the *people* who have cancer. Without my childhood training, I would've let this war defeat me. The fighting spirit was planted deep in my soul a long time ago and without it, I would've simply given up and succumbed to the outcome.

On June 9, I took the Amara kids, Amber, and Joanna, a new friend from England, to the Xanadu Hotel's beach. We packed a picnic lunch and were there all day playing, swimming, building sand castles, and exploring a shipwreck that was embedded in the beach. I'd look up at the penthouse and think about Howard Hughes living there; how he barricaded himself up there with his millions of dollars to escape the germs of humanity. "Ha! If he could only look down and see us now! Amber with cancer and him on an island that was loaded with people who had cancer!" I couldn't help it; I laughed out loud.

It was nearly dark when we got home. I could see the change in Amber right away. She was quiet and withdrawn, a bit flushed; her eyes were dull. I felt her head. "Warm... it's warm." I took her temperature. "100.3... Oh, God, please just let this blow over." I could not even *think* about sliding away from our healthy path. I desperately wanted to erase this reality... to imagine her healthy and have it be so. It was not.

Amber learning to endure the daily "blood pulls" and injections by injecting "Good Guys" (grape juice) into her stuffed animals

# Chapter 11

## *The Turning Point*

*"We cannot direct the wind*
*but we can adjust the sails."* —Author Unknown

### *June 11, 1:10 pm*

*She's sleeping now. Oh, how sleep has become our refuge, a safe place to escape from this all-consuming world of cancer. I gave her some aspirin at 11am. Her temperature seems to have broken. To me, she seems listless and cranky, but she hasn't complained that she feels sick yet. "How do you feel, Amber?" "Good." And each time she says it, I am still amazed.*

*In the past couple of days, the metastasis that was there when we left the US, then shrunk as she began Burton's treatment, seems to be growing again. It spread to the other side of the surgery scar and toward her ear. Although it doesn't hurt when I press on it, that doesn't mean a thing. I remember the first lump didn't hurt her either. I must make an appointment with Dr. Clement as soon as possible.*

*She's getting tired of the injections. "I'm gonna run away from this place!" I can't blame her. I wish both of us could run fast and far away, leaving it all behind. Despite her frustration and increasing apprehension, she's been incredibly strong and courageous. "You know, Mom, I'm afraid when you put the 'Good Guys' in, and they won't do anything, and the 'Bad Guys' will eat me up!" What a hideous thing to face at four years old! I remember that age. The world around me appeared as though it was magnified a thousand times. Everything is huge: Feelings, events, images, fears. We feel so tiny, helpless, and at the mercy of those around us.*

I had Dr. Clement examine Amber. She had a slight temperature and her tonsils were swollen. "Tonsillitis," he said each syllable slowly and with a hesitant caution. I knew what this meant. "So cancer isn't the *only* thing her body has to fight; now it's tonsillitis, too." The metastasis was growing again. I know Dr. Clement didn't want to worry me, so he didn't say it; he didn't have to. By now, I could see his diagnosis in his eyes. He prescribed Amoxicillin and tried his best to reassure me.

Her morale was sinking fast. She was tired, discouraged, and ready to give up. Though both Gary and I did our best to make a game of the therapy or treat it matter-of-factly, we were running out of ideas... of ways to help her cope. I mentioned this to Arla and she spoke with Dr. Burton. He offered to give Amber a couple of mice from his lab to keep as pets. Hopefully, they would raise her spirits and give her a reason to go on... to endure the numerous blood pulls and shots.

Dr. Burton had increased the therapy from one blood pull and four shots to two blood pulls and eight shots every day. He wanted to monitor her immune system more closely and arrest the small metastasis that now grew under her scar. Though it flattened two weeks after our arrival, it had now returned. I forced myself to stay in the present and NOT look forward. The future was bleak at worst, uncertain at best. "Now" was all we had and so I immersed myself completely in it.

### June 12, 9 pm

*While we were at the clinic this afternoon, Dr. Burton took us into his lab and showed us the mice that he uses for research. Row after row, containers of mice filled the room. I was surprised at his sensitivity. He reached into one of the cages, captured a tiny mouse, and turned to Amber. As he placed it on the floor, he said, "See how this baby runs when I put him on the floor?" He scooped it up, put it back, and chose another, a larger one this time. He placed it on the floor. It didn't move. "The adults won't run; they're immobilized. They've learned the limits of the cage."*

*I can see that he truly cares for Amber and he knows that she is discouraged. "Do you want to take some home?" "Really? Oh... yes!" She clapped her hands with joy. Burton was touched. "After you have your blood pulled tomorrow morning, come back here and I'll have two of them ready to take home." That's all she's been talking about ever since.*

*This afternoon while I was shopping at Winn Dixie, I met Mary Hofbauer. Her son, Joey, is seven years old and has Hodgkin's disease. Apparently, Joey's story has been all over the newspapers; his story parallels Chad's. After the diagnosis, the doctors had a protocol meeting with the Hofbauer's. Although the family gave them no reason, the doctors stated that they would take "strong action" if they didn't "go along" with the protocol. Mary agrees that this situation is unfair. Parents should have the right to choose whichever cancer therapy they feel is best for their child as long as they have carefully researched all of the therapies and protocols.*

The bout with tonsillitis was beginning to take its toll. The metastasis was stabilized at 2 cm. Part of it had turned purple. "Necrotic," Burton said. Her hair was stubby now; I prayed that soon it would cover the tumor site and help me pretend she was healthy, *not* battling cancer. The growing tumor and nearly bald head were the physical symptoms; the ones inside were harder to see.

Amber was doing her best to continue the fight. She had her days of feeling low, but she expressed herself differently than an adult would. She could not identify, then explain what she was feeling inside. When she was tired, she got cranky and then her bad feelings came out. Most of the time, she handled her struggle the way a saint would; she rarely complained. When I asked her, "How're you feeling?" Her answer was always, "Good." Putting myself in her place, I would've given up long ago.

I decided to interview Amber since she was getting such a kick out of watching me interview the other patients. I thought it might be a fun and round-about way to find out what she was *really* feeling, without probing too deeply.

**June 18, 1 pm**

- **Me:** *What's your name?*
- **Amber:** *Amber.*
- **Me:** *How old are you?*
- **Amber:** *Four.*
- **Me:** *Where do you live?*
- **Amber:** *The Bahamas.*
- **Me:** *How do you spend your days... what is your favorite thing to do?*
- **Amber:** *Ummmumum... go swimmin'!!!*
- **Me:** *What type of cancer do you have?*
- **Amber:** *Sore... a sore tonsil.*
- **Me:** *Do you know where your cancer is... where it's located?*
- **Amber:** *(she points behind her right ear)*
- **Me:** *Do you have any symptoms... how do you feel?*
- **Amber:** *Good.*
- **Me:** *How do you feel about Dr. Burton's therapy?*
- **Amber:** *Good.*
- **Me:** *How do you feel about the shots?*
- **Amber:** *Not very well.*
- **Me:** *What do you think about them?*
- **Amber:** *Good.*
- **Me:** *What do you think about the blood pulls?*
- **Amber:** *Good.*
- **Me:** *How do you feel about having cancer?*
- **Amber:** *I... I want to try and NOT GET cancer.*
- **Me:** *How do you feel about Yale-New Haven?*
- **Amber:** *BAD! I didn't like it when they took my bone marrow.*
- **Me:** *Can you tell me what happened?*
- **Amber:** *You had to leave.*
- **Me:** *I had to leave?*
- **Amber:** *Yup... out the door.*
- **Me:** *Do you remember what happened when you got operated on?*
- **Amber:** *It didn't feel so well, that operation that I had. I remember when I took my gas... I had to breathe the gas in.*
- **Me:** *What else do you remember?*
- **Amber:** *No more.*

- **Me:** *Do you remember when you woke up?*
- **Amber:** *Yeah.*
- **Me:** *What did you think?*
- **Amber:** *Bad.*
- **Me:** *How'd you feel?*
- **Amber:** *Bad.*
- **Me:** *What would you say to other little kids who get cancer?*
- **Amber:** *I would say: If you go to your doctor's, GET WELL.*
- **Me:** *Where?*
- **Amber:** *At the clinic.*
- **Me:** *Do you feel better going to the clinic or Yale-New Haven?*
- **Amber:** *CLINIC!!!*
- **Me:** *Why?*
- **Amber:** *I like taking blood pulls instead of staying in the hospital all day.*
- **Me:** *Well... I think you're a pretty brave girl, you know that?*
- **Amber:** *(nods her head enthusiastically)*
- **Me:** *Are you gonna eat your ice cream?*
- **Amber:** *Yup! I'm gonna wait 'til it melts, then drink it!*

Many of the patients I met broke my heart all over again. I couldn't ignore their pain just to keep myself from feeling it. I was caught in this web of cancer. Yes, I did want to break loose sometimes, but I knew this was my destiny... my Life Task. Those words were popping into my head more often these days. "Life Task." I was linked to cancer, to Amber and all of its victims, its course in the history of man, and the role I was meant to play in it. The "why" was not yet clearly defined; I was still working on the "how" and so I documented *everything* —my journal, photos, movies, audio recordings, interviews, newspaper articles, medical records, Amber's drawings. I knew I would need them someday but didn't know why.

Pam Bargren was a lovely young woman and a mother of two children, Kimmy and Chad. She moved down the hall and her husband, Wayne, asked me if I would pull her blood since she was too weak to make it to the clinic. The first morning I walked into her apartment, she was lying on the couch with a scarf tied around her head to hide her baldness. She weighed less than a hundred pounds. Dark circles were under her eyes, but the smile on her face was wide and welcoming. She struggled to sit up. "Hi, you must be Patti. C'mon in. Can I get you anything? A cup of coffee maybe?" I knew she couldn't. "No, thanks, that's all right. I just had one." We made small talk while her husband, Wayne, and her friend, Carol, stood by. It was early and the children were still sleeping.

I lifted her arm to inspect her veins; her arm was black and blue and loaded with what appeared to be tumors. "Where is the easiest place to draw blood?" "Well, I'm not sure... maybe here?" I felt her vein, then prepared her arm and tried to stick her. No luck. On the second try, I found a vein and got the blood I needed. Her veins felt like spaghetti and I was chasing them around her arm with the needle. The chemotherapy she had received nearly caused them to collapse.

The look in Wayne's eyes mirrored my own. He stepped into the hall to talk to me. "Patti, I have to go back with the kids to the 'States on Monday. Carol will be staying here with Pam. I'll give you my home and work numbers. Please... call me if you need anything. And... thank you." I could see that he didn't want to leave his wife but he needed to get back to his job to earn the money to pay for all of this. I realized then how much cancer affects *everyone* and not just the person who has it.

## June 22, 10 pm

*Charlie and Debbie have moved into 404A. They came from San Diego. Charlie is a handsome young man in his early twenties, strong, virile, and full of cancer. Until this, he was a professional boxer. Knowing his chance of survival was slim, he offered himself to the medical establishment to be used as a guinea pig. They tried all kinds of experimental treatments to stop the cancer from spreading, but it was relentless. He is left with a small section of one lung. I can't believe he's not bitter or angry. He seems to have accepted his fate of death while living the rest of his life to the fullest. He came to the Bahamas for one last try at life. He hasn't given up yet. He is still a fighter.*

*Gary is doing odd jobs around the island to help us out. Money is running low and I don't know how far I can stretch it. I haven't received any child support from Michael since we've been here. Thank God for Gary. He left his job and even his own son to be with us as we face this life and death struggle. He's such a hard worker, yet he never complains about it. He helps so much with Amber, too. I'm glad that Amber has had the chance to know a father's love, even if it isn't her own father.*

My submergence into the world of cancer was so overwhelming, I needed to escape. I found one way to help me do this... to leave CancerWorld behind, if only for a few hours.

Gary agreed to stay with Amber while I went out. I'd wait until she was sleeping, then I'd get dressed up and walk across the street to the Princess Casino. From the moment I opened the door, I was transformed from "Patti, the mother of Amber, cancer, deformity, blood, pain, and endless hours of agony and hopelessness" to "Patti, the pretty, sexy, hungry for love and adventure, wild times, take-me-away-from-this-hell woman." Transformation complete, I'd stroll from table to table watching the croupiers, imagining myself in their arms entranced by love. I was even willing to settle for lust, disguised as love. Going unnoticed, I'd continue my stroll, stopping to watch the rich men sitting behind their stacks of chips, casually flinging them across the table to the dealer. I developed a pattern: Stop, watch, try to catch a man's eye, then move on without success.

The casino was filled with noise... lots of noise to drown out any thoughts that were uncomfortable. My senses were saturated with cigarette smoke, cheap cologne, expensive perfume, big diamond rings, necklaces, flashy watches, manicured nails, nice clothes, drinks, people screaming numbers, music, and laughter. "Nobody is having a bad time *here*." Filled with longing, I'd slowly walk back home and into the world I could only escape for a night.

I'd quietly unlock the door and tip toe over to my bed. Amber would be still sleeping; Gary would be waiting. I couldn't really expect him to understand, but I did. My daughter was dying before my eyes while I battled to save her life in vain. In my heart, I knew she was dying and I had to watch her—*I had to*—except when I went to the casino. There, I could separate myself from my painful reality and soothe my soul or drown it out, if only for a brief time. Satisfied, I'd slip in the door, back into my "mommy" mode, out of my dress, and into bed.

In the morning, I resumed my daily routine. My secret life helped me to adapt to my real one; it gave me the courage to make the best of a bad situation; be the best at whatever I did. I became so skilled at giving Amber her shots that I could do it anywhere. The shots had to be given exactly an hour apart. In the supermarket, the timer would go off, we'd go to the corner of the produce section, I'd lift her dress a bit, and quick as a wink it would be over. At the movies, in church, at the beach, walking down the road... wherever and whenever the timer would go off, I'd give her an injection. I even gave them to her *right through her clothes!*

Life on the island was... well... like life on any island: The reason you were there set the tempo for your daily activities. I was there to save Amber's life; give her the cancer therapy of my choice —that made sense—in the only place it was allowed to be practiced. I wasn't a tourist on vacation getting away from it all, relishing the solitude, spending my days in tune with the rhythms of nature. I was working and fighting against time, cancer, and the politics that engulfed it. Our days were controlled by the strict routine of blood pulls and shots. Yes, we were living in Paradise, but what brought us here was Hell. I had to be content with a compromise: Purgatory. I would try to make our life at least bearable and fill it with moments of joy punctuated by pain.

Our daily trip to the local post office was like an addiction. It was my connection to the world beyond the island, a world that seemed far, far away or maybe didn't exist at all. After our morning ritual of blood pulls and shots, I'd strap Amber into her seat on the back of my bike and we'd ride to the Town Centre to check "General Delivery." By now, all the locals knew who we were and why we were there. They accepted us into their culture... into their world. Everyone knew Amber by name.

I'd lift her up and sit her on the counter. Smiling from ear to ear, she was eager. "Mornin', Amba. What con we do for ya today?" The air was thick with their Bahamian accent. "Hi. Do you have any mail for me?" "Hold on... lit mee look." While we were waiting, the other postal workers would come up to talk with her. "Hey, girl... how's those dance lessons comin'? Did you start your class yet?" "Nope. My Mom's gonna take me on Saturday though, and then I'm gonna be a ballerina!" "Oh... and what a prittie ballerina, too!" On good days, we get maybe a letter or two; most days, nothing. I hoped for a child support check from Michael or maybe a letter or card of encouragement. "Oh well, come baack and see us tomorrow now, okay?" "See ya!" she said as she scampered outside. I'd turn around to wave; they'd be shaking their heads in compassion and disbelief. It was unusual for a child to have cancer in the 'States, but unheard of in their Bahamian culture.

Just like all the other mothers, I brought my daughter to Saturday morning dance class. We collected in a large mirrored room. The teacher spoke to us briefly, "...Registration form... fee... loose clothing... time to pick them up..." Amber milled around nervously, wanting to separate from me, but not go too far. She wanted to be like all the other girls and in *her* mind she was. But the walls of mirrors told a different story.

"Mom, I don't wanna wear this." She handed me her hat. I silently gasped. "Oh, no! They'll see it now!" I collected myself and tried to persuade her. "Are you *sure,* Amber?" "Yeah, Mom, none of the other kids have a hat." She skipped away to rejoin the group of girls who were now holding hands in a circle. The metastasis... The *new* Lump... the tumor... was now large and getting larger. It was lumpy, red, and so obvious. In the mirrors, it multiplied. No matter where I looked, *there were tumors everywhere;* some went on forever. By now, I'd learned to look beyond it to see Amber, but they could not.

The children were almost hypnotized by it. I watched as they stared—some of them curious, others were fascinated, all of them wanting to know more. Their bodies were moving along to the music and they found it hard to focus for long. When the lesson ended, we collected Amber's things and filed out the door with the rest of them. *"Eeeew! What's THAT?!"* "How *ugly!!"* Their mothers would quiet them, tell them, "It's not polite..." I knew they were just being kids, they weren't being rude. I gently explained, "It's cancer." The kids said, "Oh." They were satisfied; that explained it. The mothers were aghast as they pulled their little girls closer, hoping it wasn't contagious.

Her dance class had given her hope. She saw it as the first step to prepare her for her career as "Ballerina of the World." "Mom, when I grow up, I wanna be a ballerina!" She really meant it. I saw the dance lessons as, "Not much time left, I have to give her as many once-in-a-lifetime experiences as I can. We don't have a minute to waste." But she saw them as a beginning and I was glad for that.

Our links to the outside world were Linda Bouvier and Judy Doherty, the reporters that followed Amber from the beginning. They had been publishing periodic updates from the letters or telexes I sent about her progress, Burton's therapy, and our situation on the island. *The Associated Press* spread the news around the world. People everywhere had adopted Amber as their own. She belonged to the world now and I was only her protector... her keeper... her mother. She was a rising star and I did nothing to stop her. This was her destiny... *her* Life Task.

Despite our difficulties, there were some benefits to our isolation on the island. We were among "our kind" of people: Those who had cancer and various deformities (battle scars) from their fight. I didn't have to hide the tumor just to avoid the stares. I wasn't constantly reminded of what "normal" was. I didn't have to see perfectly healthy children doing perfectly normal things. Oddly, I began to feel at home.

### July 7, 4 pm

*Since my last entry two weeks ago, a lot has happened. Zene, a beautiful woman in her forties, came into our lives. In her youth, she was known as "The Golden Girl." Blond hair, blue eyes, enchanting smile—a girl with a future, she'd go far in life. How could they know? Here she is in the Bahamas, filled with cancer, desperate to live, unable to care for herself. She is deteriorating very quickly. We stop by her apartment* every day to clean, run errands, keep her company, and give her shots. Sometimes, Amber gives them to her! They have become really close. They are walking the same path but in different shoes.

Last Tuesday, I saw Dr. Clement. He examined the tumor. Since her tonsillitis, it has grown to the size of a golf ball. When Amber left the room to go play with the staff, he admitted, "We're losing the fight." I could no longer deny it. He said it out loud. "How long will she live? How will she die?" "Maybe a year before things get bad. She may or may not have pain. She might get real giddy... so much so that you can't stand it." "I'd like to go home in a month, but I'll stay if Burton feels positive." "Sounds fair."

I spoke with Burton today and expressed my concern. "The tumor is growing out of control." "We'll monitor her more closely... put her on three pulls a day and twelve injections." "Dr. Burton, will you inject the serum into the tumor?" "Forget it." I went on to my next thought. "Dr. Clement suggested that we have the tumor 'de-bulked.' If they remove what they can, then her immune system will have a better chance to fight this." "I agree, but who are you going to get to do it? You left the 'States for treatment." I hoped he was wrong but knew he was not.

God, I feel so helpless! I am standing in the middle of a battlefield between two armies. On one side, the medical establishment; on the other, the unorthodox doctors. Their guns are drawn. In their zeal to eliminate each other, they completely overlook Amber and the millions of others who are trapped in the middle. They are stubborn, close-minded, unyielding, and unwilling to compromise, much less work together to fight the real enemy: CANCER. Because of their obstinance, Amber will die.

### July 15, midnight

Gary and I went to the movies tonight. Amber stayed with Charlie and Debbie. She suspected that Dr. Burton might be Santa Claus and didn't want to take any chances; she wanted to get her order in early and dictated this letter to Debbie:

*Dear Santa,*

*Please buy me a puzzle. Hey, Santa, I sure miss you back at Milford this year. How is Mrs. Claus? I want a "punch" Play Doh game. I sure love you, Santa. I need a new bike. I also want some turtlenecks and some shorts and a hood for the winter and a little sleigh. Also, a big pack of glue (the white kind), a big old house, a little flag, three kittens with mittens, and some clothes for the cats, a tiny pillow for myself with my name on it: Amber Marie Calistro. I need some school supplies, a coloring book and crayons. I need a lunch box with "Black Hole" on it and a little guy to watch me do my school work. Oh yeah, I also want a "Black Hole" thermos. I want some barrettes and some ribbons for my hair. I also want you to bring some art supplies for Patti. Don't bring Gary nothin' cause he gots enough stuff.*

*Love,*

*Amber*

*p.s. I love you and Dr. Burton is giving me treatment and making me feel better.*

Upon our return to our apartment, I put Amber to bed. Like most nights, I read her a story and sang her a song as I gently stroked her back, butt, and arms until she drifted off to sleep. Because of the growing tumor, she could no longer sleep on the right side of her head and shifted uneasily before I could hear the slow, steady breathing that confirmed her sweet slumber. "She is *perfect* except for the cancer," I silently lamented, "Oh how I want her to be 'normal,' not different. And definitely *not* fighting cancer!" I longed to return to the days of our past. They were a struggle, yes, but we were together and we *lived... we truly LIVED* through them. Now it was different. We were living our days "in the moment" and "tomorrow" was never taken for granted.

I unfolded the Santa Claus letter and read it out loud to Gary. Both of us smiled deep down inside and it pushed away the pain. Our happiness was measured in seconds, not minutes, days, weeks, or months. Our pain returned when I read: "I want some barrettes and some ribbons for my hair." We looked at each other and knew that *this* Christmas wish could not and *would* not be fulfilled. Her beautiful, black, soft, curly hair was taken by the "Hair Fairy" and would never return again.

I was desperate... clinging to the hope, however slim, that she would live. I made several calls to different hospitals in the 'States, trying to find a doctor to help us to de-bulk the tumor. Unbelievably, the doctors refused to get involved because we had left the United States to seek treatment elsewhere and because Amber's story was highly publicized. Once *The Associated Press* put it over the wire service, our story was known around the world.

A group of Canadians, including some doctors, had come down to check out the clinic and Burton's therapy. He told them about Amber and asked them to examine her to see if they could de-bulk the tumor. David Stewart, a wealthy gentleman and an altruist, talked with me and took photos of the tumor. He'd take them back to Montreal along with her medical records and consult with a medical team. I saw him as my... as *Amber's* savior. Because of his kindness, caring, and generosity, my daughter had one last chance to live and I would be forever grateful for this renewed hope and help.

As I lay down in my bed that night ecstatically exhausted, I heard the voice again. It'd been a long time and I'd nearly forgotten it. "I've been with you; I haven't left." Still doubting, but reassured, I continued to listen. "I have been guiding your every thought... every decision... every move you've made. They will try to help Amber." Whatever apprehension I had about going to Montreal, quickly vanished. We were going. It was only a matter of when.

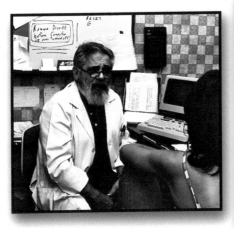

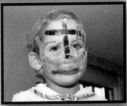
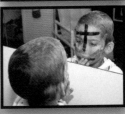
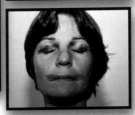

In between visits to the clinic, we rode our bike to
the beach or downtown / Dr. Burton in his office /
Gary was now working at the clinic to help us
pay for our living expenses / Amber loved to
create "tape jewelry" and play "dress up" as
an angel or a ballerina

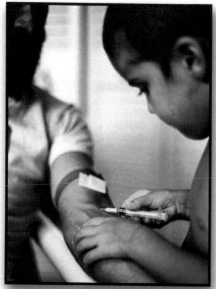

To help her cope with the daily pulls and shots, Gary let her pull *his* blood. She got it on the first stick! She was very proud of herself. Even though she was only four, she'd learned a lot in her short time.

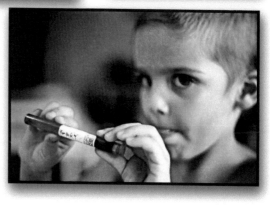

# Chapter 12

## Making Memories

*"Things that are hard to bear are sweet to remember."* —Seneca

### July 20, 4:45 pm

*I'm in flight. Amber is cuddled up in a blanket, fast asleep on the empty seats across from me. She's clutching her "Sheepy," a small white stuffed animal. As hard as it is to believe, we're on our way to Montreal! Doctors have agreed to de-bulk the tumor without forcing me to give her any additional treatment; no chemotherapy; no radiation. They respect my decisions as her mother. This is the first time Burton has asked foreign doctors to help him. Amber is now a "goodwill ambassador." Dr. Burton has gone way beyond any hope or expectation. He's paid for everything, even giving us $1000 cash to "have the time of our life!" David Stewart is covering the hospital stay and all tests. Oh, God, I am so grateful.*

*We will arrive a JFK at 5:30pm, catch Air Canada at 7:40pm, and arrive in Montreal about 9pm. The Stewarts are supposed to pick us up at the airport, take us to The Royal Terrace Hotel, and then to the hospital in the morning. Another journey… another chance to live!*

While Amber and I flew to Montreal, Gary stayed in Freeport to work at the clinic. He was enjoying his work in the lab. It made him feel as though he was not only actively doing something to help Amber, but making a difference in the lives of all of the other cancer patients as well. I admired his willingness to set aside his life in the States and support us, but I knew it was taking its toll. Gary missed his son, his family, and living a normal

173

life. The only way to cope with our life in the Bahamas, was to "live in the moment" every day, not look too far ahead, and do what we could to ease the pain of others.

Flying to our "Beacon of Hope" was overwhelming, but exciting as well. It felt as though we were in the eye of a hurricane; uncertain we were safe, yet hanging on to the hope that the storm would pass over us without damage. We'd come so far and needed to enjoy the little bit of peace and serenity that the "eye" allowed us. I knew that wishing couldn't make it so and was certain that the calm was only temporary.

Since I'd never been to Montreal, I had no idea what to expect. Though Canada was our neighbor, I knew that the culture would be different. Navigating our way through their medical system would be a challenge. Having David and his assistant, Claire, to guide us would be a godsend.

The plane from JFK was nearly empty. I settled Amber down across the seats in front of me; tucking her blanket around her and her "Sheepy" that she brought along on the adventure. She was exhausted and immediately fell asleep. I sat back to relax, have a drink, and bask in this brief respite. "The letter." I took out the letter that Dr. Clement wrote to the doctors in Montreal.

*To Whom It May Concern:*

*Amber Calistro is a four-year-old with rhabdomyosarcoma of right post auricular region. Excision-biopsy was carried out by Dr. Touloukian at Yale-New Haven Hospital, New Haven, Connecticut. This was followed by approximately 2,000 rads to the head and neck.*

*Amber has been in Freeport since 13 May 1980, receiving Immuno-Augmentative Therapy. This treatment has resulted in great improvement in her blood immune assays, but also a slow increase in a recurrence at the tumor site.*

*We are presently interested in obtaining help to de-bulk the tumor with minimal trauma to the surrounding tissues. Our results here, show that if a tumor can be dramatically reduced in size, it is likely that Immuno-Augmentative Therapy will contain any further occurrence.*

*I apologize for not addressing this letter in person, but Mr. David Stewart will probably have approached you on this subject.*

*Enclosed is a copy of all of Amber's records since her arrival here; the other results from Yale-New Haven are held by Amber's mother. Thank you very much for your help with this delightful child.*

*Sincerely,*

*John Clement, MRCS, LRCP*

We arrived on time. After collecting our luggage, we waited in line to go through Customs. It was late and I was nervous. I looked down at Amber, a bit sleepy and clutching her little stuffed dog that she sometimes used as a pillow. We inched closer to the customs officer. I caught my reflection in the glass. I didn't know the person looking back. I was skinny with sunken and tired eyes. "Next?"

We went into the Customs Office. "Good evening. Welcome to Canada. What is the purpose of your visit?" "I'm bringing my daughter here for tests." "Tests?" "Yes, she has cancer." *"Cancer?"* "Oh no, the whole discussion is about to begin," I thought. "Yes, she's receiving therapy in the Bahamas and we're here to test her for possible surgery." They seemed confused, so we spent a lot of time going back and forth, checking papers, letters, etc.

I was tired and just wanted out. I wanted to crawl into bed —any bed—and surrender to sleep. I needed to let go of reality, if only for a few hours. My mind drifted off as he said, "You can go now. Enjoy your stay." He motioned toward the door. I snapped out of my thoughts, thanked them, took Amber's hand and headed out into the night.

## 22 Juillet, 3:30 pm

*Ah yes, Montreal! It's so exquisite, fancy, old, delicate... so French! We spent the first night at The Royal Terrace. Amber was exhausted but fine. She is off Burton's therapy which frightens me. For the first time since her diagnosis in March, she isn't on ANY therapy. "Will the tumor spread... start to cause pain... open up and bleed... what?" For her, it will be a needed break; no pills, no shots, no pain, no clinics filled with people*

*who have cancer. For me, it will be a gamble, a chance at risking her life
now, to save it in the future.*

*The next morning at 9:30, David Stewart picked us up and took us to the
Hospital Sainte Justine. We went through admissions, then up to Etage
5, room #5223. After we got settled, a nurse came by and took three vials
of blood, a coagulation test, and a urine sample. It feels strange to stand
by and watch someone else draw Amber's blood; though I'm glad to be on
the sidelines for once.*

*Most of the people at the hospital speak only French. I knew the three
years of French I took in high school would come in handy someday. I
brought along my English-French dictionary for reinforcement and figure
I'll do my best to communicate.*

Compared to the constant blood pulls and shots, our stay
was very pleasant. We had three meals a day, a television in our
room, and a playroom at the end of the hall. Our room was large
and bright with windows that overlooked a park. We even had
our own private bath and shower. Amber's hospital bed was
similar to a big stainless steel crib with sides that went up and
down. I slept on the couch that was next to it, glad to be at her
side.

For the first couple of days, she went through a barrage of
tests. As I stood outside the Radiology Department, I overheard
Dr. Blanchard discussing Amber's case with his assistant. I tried
my best to interpret what they were saying. Basically, they were
concerned about the possible involvement of the mastoid area.
"The tumor may be deeper than we thought." He came out and
spoke with me. "I'm not sure how deep the tumor has gone. We'll
need to get a CT scan to have a better idea. Even though I, myself,
don't believe in Immunotherapy—at this point, anyway—
everyone has their own beliefs and I can certainly respect yours." I
got the feeling that the Canadians didn't feel threatened by the so-
called unconventional cancer therapies.

**22 Juillet, Midnight**

*After I tucked Amber into bed and stroked her to sleep, I went for a walk. I knew she was overtired and would sleep for a while. I needed to get out... to see if a world still existed beyond the hospital. I walked across the street to the park. After it started to rain, then pour, I spotted a corner cafe and ducked inside. It smelled of coffee and pastries and cigarettes. I sat down at the nearest empty table and blended into the crowd. Alone among the strangers, I finally had a chance to think.*

*"Oh, Amber, it's so hard to watch you die! You are so pure and innocent. I'm terrified of the future. Right now you feel no pain... suffer no side effects, though the new tumor is growing. You play, sing, and dance just like any other child. At times, my pain is so great, I want to turn my gaze away from you, away from the cancer that sits on your head glaring back at me. I no longer put my "all" into us; that would be investing in the future; that would be more to lose. Can anyone ever begin to understand this pain I feel? It is a physical pain. It hurts so much I want to die! I want to go with you, Amber."*

Our stay at Sainte Justine's was made easier by the staff as well as the other children on the floor. Many of them were gravely ill, but none of them were so obvious as Amber. The tumor was massive and too big to ignore. Despite its size, it didn't stop her from the simple pleasures of being a kid. She still wanted to live her life and live it the way she always did: Playing, laughing, doing all the things children do as they grow into adulthood.

One morning, after the tests were completed for the day, we went down to the playroom with our face paints. I'd done some face painting before and enjoyed it. I carried them with us wherever we went, just in case I needed to entertain some children at a bus stop, in a park, outside the grocery store, or in a hospital. The local Canadian children could not speak English, so they watched in fascination as I sat Amber down and began to transform her into a "princess." They giggled and laughed as I painted her lips bright red, put blue eye shadow on, and stroked delicate black lines under her eyelashes to exaggerate her own. "Okay, who's next?" All the children raised their hands. Amber became my assistant face painter and worked alongside me to brighten their day. Her occasional slip of the hand or smeared line wasn't noticed as they scurried over to the mirror to see the new face looking back. Lions, puppy dogs, Dracula, and more than a few princesses filled the playroom with laughter.

On Friday, we took a taxi to the Hotel Dieu (The House of God) for a CT scan, a detailed series of vertical x-rays that would help us determine exactly how far the new tumor had gone... how much had penetrated *inside* her skull. I was concerned, yet confident, about the Canadian medical system. There seemed to be a true sense of teamwork... of pulling together as one for the benefit of the person who was sick... of a willingness to explore ALL options, regardless of origin.

The Hotel Dieu was an enormous, very clean, and modern hospital. As we went up to the Radiology Department, I glanced at the bronze plaque above the door. It told me that the CT scan machine was donated to the hospital by David Stewart. I asked the technician about it. "Oh yes, Mr. Stewart has given millions of dollars to help ill children." I was so grateful that he chose to help Amber and certain that God had a hand in it.

Dr. Mecina came into the Examining Room just as Amber had changed into the hospital gown. He explained to us exactly what he planned to do. "It won't hurt a bit, Amber." He walked us into the next room. "You'll lay down on this table, the nurse will put a 'hat' on your head, and then you'll hear some buzzing sounds. The only thing you have to do is stay very, very still, okay?" She nodded apprehensively and clutched her Sheepy tightly.

They took a series of eight pictures. Dr. Mecina reviewed them with me. "You see this area here? This is the tumor... here is her skull bone. I'm not sure if there is any involvement with the brain. Just to be sure, I'd like to inject a dye that will help us to see the images more clearly."

I went into the room and explained it to Amber. "It'll be just like a blood pull." The nurse came in with a very large syringe filled with 26cc of Renographin-60. She tried to find a vein in Amber's arm without success. "Do you want me to try? I've been pulling her blood a couple of times a day for the last three months." "Yeah! My Mom can do it!" The nurse hesitated, then consulted with Dr. Mecina. "Well, it's unconventional, but let's give it a try." Amber relaxed. On my first attempt, I was into her vein. They were surprised and relieved. I was amazed at how well I knew her body, right down to her veins.

After the test, the nurse took Amber to get dressed while Dr. Mecina studied the images with me. "The tumor is about 1 1/2cm *inside* the skull." I heard a gasp; it was me. "The rest looks fine. If they *do* operate, they will take out the affected skull bone and replace it with acrylic." It sounded like he was describing the beginning of the end. Almost like "Frankenstein," she would be taken apart then put back together.

### 23 Juillet, 9 pm

*Amber is sleeping soundly. She had another exhausting day. The results of the CT scan seemed like another death sentence. Before we got back to Saint Justine's, we went for a walk across the street in a field of flowers. I had such a feeling of doom and dread, as though this was our last walk before her sentence was carried out.*

*Like so many times before, I drank in every detail of our movie... of our life together. "Her hair glistening in the sunshine... her little pink dress... sandals... tan skin. I love the way her fingers gently caress that bouquet of flowers." She continued to pick the wildflowers, then stopped and looked up while she handed them to me. "Hey, Mom, ain't I the BEST picker?" "You are, Amber. You are the best!!!"*

*Tears were beginning to well up in my eyes. I tried to keep them from spilling over. It wasn't working. "Amber, I REALLY love you, ya know." "You don't want me to die?" she said. I was surprised. She could read my mind. "Do you want to die?" "No," she said calmly. The question didn't phase her. "Amber, what do you think happens when you die?" "Your spirit lives." "That's right. No, I don't want you to die. Have you ever died before?" "No." "I have." We walked on. Amber resumed her flower picking. I returned to my thoughts.*

Since all the tests were completed, the conclusions were basically drawn: They would not operate. It would possibly do more harm than good. Dr. Blanchard let us come and go as we pleased. I remembered Dr. Burton's last words before we left Freeport: "Go and have the time of your life." And that's exactly what we did. I knew, after this brief pause in time, that she would stop living and begin to slowly die. Despite my strongest and most tenacious efforts to save her life, I would have to accept her fate and help her cross over to the "other side." At that moment, I made the choice to "live in the moment" as I'd never done before.

Burton's words haunted me. This time was the *only* time of our life and I needed to accept that. I had a meeting with Dr. Blanchard that afternoon. I wanted to know exactly where we stood. If there was no hope, I wanted to spend the next couple of days in Old Montreal living it up, instead of staying in the hospital until our flight left on Monday. With regret in his voice, he let his thoughts spill out. "I feel we'll be endangering Amber's life if we attempt to take the tumor out. There is more *inside* her head, than out. She would be deaf in one ear..." I didn't hear anything after that, I just let the words come in, swirl around, then go down the drain to a place somewhere deep inside me, forever forgotten.

I thanked the staff at the hospital and called David Stewart to let him know what was happening. "They did all they could do... the tumor has gone too far... we're going to spend a couple of days in Old Montreal before we fly back to Freeport. David, how can I ever repay you for what you've done for Amber... what you've done for me???" He politely dismissed my gratitude and wished me luck with Amber. I knew that he wanted her to live, just as I did.

Our visit to Montreal was coming to an end. I was so grateful to all the people who had helped us. David Stewart, Claire, and the Canadian doctors. We would not have been able to go to Canada if it wasn't for Dr. Burton. Not only was he treating Amber for free, but he paid our airfare *and* gave us a thousand dollars spending money for our trip! "Go have the 'time of your life' in Montreal," he reminded me. I hoped, someday, to be able to help someone else the way Dr. Burton... the way so many people had helped us.

Packing our things and leaving the hospital made me feel regretful, but when we stepped out onto the sidewalk and started walking down the street, my spirits began to lift. "Let's see where this road takes us, Amber." We found a park, played on the swings, and hopped on the bus that was heading downtown. We marveled at all the new sights of the city. When the bus stopped at a corner that looked appealing, we got off.

"Are you hungry?" I asked her, knowing the answer. "Yup! I sure am!" We found an Italian restaurant and went in. As we were walking to our seats, I could feel the heat of everyone's eyes straining to see the tumor. She didn't have her hat on and the new tumor was both blinding and bewildering. It was the size of a small tomato by now. It stuck out like a jumbo boil: Red, wet, and repulsive. Some people gasped, others turned away to whisper. I wanted to protect Amber... to instantly disappear, but acted nonchalant, as if to say, "Oh... I'm just having lunch with my daughter. No big deal." That's what my demeanor said. I raised my eyes from the menu. Though I understood their look of shock, curiosity, confusion, amazement, and horror, it still hurt to see it in their eyes. Most of all, my heart went out to Amber. "Does *she* see them, too?" My heart of hearts hoped not.

We spent two unforgettable nights in Old Montreal, a city that was centuries old. It was simply enchanting and we were willingly under its spell. We indulged ourselves completely. We ate at ethnic restaurants, shopped, strolled along the cobblestone streets, and took a carriage ride through the city. We visited landmarks, famous cathedrals, the bazaars, and subways. We did it all. We *did* "have the time of our life" thanks to Dr. Burton, David Stewart, and all the people who took us... took Amber into their hearts.

I was determined to fulfill as many of her dreams as I could. "Amber the Ballerina" would be an easy one. Claire had called ahead to order some "real ballerina" toe shoes from "Johnny Brown," a costume shop. She must've mentioned Amber's condition and her probable fate. As we walked through the front door, the owner of the shop stepped up to greet and welcome us. "Hi, I'm Patti Calistro and this is my daughter, Amber. I understand you have some toe shoes for her." "Oh, yes! They're right over here." She took Amber by the hand and sat her in a chair to try them on.

Amber anxiously watched the woman tie the pink laces around her ankles, barely containing her excitement until she was done. The second she tied the last bow, Amber was standing on the floor, then on her way to the mirror. She was speechless, but the joy she felt was not. Little squeals of delight slipped out of her wide grin. "Mom, what d'ya think??? Now I'm a *real* ballerina!" To complete the outfit, I got her a tutu. They didn't have a child's size, so I got her an adult. It was big but she didn't notice and neither did anyone else. We were all absorbed in making her dreams come true and not in the details of how.

I watched her with pride as she stood there adoring herself in the mirror, turning this way and that, making sure she saw all angles. Her adult-sized pink tutu nearly covered her whole body, her toe shoes pointed out. She embraced her "official ballerina slipper case" that the owner of the shop gave her and was wearing a smile that just wouldn't quit. At this moment, the tumor was gone, she was truly "Amber the Ballerina" now and forever.

Back in the hotel room, I gave Amber a bath and tucked her into bed. As she listened to her *Thumbelina* tape, I went into the bathroom to take the longest shower of my life. The hot water went on forever and my thoughts began to flow: "Cancer... the tumor... my little girl... my baby. How can I bear this, God? I am so human... so weak. Are You here... are You listening?" I sat on the floor and put my head on my knees. The water was pounding on my back. "I'm here. Don't look ahead. Take each decision at the time it is presented, no sooner. You will be my arrow, but I will point the way." "Okay, God, come on, *show me!* I need to *see* You to be sure You exist." I was angry and demanding. He refused to give me the miracle I'd begged for all of my life: I wanted to *see* Him! I lay down on the floor of the tub, cried until I couldn't anymore, and watched my tears go down the drain. I hoped that my sorrow would be gone forever.

Wrapping a towel around myself, I stepped through the bathroom door. I could see how God was presenting Himself to me: AMBER. *She* was the miracle—the proof—I wanted. I stood there transfixed as she lay on her back, sweet as an angel, with her tutu on, her toe shoes poking up through the blankets, and her arms around her ballerina slipper bag. I looked for her wings. I knew they were there but couldn't see them with my eyes, only my soul. "Embrace the angel. Love her completely. Don't ever leave her. Don't ever let her go." I lay down next to Amber, encircled her in my arms, and within minutes, I was fast asleep.

Sadly, we flew back to Freeport the next morning. We looked out the airplane window waiting for a glimpse of Grand Bahama Island... our home. In the distance, I could see the little spot of land that, just a short time ago, held a promise of hope. Now that I knew the truth about the tumor, that hope was fading. My mission now was to continue the fight to regain her health, but be willing to admit when it was gone and, once it was, help her to make the transition from life over to death.

Gary picked us up at the airport and had planned a nice dinner for us. His work at the clinic was going well and he seemed to be much more upbeat and optimistic. He needed to be challenged and involved rather than focusing on me and our relationship. Amber was thrilled to see him and talked his ear off about Montreal.

It felt foreign to be back at the clinic. We were only in Montreal for a week, but it seemed a lifetime away. There were many more patients than I had ever seen before. To my surprise, some of them were doctors! As I waited in the hall to pick up Amber's shots, I struck up a conversation with a gentleman from the Midwest. We made small talk. "A doctor. Oh, that's nice. What kind of doctor?" He hesitated. It seemed as though he didn't want to answer my question. I waited. "An oncologist." It was barely audible, but I heard him. "You mean, a cancer doctor?" "Uh huh." He turned his attention elsewhere. I got Amber's shots from the refrigerator.

As I rode away from the clinic on my bike, it hit me: "A *cancer* doctor has come to the clinic to treat *his* cancer, and then goes home and gives *chemotherapy* to his own patients! Something is wrong with this picture. Something is terribly wrong."

Larry McDonald, a United States congressman, had come down to the clinic with a delegation of sorts. Evidently, he believed in Burton's Immunotherapy and had introduced a bill before congress that would allow him to practice it in the 'States. The clinic was bustling and buzzing with cameras, men in three piece suits, and a little sophistication. Everyone was impressed, everyone except Dr. Burton. He'd seen all this "hoopla" before and appeared to be bored with it. Nothing and no one impressed him. "I just wish they'd let me get on with my work and leave me alone."

Kwan Yin was turning into a cancer clinic of its own. When we first arrived in May we were the only clinic people; now they were everywhere. I felt a little resentful that we no longer had a retreat from our life with cancer. Without the constant clinic reminders, we could come home and blend into the crowd or forget why we were here. Now, there was no escape at all.

I was back to my daily routine of pulling the blood of the other cancer patients. In our apartment, I pulled Amber's first, then down the hall, out to the "pool crowd," hopping on my bike and stopping at various apartments before dropping the vials of blood off at the clinic. I stopped helping at the clinic since Gary was now working in the lab. This gave me more time to spend with Amber.

### July 28, 1:40 pm

*I am overwhelmed by a sense of loss. It has been wonderful to see people recover. They arrive here ready to die—sickly, pale, and weak—then go home ready to get on with the business of living—healthy, tan, and strong. I see it over and over again. Others are not so lucky; for them it's too late. Each time I see someone leave to go home to die, I wonder, "When will it be Amber's turn?"*

*Last night, we were going to see the fire dancers at the Princess Hotel. Amber and I walked across the hall to pick up Judy and her daughter, Angela. A look of panic was on Judy's face as she opened the door. I glanced past her to the couch where her husband, Doug, appeared to be sleeping. He had a brain tumor that had grown so large that it bulged behind his right eye. I could hear him snoring loudly, but I couldn't wake him up. I went to call Dr. Clement and to get some oxygen.*

*Within minutes, the ambulance was there and took Doug to Rand Hospital. Amber stayed with Charlie and Debbie while Gary and I push-*

*started "The Bomb," an old Fiat that Dr. Burton let us use. We raced to the hospital.*

*Doug was laying on a stretcher in the hall. He still looked like he was sleeping, but I knew he was in a coma. Judy was at his side along with his parents. We waited for over an hour for the doctor who was on call to admit him. Everyone focused on Doug. "Look! There are tears coming down!" I said. Judy wiped them away, but they kept coming. He didn't move a muscle and his tears did not stop. "Can he hear us?" we all wondered. After another hour, Doug was finally admitted. He died at 4 in the morning, still "asleep" in his coma.*

*Another loss: Charlie has decided to go home to die. I knew he had decided that weeks ago, but he stayed to please his family and Debbie. "I want to go back to boxing. What good does it do to live, if you can't choose how to do it?" His wisdom is astounding! He's right, I know. Still, it hurts to see a man so good... so great... greet his fate so soon. They'll be leaving July 30 at 3:30 for the airport. Debbie came over to say goodbye.*

*Pat Curtain left yesterday at 1. When I went to pull her blood, Arla came with me. Pat had that "dying look" about her; a look that I was becoming familiar with. She could hardly speak, the whites of her eyes were bright yellow, her lips had sores on them. She was nothing but skin and bones. When Arla asked her to sign the release form, she couldn't; she kept crossing out her name to start over. God, how my heart aches for her.*

*In the week we were in Montreal and off Burton's serum, the tumor has doubled. Now, instead of golf, it's tennis... it's the size of a tennis ball. The skin that covers it is stretched so tightly that it looks transparent. I can actually SEE THE CANCER!!! It looks like big globs of cottage cheese floating in blood. It's purple and red and white. Her hair is about an inch long now; not nearly long enough to hide it. That's why her hat is so important.*

*When we go in public and she doesn't have it on, people stare in disbelief. They don't even see the little girl behind that grotesque glob of cancer. Then the questions begin. "What IS that?" "Cancer." "Oh, my God...*

*how did she GET it? Can she be cured?" I try, in my feeble way to explain... to treat it as casually as possible knowing that Amber is watching me and hanging on to every word. They press on. "She's so cute... and sweet..." I finish their sentence in my head. "... and she's going to die." Yes, she IS so perfect and there on/in her head is the PERFECT EXAMPLE OF CANCER. Such irony!*

Since my encounter with cancer, I'd had many conversations about death. None of them struck me to the core more than my own daughter's. We'd touched the subject briefly, but I hadn't fully explored it, not with Amber, anyway. Perhaps I was afraid to admit it... to say it out loud... to take it from a thought and make it a thing. I wasn't prepared to give up, let her go, lose her—not yet.

The morning after Doug's death, Judy overheard a conversation between Amber and Angela. Upset at her stepfather's death, Angela was crying and Amber was trying to comfort her. "Don't worry, Angela. We're just like roses; we 'bud out' and grow, then our petals fall off and we die. We fall to earth, but we come back again!"

I recorded my conversation with Judy:

- *Judy: Patti, isn't it remarkable, what your child said?*
- *Me: I know. I'm going to start recording her more. I feel she's carrying messages from a higher being, whether it's God, or...*
- *Judy: I wonder if she isn't some type of... like a prophet or something... a messenger from God. How would she know to say that? The words... she put it just like that.*
- *Me: So spiritual...*
- *Judy: Yes, yes... so comforting. Angela just quit crying.*
- *Me: And then what happened?*
- *Judy: Then she just took a puppet and said, "Angie, I'm your Daddy. I love you. Don't cry." Then, Angela stopped crying... and I wonder if something... some power much stronger than us didn't possess her to say that.*

From that moment on, my suspicions were confirmed. I saw Amber for who she was: A messenger from God. He spoke: "And *your* task is to deliver that message." "But I'm just a *human,* nobody special. I can't do this! No one will listen to *ME!*" "You're right, but they *will* listen to *AMBER.*"

My heart felt like it had a large, gaping wound in it and love was pouring out. People were leaving... going home to die. This therapy was their last chance at living. By the time they found out about Burton, they had exhausted the traditional therapies. Their veins were shot, their immune systems depleted, and some were mutilated beyond recognition. "I wish they could've had the choice to come here *first.*"

### July 30, 5 pm

*Charlie and Debbie left. This afternoon, they drove off in a taxi and didn't look back. I was filled with anguish as I watched Charlie and Amber say goodbye. They are both fighters. He bent down and gently kissed her cheek, then hugged her... clung to her, really. From one victim to another, though years apart, they are bonded together by the love they feel for one another, then torn apart by the tragedy of cancer.*

*Debbie gave us the key to their apartment; they left food and Charlie's spear gun. The Womack's left us food. So did Marian, Mr. Chinn, Peg Handwell, and Pam Bargren. Mr. Greenspan left, and Zene and Pat and Sid. What a life I'm living down here and I'm not sure I believe it. Seems like a dream or a nightmare or another world entirely.*

### August 3, 10:30 pm

*Amber is sleeping. I just checked the tumor. I inspect it only when she's sleeping; I don't want her to know. It seems to be split in two; the lower part is spreading towards her throat. Near the surface, it looks necrotic, but it's hard and bony underneath. She is congested and has a cough. She seems to bleed more at the injection sites. Apart from that, she has no symptoms. I can't believe it. She has a huge tumor on her head and HAS NO SYMPTOMS!*

*Money is getting so low. I have a $100 traveler's check leftover from our trip to Montreal. Michael still hasn't sent Amber's child support. Even though it's only $25 a week, it sure would help. He promised Amber that he would be down in June, then canceled at the last minute saying he had to work. I try not to talk about him in front of her. I know I'm angry at him and afraid it will show.*

*The pressure between Gary and I—his wanting to be intimate, me wanting to be left alone to focus on my daughter—was too much for me. I asked him to leave. He's moved into Charlie and Debbie's apartment. I'm enjoying my solitude with Amber again. I don't feel like I have to perform for an audience and then be judged for my performance. I can simply live, or struggle, in my case, in peace. He has been a tremendous help to us and I truly appreciate him, but I only have so much time left with my daughter and I need all my strength and energy for her. I can't be pulled in more than one direction right now.*

*I am so tired... so weary... so beat to the bone. It's been two and a half years since I left Michael in December of '77; a long and difficult journey. Since that time we've been on the move, living in too many places to count: Mom and Dad, Joey, Patti, and the church people. Moving east, we rented our two-room castle, moved in and out of Kathy's, on to Aunt Anne's, Alan's, Bambi's, the boat, the studio, then back to Bambi's again. Now we're here in the Bahamas. I want to rest... to stay in one place long enough to give Amber a house with a yard, pets, and a sense of stability. "HOME." I want to give her a home.*

### August 5, 10 pm

*"Thank you, God and Dr. Burton, for Amber's restful nights." So far, she doesn't have a problem sleeping. Sometimes while I'm watching her sleep, she'll turn her head onto the tumor, then quickly back to the other side. It's much too large to sleep on now, but she still hasn't had any pain, or discomfort, or agony. "I hope you don't suffer, Amber."*

Amber was finding her own ways to cope and her mice, Money and Nickel, were the saving grace, the island on which she could rest. Nickel had a tumor on his butt, so he was her favorite.

She'd spend hours and hours playing with them, building little cities and jungles for them to explore, and chasing them around the apartment just like she did Bambi's dogs.

Rainy days around the apartment were special. These were the times we spent playing school or dressing up. Amber loved to spend hours trying on my clothes and experimenting with makeup. Since I didn't have much jewelry, she invented her own. With a roll of Scotch tape and some crayons, she'd transform herself into a living work of art, then strut around playing "model" while I played "photographer."

I continued to document… to record the moment. As I looked through my viewfinder, I studied the face before me… the face of a wise old woman with a little girl's mischievous smile. Colored tape covered her face: green and blue on her mouth, red on her eyes, and on the center of her forehead was a big, black cross. I felt a twinge of sadness that the cross provoked, and then she was gone; off to lean—coquettishly—against the wall. "Hey, Mom, c'mon over here. How's *this?*"

I had been taking photos right along. I knew I had to document everything; if not for now, for later, but using my movie camera was different; the images *moved;* they were alive. I hadn't taken many movies since her diagnosis in March. "I *should,* I know, but I'm afraid to look at them after she's gone." I mean, WATCHING HER DIE WAS REALLY SOMETHING! "Do I want to see this *again?*" To watch one so beautiful become deformed by this cancer went beyond anything I could've ever imagined and my imagination was beginning to overtake my sense of reality.

### *August 8, 8:45 pm*

*I am depressed, angry, frustrated, and tired, incredibly tired. I want to sleep right through this. I want to sleep forever. I am too weak to go on.*

*I just spoke with Roger Kaiser and told him that I didn't have the money for this month's rent. Unbelievable! My daughter is dying and I can't pay the rent. Michael has not sent one cent. I simply can't believe him! Gary has been helping us with the money he gets from his odd jobs and the clinic work. Thank God for Gary. Where would we be without him?*

189

Our routine remained the same with few variations. The alarm rings at 6:30 am. I look over to see where she is. "Sleeping... peacefully sleeping." I gently rouse her. "Come on, sweet thing, time to get up. Let's take our shower and start the day." We act lazy and hug and kiss and roll over a couple of times, but really, we're on a very tight schedule. I rub her legs, her butt, her back; I avoid her head. We hop in and out of the shower. I dry her, then wrap a towel around her and lift her onto the counter and pull her blood. Using a 27 gauge, half-inch needle, and a 3cc syringe, I take about 2cc of blood out of her arm. Gary drops by at 7:30 and takes it to the clinic. I don't pull anyone but Amber's blood, so now the day is ours.

We eat breakfast, clean the house, then play school with the mice. Sometimes, we go back to bed for a snooze. About 9:30, Gary drops off her shots. They're labeled, "9:30, 10:30, 11:30." We go back to the clinic around noon for another blood pull, then I drop her off at the Amara's to play with the kids while I ride into town and run errands.

At 1:30, I pick up her shots (one or two), then bring her back at 3 for another pull. I'm back at 5 for more shots: "5:00, 6:00, 7:00, 8:00." By the end of the day, she's had it. Ten shots and three blood pulls later, she was ready for a little rest. After a lullaby, story, record, tape, or just talking, she falls off to sleep.

The isolation on the island was becoming unbearable. I had to decide whether to take Amber back to the 'States and face certain death, or stay here, in Freeport, living a pain-free life. I made the decision to stay. To do that, we'd need more supplies. Amber stayed with Gary, while I went back to Milford for a few days to collect back child support payments, check on the studio, and touch base with Linda and Judy.

### August 20, 1:45 pm

*I'm here, in Milford, sitting at my work table in Studio 3, looking down at the traffic below, people walking here and there, all of them with a purpose. "And life goes on." I went to the Milford Citizen, the New Haven Register, and Channel 8, asking for letters from the public to*

*Amber to help boost her moral. I also updated them on her treatment and our situation in the Bahamas.*

*I got back to the studio just in time to wipe off the layer of dust for the meeting at 7:30. It was an open meeting about cancer. Many different people were there: A nurse who works with cancer patients at Yale, some former patients and companions who were at Burton's clinic, two women who have cancer, some of my close friends, and many others. Our discussions took us well into the night. Seems like cancer is a very hot subject.*

*This morning, I went to The Fairfield Advocate and spoke with Jim Motavalli. He's writing an article about Amber and the "cancer cover up." After that, I went to the copy center to pick up the patient / companion newsletter I had printed, then drop off some film at the New Haven Register. They wanted some recent photos to accompany the update they're writing about Amber.*

*I met with Michael. He refused to pay the child support he owes: Over $450. "Why should I? You're getting along just fine on donations." "But Michael, you're her father, for God's sake. You are responsible for Amber, not Gary. He's been supporting us, not donations." No use; I can't fight him, the system, and cancer, too. My energy must be saved for the battle that lies ahead. I'm leaving for Freeport tomorrow. I miss Amber and Gary.*

Leaving the US was difficult but I knew my heart was in Freeport and Amber's best chance at survival was, too. I returned to the same nightmare I had left: People with cancer who were here as their last hope; many of them dying; isolation from our loved ones, conveniences we take for granted in the US—gone, pulling blood, giving shots, watching Amber's tumor grow and become bloody and necrotic. Even so, it felt good to be back. I was near Amber again, despite the big tumor on/in her head. For a short time, I didn't care. The only thing that mattered was that she was alive and had no pain. And I was near her again.

Gary had taken good care of her while I was gone. Really, he was the only father Amber knew. Both of them were like a couple of kids. Sometimes, I had a hard time figuring out who was the kid and who was the adult. I loved to watch them play. I was grateful for his company, but was sure I didn't show it. I knew I could count on him to be there for Amber and she knew it, too. Despite our relationship struggles, we were still a family.

### *September 6, 7:20 pm*

*Today, Amber and I talked.   She chose the subject.   I recorded the conversation.  The life she was living seemed to take on characters.*

- *Me: O.K., Amber, what were we just talkin' about...
  robbers, right?*
- *Amber: Right. If a big monster came and tried to ate us,
  would you shoot him?*
- *Me: No way!*
- *Amber: I would... would you?*
- *Me: How could you do that?*
- *Amber: Like this: When he was comin' near me... really...
  like about that far from here, I would shoot 'em... and he
  would be dead. Wouldn't you?*
- *Me: Wouldn't you feel bad?*
- *Amber: Why? I wouldn't! Monsters could eat ya. And I
  don't want monsters to eat me.*
- *Me: Hmmmmm... that makes sense.*
- *Amber: Doesn't it?*
- *Me: Uh huh.*
- *Amber: What if he ate you, what would you do?*
- *Me: I'd be dead. I couldn't do anything.*
- *Amber: If he was comin' near ya, what would you do? Take
  a boison (sic) apple? Or would you shoot him?*
- *Me: Take a poison apple.*
- *Amber: Where're ya gonna get it?*
- *Me: From my poison apple tree.*
- *Amber: Where is it?*
- *Me: In my backyard.*
- *Amber: Where? (giggles)*

- **Me:** Behind my house.
- **Amber:** Where's your house... what one... and where is it?
- **Me:** I'd buy one.
- **Amber:** (giggles) Oh! I have a good idea how to do it!
- **Me:** What? How?
- **Amber:** Kill 'em... lock 'em out. What if he eats the house? I would just shoot up the roof... wouldn't you?
- **Me:** Uh huh.
- **Amber:** I'd sneak out the window and go "POW!!!" and shoot up into the air... and a bow and arrow goes right stickin' in him, right?
- **Me:** Right!
- **Amber:** I would do that.
- **Me:** Hmmmmm...
- **Amber:** Would you?
- **Me:** I'd follow behind you while YOU did all that.
- **Amber:** How come?
- **Me:** It would be very entertaining.
- **Amber:** Would you be afraid that a monster might get you?
- **Me:** Yeah... wouldn't YOU be?
- **Amber:** Oh yeah! What if Gary gets killed and we're still alive? What would you do? Oh!
- **Me:** I don't know.
- **Amber:** Umm... mum... mum... go into the bushes and hide on 'em. We'll go past 'em and go back to our house and we'll see if we can find a boison apple and give it to 'em and say, "Eat this 'cuz it'll taste gooood." Right? Do it very sweetly, right?
- **Me:** Right! Boy! You do that pretty good... just like a witch.
- **Amber:** We could put on witch hats and everything... a broom... we could dress up like a witch and then we'll take the apple with us. We'll go give it to him and say, "No sense, my dear, just eat it." And he will eat it and he will DIE! (laughter) We'll say, "Close your eyes; it will taste gooood. Take a chunk of it, and swallow it, and you will die." (giggles) We'll trick 'em like that, right? Doesn't that sound like a good idea? Oh, no! There's a monster back there! POW!!!

- *Me: He's coming, Amber! Look at him... he's right by the chair!*
- *Amber: POW! POW! POW!*
- *Me: He's not dead... oh, there he is! Get him!*
- *Amber: POW! POW! Let me get some fire! Is he gettin' dead?*
- *Me: Yeah, now what are you gonna do with him?*
- *Amber: Leave him there.*
- *Me: Yuk! He'll rot and stink!*
- *Amber: Throw him down the chute!*
- *Me: What chute?*
- *Amber: The garbage chute!*

I was still involved with the patient/companion group I started and it seemed to be helping them, especially the newcomers. Since Burton's therapy was run from a clinic, not a hospital, each patient was required to have a companion to live with them to help with blood pulls, shots, housework, shopping, etc. In addition, they needed to arrange to live in one of several nearby apartment complexes or hotels. Most people were used to being at home and going to a doctor's office or being admitted to a hospital for treatment. The group made the adjustment easier; it gave them the contacts and resources to get them up and going. Fighting cancer was hard enough. I understood that. Besides, running the group made me feel worthwhile, like I was doing *something* to ease the pain, if not stop the madness.

Now that I had decided to stay in Freeport, I set about making our lives more permanent. I knew that apart from becoming a ballerina, more than anything, Amber wanted to go to "real school," not just preschool. I asked around town. "Sunland School." I heard it repeatedly. It wasn't far from our apartment, so I set an appointment and rode my bike over to speak with the principal.

The school was lovely. It was a yellow building with large, cartoon-like paintings all over the outside walls. The playground was well stocked with plenty of equipment: Swings, slides, etc. Palm trees surrounded the grounds and shaded the large playing field.

Hoping to make this Amber's school and fulfill her dreams, I walked into the principal's office, introduced myself, and explained why I wanted her to attend. "She has cancer and may not have long to live. Before she dies, I want to grant her this one last wish. Will you help me?" "I'd be delighted to have Amber attend school with us." He gave me a list of supplies and told me where to get uniforms.

I couldn't pedal the bike fast enough to get home to tell Amber. *"REAL SCHOOL... I get to go to REAL SCHOOL???"* I loved to see her happy, especially after enduring so much pain and uncertainty. Living with cancer in a foreign country was difficult and we did our best to cope... to transform our anguish into happiness and some sense of "normal." At some point, I'm not sure when, my mission switched from trying to save her life to helping her live whatever life she had left to the fullest. We rode our bike to the Town Centre and got all the school supplies on the list as well as her uniform. She could barely contain her joy; she wore her uniform and fondled her new purchases for most of the weekend.

Monday morning bright and early, Amber was in her uniform and waiting at the door; book bag on her back; lunch box in hand. "Come on, Mom, let's go. We're gonna be late!" She grabbed my hand and pulled me out the door, down the hall, to our bike. I aimed the bike towards the school and pushed those pedals as hard and as fast as I could. At this point, getting her to her dream was as important as saving her life or making sure she would live the rest of it to the fullest.

She was so thrilled, she could hardly stop moving while the principal introduced her to her teacher. She tried to overlook the tumor, but I could see her nearly jump back at the sight. While Amber busied herself in the playground, she expressed her concerns. "What should I tell the parents when they ask, 'Is it contagious?'" I told her it wasn't, but could certainly understand her asking. I explained what I knew about cancer. She seemed satisfied. I told her about our daily routine of blood pulls and shots. Since I would be there so often to administer the therapy, she invited me to help with her class.

On the playground, depending on the angle, Amber looked like any other child. She stood in line at the swings, the slide, the hopscotch, unaware of *what* was the focus of all the attention. *She couldn't see it because it was on her head.* Thank God she couldn't, except when she looked in the mirror. The tumor had grown to the size of an orange. It was massive. Her skin stretched to accommodate it and, as a result, was so thin it was transparent. It appeared to split in half with a valley down the middle. You could actually *see the cancer.* It was bizarre. The other children were naturally curious, but followed Amber's lead. "It's just a bump, that's all," she matter-of-factly dismissed it. *She* had grown accustomed to it, though they had not.

Most of the time, cancer is hidden *inside* the body. You don't see it, therefore it doesn't exist. In Amber's case, the tumor nearly hit you in the face. People noticed *it* before they noticed *her.* You couldn't ignore it, I couldn't pretend, and she became the victim of prejudice. How I wanted to break the silence about cancer and educate people to the reality of it! I wanted to do it instantly, so my daughter wouldn't have to suffer the effects of public ignorance. She could spend the rest of her life—however little that was—being accepted, cherished, and loved by all who had the honor of meeting her. I knew that my efforts to educate had to wait. Tending to Amber came first.

Despite my decision to stay in the Bahamas, I was desperate to find a surgeon to de-bulk the tumor... to give Burton's treatment a fighting chance. Calling from the Bahamas was unreliable and very expensive. I sent Michael a telegram: *"Cancer spread to the lymph nodes. Needs surgery. Situation urgent."* He responded: *"Touloukian out of country til end of month. Shall I try to find another surgeon?"* I tried to phone him to let him know how desperate the situation had become and to search—beg, if he had to—to find help. I couldn't get an answer. Frantically, both Gary and I called at regular intervals. A week later, Michael's phone was disconnected.

My life became a balancing act. On one hand, I was trying to live a normal life with my daughter: Dance lessons, school, trips to the beach. On the other, I was trying to keep the cancer from killing the only family I had ever truly known... the only bond that could never be broken.  I walked through my life on a tightrope; afraid to look too far ahead.  I dreaded the day when the first symptom appeared.

"Mom, I can't hear very well out of my right ear. Look inside and see if it's waxy, will ya?"  My heart stopped and so did my world.  Like a puppet master, I picked myself up—strings still attached—and began to manipulate the act of living.  My inner strength was gone; I had to call on something... someone... outside myself.  "God, I can't do it but YOU can. Please help me to live through this. I've never done this before. I am so weak... so human."

### September 14, 11 pm

*Today, while Amber was napping, I went into the bathroom, closed the door, sat on the floor and cried.  I cried until my tears ran dry.  As I sat in the darkness, I had a vision of us standing on the edge of a cliff.  The waves were crashing into the shore below and I could feel their thunderous pounding through my feet.  I'm holding her.  She's weeping. I'm trying to comfort her... reassure her... make sense out of the senseless. She is going to fall, I know.  She's not afraid of falling; SHE knows she can fly.  She's afraid to leave me behind to suffer my loss.  I feel the gravity of the earth pulling her from my arms; it's much stronger than my ability to hold on... to save her.  "How can I just stand here, watching her fall to her death?"  I feel the force tugging, pulling, ripping her out of my arms.  I want to jump with her, but my feet are stuck to the ground. A lightning bolts hits us.  I can feel it's burning energy as it splits our embrace apart.  I'm blinded by its flash and when I open my eyes, I see an angel.  "It looks like... AMBER!"*

*Lately she's been talking about ME dying.  She must be feeling the pain of impending separation.  One day, out of nowhere, she approached me— lips quivering, tears in her eyes—and asked, "Who's gonna be my Mommy if you die? Who will take care of me?"  I held her in my arms and rocked her.  "Gary will, honey. Gary will."  I knew that we would never come to that, but I also knew that she was asking for comfort... for reassurance... for a way to wrap herself around her fate and mine.  "It'll be okay."*

*This morning, she told me her dream: "Mom, I had a dream last night that I was five and I didn't see you for a while. Then I was twenty... big, like you, and I saw you!" I wonder, "When she dies, will I ever see her again? Part of me will die, too. Will I ever learn to live again... live without her? Why is she dying? What is the purpose for my loss? WHY IS THIS HAPPENING???"*

Though I struggled to hold on to a sense of control, I felt victimized by cancer... by society... by Michael. I wanted to forget him... just let him go. But for Amber's sake, I couldn't... I wouldn't. Gary was trying his best to be a father to Amber, but I was sure she felt rejected and abandoned by Michael. I could grant every wish but one. I couldn't change him into the loving, caring, unselfish father she needed by her side right now.

### *September 17, 10:45 pm*

*Gary just returned from the phone booth. He called Michael and finally got in touch with him. Evidently, he moved but neglected to tell us. He hasn't done a thing about getting a surgeon to de-bulk the tumor, sending Amber a letter or card, child support—nothing! "I had a reservation for the 28th, but I had to cancel it. I'll be down sometime in the future. Then I can see what's going on; whether you need a car, or money, or what." His arrogance is astounding! I'm glad Amber doesn't have to see it.*

Gary flew back to the 'States to see Todd and get some household supplies for our lengthy stay in Freeport. In the meantime, Amber and I moved into his apartment since we couldn't pay the rent in our own. We made moving day a game we played and we played this a lot in our lives: Whittier, California to Unionville, Connecticut to Canton to San Gabriel, California to Whittier to our car to Altadena to Milford, Connecticut to Ansonia to Totowa, New Jersey, West Haven, Connecticut, to our car to Milford to Stratford and to the Bahamas. Fifteen places in her short life of four years. It was hard to believe and difficult to accept.

We packed up our belongings and loaded up the shopping cart that people used for heavy loads in the apartment complex.

Amber climbed on top. I "drove" her down the halls, into the elevator, and up to the fourth floor to Charlie and Debbie's old apartment. Walking in, I was reminded of Charlie. Oh, how my heart ached at the memory of this vibrant, vital young man who had his whole future before him and his beautiful woman at his side; his life... his future needlessly was snatched away. I simply could not forget him or the many others that faced the same fate. My Life Task was beginning to unfold though I didn't know it at the time.

School was the center of our lives; therapy came second. When the time came for her shot, I'd peek around the corner of her classroom and give her the signal. She'd follow me into the teacher's bathroom, I'd lift her skirt, drop her panties, and pop one in. Then she hurried back to class; she didn't want to miss a thing. Blood pulls were a little trickier. I'd put her on the bathroom counter, draw her blood, send her back to class, take her blood to the clinic, wait for her shots, then ride back to school. My timing had to be perfect.

I was SO glad that we'd brought our bicycle for transportation. It was the same trusty blue bike that I bought at the thrift shop in Whittier for $13. It had taken us through rain and snow and now the searing Bahamian sun. We survived the summer, but now, with Amber getting sicker, I hated to have to ride her on the back in the searing sun, though she didn't seem to mind. She loved riding along the streets of Freeport waving to the people she knew. When she was tired, she would put her head on my back, pull the hood of her sweatshirt over her head, wrap her arms around me, and fall right to sleep.

My split personality was becoming more obvious. I felt schizophrenic, like I was two completely separate sides of the same coin, just like my childhood: "Patti A and Patti B." I could drift between the two in an instant. "Side A" was coping really well; it didn't bother her a bit. She took care of Amber, of other cancer patients, of herself. Her life was normal. She could laugh, be optimistic, responsible, friendly, have hope for the future. "Side B" was hiding. I suspected her existence, but I never really met her. I could see her self-destructing habits rear their ugly heads, every so often. I came close to knowing her several times, but it would be years before I was introduced. In the meantime, "Side A" was the *real* me; "Side B" only a shadow.

### September 19, 2 am

*Last night, and again tonight, Amber told me that her "bump was hurting." She woke up an hour ago, crying in pain. "Where does it hurt, Amber?" "All over my head, Mom. All over my head." I gave her some aspirin, then rubbed her back until she fell asleep again. Then I lay next to her thinking... thinking... thinking. I've decided to take her back to the 'States as soon as possible. If I go to an emergency room, they'll HAVE to treat her. I know she needs to have this tumor de-bulked NOW. It's huge and growing out of control.*

*She's so beautiful and precious. She's all I have, Lord. I don't want to lose her. The pain... the thought of it... is more than I can bear. Will I survive her death? Amber... oh, Amber. I hope you don't suffer. God, it's the only thing I ask: PLEASE DON'T MAKE HER SUFFER... PLEASE!!!*

Like some sort of morbid word game, I had to pick and choose my words very carefully. I had a lot of practice before now, so they came out spontaneously, as though they reflected my true thoughts. The Bahamians were more direct. They could not understand how a child could have cancer. Everywhere we went, the subject came up. "What's that... a boil?" "No, it's cancer." *"Cancer? Your baby got CANCER??? I didn't know babies got cancer! She gettin' better???"* "We take things day by day and leave the rest to God." Or, "She's getting better and better every day." I twisted the truth. She *was* getting better spiritually, if not physically. "She gonna die?" "We're all going to die someday. Some sooner than others. We just don't know when our time is up, do we?" I didn't want Amber to listen to this, so I politely excused myself and went on with our day to day living.

### September 22, 9:15 pm

*This evening while Amber was in the shower, I decided to clean the mice's cage. I heard the water falling on to the floor of the tub, then gasps. "MOMMY!" I ran to the bathroom, pulled back the shower curtain, and saw a trail of blood dripping down over her shoulder. My body was just a shell; inside I collapsed into a thousand pieces, but for her sake, I held myself together. "Hey, girl, what's this?" "I don't know. My bump just started bleeding."*

*I looked closely and could see blood coming out of the crack, the split in the tumor. I quickly took a washcloth and put pressure on it until the bleeding stopped. I hoped she couldn't feel my hand quivering and changed the subject. "Hey, those mice had a pretty messy cage, you know. Next time, you get to clean it and smell their poops! Did you tell Joanna about your new school?" "Yeah." "Well, what does she think?" As Amber rattled on and on, I washed the blood off, dried her, put her jammies on, and lay down next to her to read. I was grateful for another night together. There won't be many more.*

I was at a crossroads. To the left, certain and painful death; to the right, *un*certain and painful death. "Do I leave the Bahamas and take a chance on finding a doctor who will help her once we get back to the 'States, or do I stay and hope to find someone *before* she leaves Dr. Burton's care?" So far, we had no success finding a doctor to help us... to de-bulk the tumor so that the immunotherapy would have a chance. Communication to the mainland was tenuous. It was difficult, if not impossible, to make calls from a phone booth.

I spoke with Dr. Burton. He agreed that the time to de-bulk the tumor was *now*. We didn't have the time to waste. Burton was frank. "Who the hell are you gonna get to do it? No one's gonna touch her. She's 'hot'... too much publicity... you went outside the establishment for treatment... their careers are at stake." "But she's *innocent!*" He shook his head in disgust as if to say, *"That* doesn't matter, Patti." He knew all too well about the politics... the money... the profits at stake. I had no idea. I was just a mother who was trying to save her child's life.

With regret, we made plans to leave the clinic. The pain that she was now beginning to experience frightened me; I wanted her to be near a well-equipped hospital with advanced pain relief techniques. Dr. Burton called a doctor in Miami who would examine her to see if he could recommend a surgeon. I scheduled a gap of several hours between the time we landed in Miami and left for New York to see him.

I packed what I could take on the plane, locked the apartment, and paid our last visit to the clinic. It was very sad. I could see in Dr. Burton's eyes, that he had grown to love Amber and wished he could've done more. I know he felt like a failure, but I tried to let him know how much I appreciated all that he'd done for us. He hugged her. In that embrace, I saw a man who had spent his whole life wanting to save humanity and a little girl who was the epitome... the symbol of cancer. I left thinking, "God! If he only had a fully staffed and funded clinic in the United States, the wonders he could do!"

The clinic staff tried their best to be cheerful and optimistic. "Take care now, Amber." They'd take their turns hugging her, then turn away so she couldn't see their tears. All of them desperately wished they could make her well, help her live a full and happy life. Each of them showed us kindness, caring, professionalism, and a side of humanity that we missed in most of the doctors we'd seen in the 'States.

The last stop was Dr. Clement. He was a strong man, but I could see him teetering on the verge of weak and vulnerable. "I'm sorry we couldn't do more for Amber. I've written this letter; maybe it will help." He paused, then handed it to me. He bent down to Amber. "You take care of your Mom now, Amber." Our eyes linked but didn't linger. There was no time to waste. We left his office, walked out the door of the clinic, and got into the taxi that was waiting to take us to the airport. As we sat in the back seat and watched the clinic... the Freeport we'd grown to love go by in a blur, I took out the letter and read it to myself.

*Dear Doctor,*

*I should be grateful if you would see Amber Calistro, age four and a half. Amber has rhabdomyosarcoma of right post auricular region, excised in March 1980, in Connecticut.*

*Amber's mother has elected for a trial of immunotherapy for the recurrence of the tumor, and it seems there has been some control of the tumor. However, the amount of tumor is such, that it seems most unlikely to be successful. We are, therefore, most interested in a surgical attempt to de-bulk the tumor, and be most grateful for your help.*

*Yours sincerely,*

*John Clement*

Our stay in the Bahamas had come to an end. Although Burton's serum had controlled the initial metastasis, her ordeal with tonsillitis taxed her immune system and drove the cancer out of control. From that point on, we were struggling to stay one step ahead of the "man-eating monster" that was threatening to eat my baby alive. David Stewart and the Canadians had reached out far beyond the borders to save Amber's life. It was certainly an enormous effort on a worldwide scale. Everyone who knew—or knew of Amber—wanted to help her live.

I replayed our time in Freeport as the taxi sped along. All the people we'd met during our five month stay were now part of our past: Patients, companions, Burton, Clement, the staff at the clinic, the locals at the Town Centre. So many of them cared for us... cared for Amber. They helped us to forget the tragedy of cancer, look beyond it for the goodness that life had to offer, and to cherish the people that came into our lives. However briefly, our paths had crossed, and we gave to each other a gift that would last: Our love, the memories we shared, and our time here on earth. This little girl was a great teacher; she taught all of us about the true meaning of love and life: Live life to the fullest and "in the moment," for this is all we have.

While we flew to Miami to see the two doctors that Dr. Burton recommended, Gary stayed behind to finish his work at the clinic and close up the apartment, then head back to Milford to search for a surgeon to help us de-bulk the growing tumor. After our doctor visits, Amber and I would meet him there.

We knew it would be difficult to find someone who would put aside the politics of cancer and the glare of the public eye and do all they could to save Amber's life. We had grave doubts they could... they would. We were now in the news and out in the open. More importantly, the fact that we had gone outside the "Medical Establishment" for additional therapy was a hurdle that no American doctor we'd contacted from the Bahamas would overlook or work with or accept. "Beg if you have to," I said with sadness at our parting. "I love you, Gary. I can never repay you for all that you've done for me, and especially for Amber." "I'll do whatever it takes to find a surgeon," he promised. I knew he would keep his promise; he always did.

We boarded the plane for Miami. I was nearly out of hope, but unwilling to let her die. Forward was the only way to go. As the plane lifted off the runway, I could feel my spirits begin to sink. The sound of Amber's voice lifted them up and kept me from drowning in my own self pity. "Mom, look! There's the clinic... Kwan Yin... our Naked Beach!"

Our future was uncertain and unyielding, but for now, I *did* have Amber, this moment, and our beautiful memories. No one could take my memories away.

Making memories
in Montreal

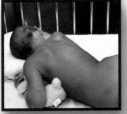

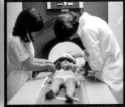

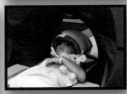

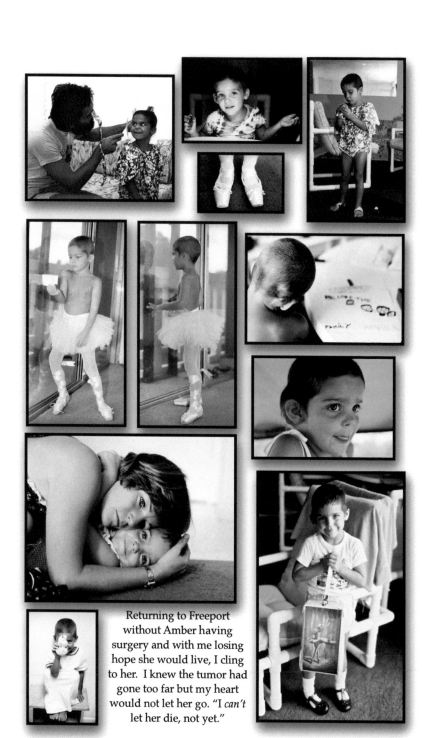

Returning to Freeport without Amber having surgery and with me losing hope she would live, I cling to her. I knew the tumor had gone too far but my heart would not let her go. "I *can't* let her die, not yet."

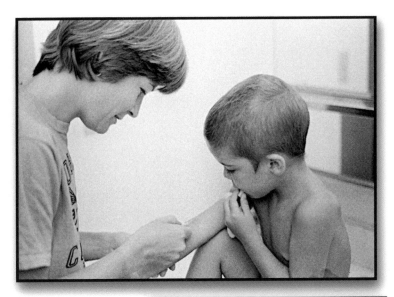

Amber continued to amaze me. Each day was filled with blood pulls and shots, yet she still kept her positive, sweet, uplifting attitude. It was hard to live this life day in, day out... to watch her endure. But when I thought of all that *she* lived with, *my* pain was insignificant.

In late August, Amber began to get discouraged. To lift her spirits, Dr. Burton gave her a couple of mice from his lab. She named them Money and Nickel. The moment she got them, her life... her spirits were lifted.

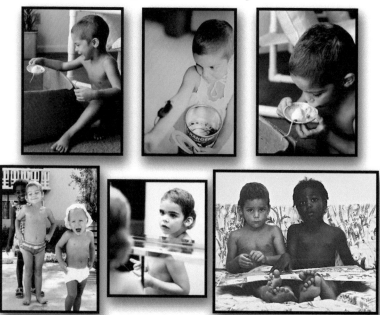

As the tumor grew, so did my determination to fulfill Amber's dreams. I signed her up for dance class and to go to *real* school—Sunland School. She was thrilled!

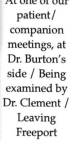

At one of our patient/companion meetings, at Dr. Burton's side / Being examined by Dr. Clement / Leaving Freeport

# Chapter 13

## *The Key to Heaven*

*"God pours life into death and death into life without a drop
being spilled."* —Author Unknown

Upon arriving in Miami, I was in a time crunch. I had less
than an hour and a half to get our luggage, store it in a locker, and
catch the bus to the section of town where Dr. Mencia's office was
located. This was my first time in Miami and I had no idea where
we were. I finally found a map and, with the help of an airport
worker, was pointed in the direction of the correct bus stop.

The bus was loaded with people. Amber wouldn't wear her
hat and no matter what I said, the answer was always the same:
"No." I wanted to sit in the last row so that no one could sit behind
us... no one could stare. I checked it out. "Full." Three rows from
the back, two seats were empty. We headed for them. As we sat
down, I could hear the teenagers behind us whispering. "I hope
Amber doesn't hear them." I made small talk with her, hoping to
drown them out. It was a very long ride. At times, I felt
compelled to explain, but I didn't want to put Amber through it;
she'd been through so much already. Some people had no regard
for her; they would say anything at all with no thought to the fact
that *she was there, she was listening, and SHE was the one with the huge
tumor that was eating her alive!*

Two buses and a transfer later, we were dropped at a corner.
According to the map, it was a long way from Dr. Mencia's office.
We had to walk the rest of the way and we didn't have much time
before our scheduled appointment. With the midday sun beating
down on us, we picked up our pace. Amber was tired and hungry
and started to cry. "Mommy, I can't walk anymore." "That's O.K.,

Amber. I'll carry you." I gave her a drink of the juice I'd brought, then I scooped her up. We had quite a distance to go, so I shaded her from the sun with my hat, and kept on walking. Almost instantly, she fell asleep. Oh, how I longed to give her a good life, free from the pain, struggle, and cancer. I raced down the street as if *that* life was waiting for us, not the one ahead.

Again, I was drifting above our lives, looking down. It was like watching a movie. I saw myself walking, nearly running down the road in the hot sun. I checked my watch. "Twenty minutes to go. God, I hope I make it." There was a backpack on my back, a large bag on one shoulder, Amber's head on the other, moving in time with each step. "I'm hot... tired... thirsty... I want to rest. I want to remove my heavy load; not only Amber, but the weight of the world as well. I want to give up. Damn! I don't want to be doing this! *What is driving me on???*" With all of my heart, I wanted to stop. But my legs kept moving. They were sore but I couldn't feel them. "I am here. I am moving you forward. Think your own thoughts; feel your own feelings. I will help you choose... speak for you... move you in the right direction." I heard Him, but I didn't see Him, and I *still* felt all alone on the streets of Miami. Nothing changed—not the hot sun, the weight of my daughter, or the fact that my legs were beginning to ache. In a moment, we were on Kendall Ave. and walking up to Dr. Mencia's office.

I stepped from the desert and into a cool oasis. It smelled like a doctor's office. "Typical," I thought. Amber woke up. I gave her a drink of water, fed her a snack, and waited. Thirty minutes later, we saw the doctor. I reviewed her history as briefly as I could. He studied the tumor without regard for the person it was attached to: Amber. He read Clement's letter, then turned to me. "Do you intend to stay around here? I don't want to just be a technician. I won't just do the surgery and that's it. I want to take care of the whole child... take her to an oncologist and see what *he* thinks would be best for her." "But I don't *want* to give her chemotherapy... no sense putting poisons in her body." "You're not a doctor." "No, but I'm educated." "You're not 'up' on the latest treatments for cancer." "Yes, I *am.*" Clearly the conversation was going nowhere and *fast.* He wasn't accustomed to his patients asking questions or challenging his advice. "Why won't you just de-bulk it, that's *all?*" He flatly refused to answer my question and "politely" finished our visit.

I left his office feeling spunky and indignant. "At least I held on to my principles." Another side of me responded. "So what? What good did it do you or Amber?" I stuffed "Patti A and B" deep into my soul for the time being. I didn't have time to dwell on myself; I was back in the 'States to *save Amber's life,* not take a stand. On to the next hope, the next appointment.

Jackson Memorial Hospital was enormous. I hadn't been in such a large medical facility since Montreal and before that, Yale-New Haven. It was overpowering. Dr. Fix could see that we felt a little intimidated. He did his best to put us at ease and bolster our spirits. "I agree. She does need surgery. Since I'm a radiologist, not a surgeon, I'll have to consult with one on staff. I'm willing to work *with* you, though. Whatever therapy you choose, I will respect your decision." I was pleasantly surprised, even encouraged, at his willingness to cooperate and consider my point of view. I walked to the receptionist with a bounce in my step.

"Excuse me, can you tell me how to get to Miami International Airport? Where can I catch the nearest bus?" She looked at Amber who was, by now, exhausted and frail. "Are you *sure* you want to take a *bus* there?" As we were talking, a man came up. "Excuse me, I overheard you talking. I'm waiting for my wife to finish radiation treatments, but if you can wait, I'll be glad to take you to the airport." To say I was grateful, would be an understatement. What I felt was beyond gratitude; I felt the grace of God and saw Him in this man. "Thank you," I muttered, "I *really* appreciate that." We got to the airport with time to spare and sat down to eat dinner and watch the planes taking off and landing, one of our favorite pastimes.

### *September 29, 9:50 pm*

*I went to Yale today to see Dr. Touloukian. I felt as though I had received the education of a lifetime in the six months since we last met. I know he did his best with Amber; he was the only one at Yale who believed me. He will not do the surgery, but gave me the name of a surgeon he trusts: Bernie Siegel. He spoke very highly of him.*

*He also opened my eyes about cancer and what to expect: The sights AND the smells. He tried to be gentle, I know, but how do you gently chop off someone's arm with a butter knife??? He doesn't see much hope for her survival. Quite frankly, neither do I. But as feeble as my hope is, I must keep trying. I am not ready to let her go. I am not ready to let her die.*

I made an appointment with Dr. Bernie Siegel. Upon entering his office, I knew this man was different; but the skeptic in me said, "Don't even hope." The atmosphere was casual. Magazines about health, including *alternative* health magazines, were lying on the tables. "This feels like someone's living room," I thought in disbelief. His receptionist was warm and friendly. "Bernie will be right with you." *"BERNIE?* Even *she* called him Bernie. I wonder if he's a *real* doctor." Having "been through the wringer" with doctors for the last year and a half, my expectations were fairly low.

I expected to be waiting forever in the Waiting Room, just like I had countless time before in countless other doctor's offices. Old, *way* outdated magazines would be next to stiff and uncomfortable chairs. The receptionist would be preoccupied with her coworkers (what they did over the weekend, how their kids were, spouses, boyfriends, etc.) and only look up as a second thought or as though I was interrupting. "Can I help you?" in a snotty, rude, why-did-you-interrupt-me tone. Of course, I would have to have all of my paperwork filled out correctly and all the proper documents in hand. Then I would be told to sit and wait... and wait... without any further words or updates or apologies from them. My time meant nothing; I was there to wait.

From there, I'd go into an Examining Room with Amber in tow and wait for the doctor. He/she would walk in, say, "Hello," then set about the business of examining her tumor. After wiggling it, pressing it, and measuring it, a pronouncement would be made. With little or no regard for Amber, the person, they would tell me what they thought was the best solution... the wisest protocol. Any questions I had would be met with disdain and their self-righteousness would attempt to dominate the conversation. But for a few exceptions (who redeemed their colleagues in my mind), this was my experience with "Medical Establishment" doctors. Definitely *not* with Bernie. He was different, even human.

We were invited into the back and led down a hall to an Examining Room. I was delighted at the difference. The door opened and a good looking gentleman in his forties walked in. "Hmmm... kind eyes... a nice smile... a *bald head?"* "Hi, I'm Bernie Siegel." He shook my hand then looked down at Amber. *"You* must be Amber." They shook hands and were instantly connected. Without giving me another look, he started talking... and talking... and talking with *Amber!* I was rightfully in second place. Amber was the one; it was her life, not mine, and Bernie knew it. This meeting was hers. He was not in a hurry and I patiently waited until they were finished before I briefed him on Amber's journey. Then he examined her. He touched her so gently and with such care, that she seemed be one of his own. I was nearly moved to tears but held them back. I had to; I couldn't let anyone see my soul.

From Bernie's lips, a miracle. "I'll do the surgery. I'm willing to take full responsibility for Amber's life while she's on the table. I'll treat her as my own," he assured me. "What about the publicity... the controversy... the pressure from the 'Medical Establishment'?" He smiled. "I don't *have* to be a doctor." Taken aback, I was pleasantly surprised. He said it so casually and without forethought, that I knew he meant it. I was very impressed and so was Amber. She could see that he cared. He seemed to be a human being, just being *human.* He was not a doctor... a robot... a machine. Bernie actually *cared!* His philosophy of life, cancer, and death was so refreshing and unusual, I hardly knew what to think.

"I want to admit her to St. Raphael's Hospital on Monday, run some tests, and bring in a team of specialists to see exactly how far the cancer had spread and whether surgery is even possible." Finally, I could let go, fall into someone's arms—if only figuratively—and let them take charge of our life... of Amber's life.

A wave of joy mixed with trepidation washed over me, but I needed to surrender. I willingly followed his orders and thankfully gave up control.

### October 4, 9 pm

*The room is dark. I'm sitting next to Amber's bed. The light from the hall is streaming in, hitting my pen and paper, illuminating these words and my thoughts. If I close my eyes, my mind races ahead to look at the future. It will come soon enough and it's too frightening to face, so I stay awake until I can't anymore. Then the only peace I have left—sleep—works its magic.*

*We checked into St. Raphael's this morning and had a very busy day. Amber had a headache earlier and the nurse gave her some aspirin with codeine to help her sleep. Thank God. Sleep is HER only reprieve as well.*

*She went for a CT scan, a few x-rays, and various blood tests. The scan shows that the tumor has invaded a 3-4cm section of her mastoid (the bone behind her ear), and part of the petris bone. Her face has drooped on the right side. Alvin Greenburg, a neurosurgeon, said, "The seventh facial nerve that controls the facial muscles is affected. Either the tumor has invaded it or put pressure on it." He suggested a team effort: A plastic surgeon, an ear surgeon, Bernie, and himself. He added, "This will be a major undertaking... an all day operation... at least twelve hours." I asked if I could watch. I didn't want to leave her side, even if I couldn't be in the operating room and had to watch her on camera. "We can videotape parts of the operation that would not be done under the microscope, but we don't have the facilities to tape the gross dissection."*

We did our best to enjoy our stay at the hospital, but the pain was more frequent and more intense. The tumor was so visible... so huge... so necrotic, bloody, and glaring. I could not believe she was living with this "beast" both inside AND outside her skull! Between the waves of pain, we played with her dolls, walked around the floor visiting with the nurses, or went to the playroom to play with the other kids. I was running out of ways to distract her and found myself feeling increasingly impotent... more inept and small.

Bernie and Greenberg were still optimistic and so, as faint as it was, my hope had not died. As long as there was a sliver, I would not let her go. She had to have more blood tests and an angiogram to show us a map of her blood vessels, veins, and arteries. If any major arteries were feeding the tumor, surgery was out of the question. She would die on the table for sure. The next step was a meeting between the four surgeons. Later, I would hear their recommendation. "Will she live... or will she die?" For the first time since our journey began, the answer to this question would be carved in stone with no room for doubt... no possibility to erase it. One way or the other, we would know if she would live or die. Period.

The changes Amber was beginning to go through... my God, the changes. The right side of her face didn't work anymore; it just stopped. When she laughed or cried or talked, only half of her face moved. "Mom, I get *SO* mad! I try to make *this* side of my face go up," as she points to her right side, "and it won't!" She pushed up on her right cheek... as if forcing it would make it move. I tried to encourage her... to see things through her eyes... to make a game of it. "Well, Amber, your face is tired and it just wants to rest for a while." I'm not sure she was convinced, but she played along anyway.

The tumor was grotesque. It was HUGE—about the size of a grapefruit—necrotic, bloody, full of pus, and crusty. Like cottage cheese and blood under a thin membrane, it was nearly unbearable to realize that it was *IN* Amber and it was relentless in its crusade to consume my beautiful little girl. It was painful just to *look* at it, much less *feel* it. I could not imagine what it felt like to her, but I tried. "Cancer is the multiplication of cells. Uncontrolled, they go haywire, invading everything in their path: Muscle, tissue, nerves, skin, bones. Nothing is spared. *That tumor is literally eating my little girl alive!!!*"

*October 5, 8:10 pm*

*This afternoon, after Amber went to sleep, Gary and I left her in the care of the nurses and went out for a little while. In addition to the doctors, the nurses are truly amazing: Kind, caring, they embrace Amber as their own. I needed the fresh air and to know that life existed in spite of cancer. We left her a note: "We are going to get some surprises for you. Be back shortly. We love you! Us."*

*We drove to a nearby shop, The Yale Co-op. As I stood near the counter waiting for Gary to pay for his things, I heard the voice again. It was the same familiar voice of guidance that accompanied me throughout my life. But now I knew it was God. "Turn around." I did. I looked around to see if anyone else heard it. People were milling about as usual. "Look over there." I scanned the shop. My eyes stopped at a large, shiny, brass key. "Give this to Amber. It is the Key to Heaven. Tell her that she won't have to knock, she can open the Golden Gates herself." I did as I was told.*

*When we returned to our room, she was just waking up. "Hey, girl, how're you doin'?" "Good. Where were you guys?" "We went to get you some goodies and presents." We poured them onto her lap. It was like Christmas. "Amber, God told me to give this to you." I handed her The Key. "Oooo... it's so shiny." She held it and stroked it with reverence. "Whenever you feel like you're going to die, just hold on real tight, and this will open the Gates of Heaven." Her eyes lit up. "REALLY???" "Really."*

*Life and death are not as serious and solemn to children as they are to adults; that only comes with age. She can easily relate to fantasies, games, drawings, and symbols. The Key to Heaven is a good, tangible, connection to God... to His house. It is something she can understand and cling to as she crosses over "the threshold" between life and death.*

### October 6, 11 pm

*Gary came in this morning while Amber was getting some tests and brought some balloons with him. He spelled "AMBER" and "TODD" on the wall. When she came back to the room, she squealed with delight. "Mom, look what Gar did!" He also brought her "Barbie Party" from Bambi's and some fresh clothes for both of us. He even ironed my dress!*

*He's been so good to us throughout this ordeal. I owe him my life. He will always have my heart.*

*Bernie introduced us to a technique, pioneered by Susan Bach, called "Spontaneous Drawing." It would help us to better understand Amber's deep, inner feelings; it is a way for her to express them without using words. He explained. "You can read her drawings—the objects she chooses, their placement on the paper, the color, shape, and number. Red depicts anger or rage; while black is the color of grief. Yellow indicates energy. Orange reveals an openness to change. Brown, blue, and green symbolize health. Purple shows a person's spiritual side. A lot of white in a drawing means that a person is covering something up." I was intrigued. He went on. "The position of the objects on the paper also offers insight into a person's feelings. Drawings that are concentrated in the bottom right quadrant of the paper, shows that a person is preoccupied with the near future. While figures in the upper right, show concern over the present. The bottom, left indicates thoughts about the past; while the top, left illustrates feelings about the distant future or death."*

*We went into Amber's room. He handed her a blank, 8 ½ x 11" piece of white paper, eight crayons (the basic colors) and asked her to draw a picture. Later, he interpreted for me: "You see in the upper left corner, she drew her name in green, surrounded it with a purple circle, framed it in black, and put many multicolored circles radiating from it. I interpret it as her seeing herself as healthy—spiritually, but the event of her death is sad and she has many mixed emotions about it."*

### October 7, 10:25 am

*Amber is downstairs in Radiation getting an angiogram. This morning at 6, she got an injection of Seconal and Atrophine. She fell into a deep sleep until 8, when they took her to the x-ray room. She was groggy, but recognized me. "Hi, Mom..." She gave me a faint smile and then she closed her eyes again. She had a slight fever, but seemed to be at peace.*
*Last night at 11:30, she woke up holding her head and writhing about, screaming, "Oh, God! Why are You making my head hurt??? Please help me!!! Pleeease, GOD!!!" Gary and I tried to comfort her. We got some codeine from the nurse and gave it to her. Half an hour later, she was in a*

*dreamlike stupor. At this point, I think that's where she belongs. Just enough to be out of pain but lucid.*

*Bernie came by earlier this morning to deliver the "sentence." "After talking with Dr. Mombello, I feel increasingly inclined NOT to attempt surgery. What will it do for her?" He feels she is ready to die, especially after looking at her drawings.*

*After he left, I sat in our empty hospital room absorbing every detail. I looked at her bed and imagined her there, next to her Sheepy who lay waiting patiently for her return. Then, my eyes followed the path around the room. "The balloons on the wall... the window with the shade pulled down... Barbie's Party... her school books... cards from friends and strangers... THE KEY." My eyes were transfixed. "Let her go... let her die... let her come to Me." Reluctantly, I surrendered to God's will.*

*With no choice left, I must accept her fate... her destiny and mine. Hope for her life is replaced by apprehension of her death. I cannot hold her back. I need to learn how to help her over the threshold between life and death. I need to allow her glory to shine... her purpose to be revealed... her life to have meaning and impact for those of us left behind. I need to let her die.*

*I walked down to the chapel to have a conference with God. "God, I need to SEE You, not just HEAR You. Please show me that You exist. I need proof. Help me guide Amber through the agony of cancer, to her death and beyond... to come back to You." He wouldn't appear on command, or demand, or even talk to me when I wanted Him to. I had no control; it was the other way around. I would have to stay open to listen, believe on faith alone, and if He chose to give me a sign, He would.*

Our last chance at living was over. I had given her life, struggled to make it better, fought to save it, and now it was time to let her go. I needed to give her up to God and make the rest of her life as fulfilling and painless as possible, treasure each second —for it could be our last, and help prepare her for the spiritual journey she was about to undertake. "Document everything... *everything.* Don't miss a word. Each one is priceless."

Fanatical, that's what I was. I bought a case of cassette tapes and started recording every waking moment with Amber. Her experience was so incredible... so unbelievable... I wanted to preserve it. I didn't want her death to erase her life. It had meaning and purpose, but I wasn't sure exactly what it was. I suspected it had something to do with her life with cancer, but more so, her death because of it and the precious few years she had on this earth. I'd never had anyone close to me die, but I knew Amber's death was special—an event—and my whole life revolved around it.

## *October 8, 3:10 pm*

*We checked out of St. Raphael's this morning. The staff and the surgeons who came to our rescue and fought so gallantly to save her life, now stepped aside to let fate take its course. Dr. Knowlton, a radiologist, offered to work with us to make the rest of Amber's life as pain-free as possible. He will give her radiation as needed, to help ease the pain she is expected to have as the tumor grows. Everyone here has been so kind and caring. They treated Amber as their own.*

*Right now we're at the Laundromat. Gary is watching me as I sit on the hood of my Volkswagen with my typewriter before me, typing away. Amber is asleep on the back seat. This journal is my only solace. It is the only place where I can say my deepest thoughts and feelings without being judged or condemned. I need this secret, sacred place to set down my load, if only for a short time. I need to rest in a safe, quiet place, undisturbed and without measure.*

*Earlier, we went through such an ordeal with Amber. She is having intense pain in her ear and head. Sometimes, I want to knock her out and chop this tumor off myself! Her cries and screams pierce my very soul. I feel I am dying with her. "Mom, I don't want to die. I want to help you. I don't want to leave you. OW, Mommy, OW! Please stop paining bump! Pleeease!!!"*

*I know she doesn't understand what is happening to her. How could she? Although I understand it, I cannot ACCEPT it. I WILL NEVER*

*ACCEPT CANCER. If it's eating Amber alive, it's eating other people alive, too. They are just as precious to their loved ones as Amber is to me. No one who is touched by cancer will ever accept it as "just a part of life." That would mean this pathetic, useless, insignificant THING... this tumor... this perfect example of cancer, has won The War. I will let Amber die now only because I HAVE to, but I don't have to accept defeat in The War on Cancer.*

*She just woke up and is helping me type. "Mom, will you type some messages from me?" "Sure, Amber. Fire away." "Amber loves Patti. Amber, I will get the bubbles. I'll buy you a rose, if you buy me a cup of coffee. Amber and Todd love each other."*

It was good to be back to see Todd again. Though he could stay with us only on weekends, it gave us an opportunity to be reunited as a family. Our days on Sea Wing were too short and the ones we had left were numbered, so we wasted no time building memories. Todd had known and loved Amber before the tumor and it made no difference now. He still didn't see it as grotesque or repulsive; he saw it as Amber... simply a part of Amber, his sister.

We wanted to get married—all of us—so we went to the local KMart and picked out four rings. That night, we lit some candles, sat around in a circle holdings hands, said a few ritual things, clapped our hands four times, and pronounced ourselves "married." Then we kissed and hugged and celebrated by indulging in ice cream.

Linda and Judy were keeping the public informed. The articles they wrote touched the lives of so many people; most of them were strangers before this. Again, I could feel how all of us were connected... linked together by cancer and by Amber.

We resumed our daily routine of checking the mail at the post office. *Everyone* knew "the little girl who was dying from cancer," from the postal workers, to the checkout girl at the grocery store, to the folks at "Maxine's," our favorite breakfast place. Once again, the town of Milford had opened their hearts for Amber. Though it was a small town, it had a very big heart. People reached out and did what they could to make our life better. Everywhere we went she was recognized.

I did want her to be famous, but not from *this*. I wanted her to be known and loved as "the little girl who was such a fantastic model." I wanted her to be admired for her *beauty*, not the overwhelming reality of her ugly, grotesque *tumor*. She would take their breath away with her radiance and goodness, not make them gasp from fear at the sight of her. Her life now was *exactly opposite* of The Dream... My Dream... the fantasy I had all those years ago.

Her death was imminent. She was on her way to Heaven and I stepped aside to let her pass me by. I was not alone. Millions of people who had joined Amber's fight were with me. Those who stood by her and prayed that her life would be spared, now stood on the sidelines with me, honoring her courage and dignity as she bravely walked to her death. Amber belonged to all of us. "Amber is not your child. She came *through* you, but *from* Me." I realized why I felt more like her guardian than her mother. I was simply the doorway through which she came into the world. "Amber is My messenger. She is *living* My message to the world and you are going to deliver it."

I was certain that no one would listen to me, but everyone would listen to Amber. And they did. People everywhere were listening. Although there were wars going on, natural disasters, a presidential election, crime, the trappings of lust, power, and greed, sports events, and people wrapped up in their own lives, Amber was touching them. I needed only to read their letters to see that.

*"... Don't give up hope. Everyone is thinking about you; you are a very special little girl because you have shown all of us that age and size do not matter, when it comes to true spirit of the heart and having courage. I love you, Amber."* —Marie Saddig

*"... I know your head doesn't feel good. But just wait 'til the Lord lays His hand on you."* —Love, Fay

*"**A**... is for the apple of your eye.*
*  **M**... is for the moonbeams in your smile.*

*B... is for the beauty that you hold.*
*E... is for every laugh you share.*
*R... is for the rainbows that you climb.*
*Put it all together and what does it spell? AMBER. God's special child."*
—Ann Dalbero

*"... I hope this letter makes you feel happy, because if it doesn't, throw it away."* —Jim Laughlin

*"... We all hope you live. If you die, we will all remember you from this day on."* —Sincerely, Tom Herth

*"... I hope they can find a cure for cancer. The whole world is depending on it. I am depending on them, too, because my grandfather has it. Well, I hope they can cure it."* —Blaise Wozniak

*"... I feel bad about the hole (sic) thing."* —Sincerely, Carol McVerry

*"... Amber, a girl in our class brought in an article about you and we were very sad and hope you feel better and get rid of your tumor. Do you feel uncomfortable? We all want you to get better and we don't want you to feel lonely. Amber, we hope you live."* —Sincerely, Erica Caruso

*"... Your illness is for all of us to feel and look at. I'm certain you touched all of our hearts. How much you've done for so many; in so little time. I pray to God that each and every day of my life, I wake up thinking of you and how brave and beautiful you and your Mom are. I'll keep you in my heart and prayers each day of my life, and I thank you for making life better for me. God bless you."* —Joanne T. Tew

*"... Wishing you the courage to accept the will of God, and some relief knowing others are with you in thought."* —Sincerely yours, Katherine La Torraca

*"... We can't imagine what you all must be going through. We only know how much we want to help. We all fell so much in love with Amber, right into her spell, as I'm sure everyone does, who meets her. We care so much*

*about what is happening in all of your lives. Just let us know what to do. There has to be more."* -- Lisa, Bob, and Carly Evans

Without these letters, I would surely have gone insane. People embraced Amber as their own even without ever meeting her in person. Because of them, I could endure and surpass this terrible situation and her inevitable death. The burden was so heavy, I felt as though I would collapse under its load. Then I would read a letter; it would lift the weight and make me stronger. I knew I couldn't do this alone; I was weak and my faith was shaky. I only hoped that God was truly the one behind the voice that was my constant companion.

### *October 9, 10 pm*

*This afternoon I broke down. It was the first time since this whole mess began, that I let her see my fear. "I'm scared, Amber." "Of what, Mom?" I tried to regain my composure. "Amber, do you feel like you're going to die soon?" She shook her head. "No... I think Gary will die first 'cuz he's the oldest." "Are you ready to die?" Softly, and without hesitation, she said, "Yes." "You know, it's O.K. to die." She looked at me knowing that I was giving her reassurance and approval. She did not shed a tear through the entire scene. Instead, she put her arms around me, gently patting my back, as I cried on her shoulder. "It's okay, Mom, I'll protect you from the world."*

*I didn't interpret her seeming lack of emotion as "covering up." Rather, I felt a calm, peaceful acceptance of her destiny radiating from her. "Amber, I want to be honest with you about my feelings and you can be honest with me. Tell me if you have a question, or if you're scared, or if you need me to do something." "Sure, Mom, O.K." The air seemed clearer and we went about the business of living another day.*

I knew I couldn't burden her with my own sense of grief, fear, and sadness. I also knew that I needed to make this experience as honest and profound as I could. Hiding *all* of my sad feelings would be unfair to her, so I let just a few come out, only for a very brief time, and not very often. I wanted her to know the *real* me and not spend all of our precious time together in a sort of surreal, suspended state of disbelief and denial, never speaking the truth, even if it wasn't very "pretty."

We tried to pace ourselves. Between Amber's frequent sessions of pain, we lived a "typical" life: Sleeping, dressing, eating, walking on the beach, visiting friends. These times of normalcy were broken by extraordinary reminders that—*no way, our life was NOT normal.* It was not normal to give birth to a child and then, only a few years later, help them to die with grace and dignity.

In the car, on the way home from visiting the Murray's, I nearly lost her. Gary was driving with me riding "shotgun"; Amber and Todd were in the back. We were on the highway moving along, listening to *The Muppet Movie* tape, singing, and being a family. Todd stopped singing. "Dad, Amber's bump is bleeding!" I held my breath. I *acted* calm. "Let me see, Amber." I released my seat belt, turned around on my knees, and gently caressed her head. Blood was pouring out of the tumor. For a split second, I thought, "Should I let her bleed to death? At least it would be better than letting her get eaten alive by the cancer. Should I stop it?" I asked Todd for his sweatshirt and applied pressure to the tumor. The bleeding stopped. My mind raced ahead to the future. "When will it happen again? Next time, will I be able to stop the bleeding? Will I *want* to stop the bleeding?"

### *October 10, 3 pm*

*We went to the store to get a stroller for Amber; she is very weak and can barely walk now. She is not eating well; mostly sweets: Candy, cookies, soda. I rarely let her have them when she was little. "They'll rot your guts," I'd say. But now, WHATEVER she wants to eat is okay with me. I am not denying her anything. "Rotting her guts" is no concern at this point.*

*Understandably, she wants to be held all the time. She's whiny, whimpering, and sad. She doesn't want to close her eyes or be without me. Her eyes, especially her left one, are bothering her. The tumor is quite ulcerated and smelly. It's spreading down her throat, along the*

226

*back of her head, to the base of her skull. It's also penetrated her ear. And to think, there is just as much INSIDE as out. Oh, God...*

*Amber is sleeping now. She was up all night tortured by the pain. "Mommy, why does God give me this pain? Please help me! OW! OW!!! Pain, go away!!! PAAAIIINNN!!! Her words cut through me like a dull knife; like someone is reaching into my body and pulling out my heart. Amber is my heart.*

### October 11, 2 pm

*GARY FOUND A HOME FOR US! Finally, we can unpack our suitcases and move out of the studio. It's an actual house near the beach. Since it has three bedrooms, Amber can finally have her "Rainbow Room"! I am so grateful for Gary; he made it possible to fulfill her last wish: Her very own Rainbow Room.*

It didn't seem possible, but life was looking good. We had a home... a place to relax, put away our things, and let Amber die in peace. With renewed enthusiasm, we took the donations that the people who'd followed her journey had sent and went to the mall. I was sure they would want her to indulge.

The first stop was the toy store. Gary pushed the shopping cart while I pushed Amber in her stroller. "Gar, I want *that!*" as she pointed to a doll, "And *that* one, too!" "Sure, Amber, anything else?" Whatever that money could buy, she got. I knew, after she died, that I would be giving most of her things to other children, spreading the good around.

Our next stop was the department store to buy furnishings for her room. We were in the Linen Department. She'd just picked out her bedspread—a flowered one with maroon ribbons through it—when she began clutching her head. I felt the earth begin to tremble just the way it does before an earthquake or a volcano erupts. "Mom? My head's starting to hurt..." In my excitement over our shopping spree, I didn't come prepared for the pain—no aspirin, no codeine. Her anguish increased, and with it, her cries. Gary grabbed the bedspread and ran to the checkout counter. People were looking now; searching down the aisles for the source of the screaming. I took her into my arms and we made our way through a shocked and curious crowd. I raced down the corridor and into the cold, crisp, autumn wind, with Amber sobbing in my arms. I zoomed into the future—The Movie—and then into the past. "Miami... this is just like Miami. She's in my arms and I'm racing to relieve her suffering."

The kindness of the public was heartwarming. People continued to send us cards and letters with ideas and suggestions that would help make Amber's transition easier for her; more memorable for us. Quite a few mentioned Father D'Orio. "He's a priest who lives in Worcester, Massachusetts... he's *very* close to God... he heals people." I knew the time for Amber's healing was past, but I wanted her to experience this man; to be as close as she could to God on earth, without actually dying. Gary, Todd, Amber, and I planned a trip to St. Anne's Church in Sturbridge, Massachusetts for the weekend.

As we made our way to the church, I could see that *something* was happening. The crowds were enormous! Like a pilgrimage to a holy place, people came on stretchers, in wheelchairs, on crutches—any way to move themselves forward to get to this man. The healthy were bringing the sick, old, young, babies in their mother's arms. We were swept up into the river of people... the crush of human suffering. All of us were there for the same reason: To be close to God on earth. Some had hoped to be healed. We were beyond that hope and were there to experience the link, if only for a short time, between Heaven and earth.

Gary put Amber on his shoulders so that she could see above the crowd and an usher found one of the few seats that remained near the front of the church. I stopped and let the goodness, the spiritual gifts fill me. I was hypnotized by the sight before me: The church was immense, filled with candles, incense, statues, paintings, gold, marble, and wood. It was chilly, despite the body heat that radiated from the crowd. The choir sang "Amazing Grace" as we waited for Father D'Orio to come out. My body was invisible, I was sure only my spirit remained. My eyes were fixed on the door near the altar... the door through which he would enter.

With a great "swooshing" sound, Father D'Orio stepped out, visibly moving the crowd. I could *see with my eyes* the energy this man radiated. A woman started to sing "Alleluia!" as the rest of us joined her. Father D'Orio walked among us, as people reached out to him, hoping to touch this holy man... hoping to be healed of their wounds, both seen and unseen. To the untrained eye, he seemed meek and mild-mannered, but I could see God in him. He was the nearest thing to that miracle I kept asking God to perform. "God, I need to *SEE* You." It was a plea I often made. We left, knowing that Amber's place in Heaven was reserved, and headed to the New England Aquarium. It was an attempt at "normal," if only for a short time.

With the weather turning cold, I kept a knit cap on her head whenever we were in public. Hiding the tumor—now nearly the same size as her head—was the only way we could be "invisible" and slip by without questions, gasps, shock, and disbelief. Although they meant well, the sight of this beautiful little girl with a bloody, necrotic growth on her head was just too much for anybody to digest... to accept without choking with terror. With each encounter, my heart broke a little more, for I knew that Amber could see the people and hear their questions, too.

Gary and I knew that our time at the aquarium would be the last time she would be in public... be living a "normal" life... be *living* life at all. We brought her home to die and set the stage to help her crossover the threshold between life and death... between this world and the one beyond... between the world we *see* and the world we *know*. It would take all the courage and strength I had to forego my suffering and replace it with love for Amber. "It's *her* time now, not mine."

### *October 12, 2 pm*

*Thankfully, Amber is sleeping. It's the only time she has when she isn't in pain. Bernie prescribed Morphine and I'm giving it to her regularly. He suggested that I put it in grape juice, but it takes too long to take effect that way. I called him back. He told me to pick up some syringes and inject it. I started off with 5 mm whenever she feels pain. Immediately, she begins to drift above it. The truth is, I'd rather she be somewhere floating, than touching earth and the pain touching her. I look forward to her death. I want her to be at peace and be with God. Her suffering is beyond the limits of any human, especially an innocent child.*

*She seems to be starving herself; the only food she eats is candy. Her throat hurts when she swallows and she hasn't had a bowel movement in six days. "I have a stomach ache, Mom." "Turn over and let me rub your back for you, Babe." Her flesh is slowly disappearing; her bones are beginning to show through. She is literally wasting away before my eyes.*

*This morning she woke up sobbing. "Mom, I had a REAL bad dream. I dreamt I couldn't get you. You know those rocks near where our boat used to be? Well, you fell in the water and I couldn't get you back." I held her in my arms, rocking her and soothing her mind and her fears. "Amber, I promise you: I'll never leave you. Never."*

Our days were all mixed up; there was no day or night or schedule of any sort. Whenever she had pain, I'd inject her with Morphine; she didn't even feel the shots. The sting from the needle was nothing compared to the pain from the growing tumor. Her little buns were riddled with holes from the injections from the immunotherapy and now from the Morphine. Many, many little scabs dotted her sweet butt cheeks. I remembered the days when they were pure and clear and not marked with the intrusion of needles.

I tried to imagine what her pain felt like: Someone or something is eating you alive, microscopic bit by bit, cell by cell. The process is so small in fact, that it's invisible to the naked eye. But like the ticking of a clock, it never stops. Your brain is being squeezed against your skull, ever so slowly, by this monster that lives inside your head. You cannot stop it. You are tied and bound, unable to move. And then... someone approaches you, drill in hand. Slowly, *very slowly*, they begin to drill a five inch hole in your skull. It lasts forever. You hope... pray... beg for death to come soon; but it can't come soon enough to give you any relief. This is your destiny. You have no choice but to live through it and it will not stop until you're dead.

This is Amber's life and I am forced to watch her live it; unable to stop the pain, kill the intruder, or put her out of her misery. She's surrounded by bulletproof glass. I can't break through it to save her. The only thing I can do is try to help relieve her pain, calm her fears, watch, and wait... just wait. Waiting, watching, and wishing it would end, punctuated by joy, love, and intense appreciation for her life; this was how I spent my time.

The cards, letters, and gifts continued to come. Although she was high on morphine, she was lucid and aware that people cared about her. When Gary went to the post office, she would eagerly await his return. Her "headquarters" was the living room sofa. I'd clean her up, prop her up with pillows, and pour out the bags of mail on her lap. The drugs slowed her down, but her enthusiasm was still noticeable. As if in slow motion, she'd hold up a painting that one of her admirers had painted for her and say, "Moooommmm, llloooookk aat tthhhiisss prrreetttyy ppiiccttuurrrre."

People cared and they made the time to show it. Reaching out to us... reaching out to Amber made the difference between a lonely, isolated death and one filled with love and kindness and hope. It bolstered us for what was happening each moment and all the ones yet to come. Knowing people were just outside the walls, helped me to cope with her impending death and helped her to know she wouldn't be crossing the threshold alone. *All* of us would be there to guide her, in one way or another.

Bernie was truly a gift from God. None of us had ever gone through this before. We were playing it by ear and coping with situations as they happened. He taught all of us about life and crossing over the line to death, how to make the most of each moment and this experience, what to expect and when to expect it. Most importantly, he helped us see dying from Amber's perspective, something we needed to grasp, even embrace.

On one of our last visits with him, Gary, Amber, and I spoke frankly about her approaching death. It was impossible for us to understand all of her feelings and emotions. She would be downright nasty at times. "She seems sad most of the time; rarely laughs or smiles." Bernie gently reminded us of her "Spontaneous Drawings." "Well, it *is* a sad event for her; you can see that in her drawings. She draped the purple balloon in black. Just remember, we are losing *her,* but she is losing *all of us."* Profound words indeed. They changed my outlook, my attitude, and moved me from self pity to Amber's world... to *her* perspective, not mine. This was *not* the time to be selfish or self-centered. This was Amber's time. We needed to do all we could to elevate her... to help her reach Heaven.

I left Bernie's office thinking of God's words: "Your 'Life Lesson' is PATIENCE. Your 'Life Task' is to WRITE THE BOOK... to share Amber's message with the world: That death is simply change. It is not the end of a life but the beginning of a *different* one." I *knew* I could work very hard at learning patience, but I was certain I couldn't write a book. I brought up the book in my interviews with Linda and Judy and they mentioned it in their newspaper articles. I realized from the letters I received, that people not only *wanted* the book, they *needed* it, too.

*"... I hope that you can manage to write the book and let people know that others have gone through this tragedy, and have come out of it stronger and more caring of others."* —Fred and Sue Ristow

*"... I sense that you, Mrs. Calistro, having made your peace with God, will be of great use to His ministry, however the outcome of your daughter's illness."* —Geri Kihlberg

*"... Our neighborhood bible study group met here recently and we were reading 2 Corinthians 1, about suffering, and how one can turn it into good for others. I told the group about you and the program you want to share with others. We all prayed silently for you and were touched deeply. Please let this dream come true. May Christ give you the strength and peace to carry out your good works through the Program. p.s. Your struggle has opened my eyes to the fleeting beauty of our lives and the eternal beauty we will all share in Heaven."* —Mrs. Theresa Berry

*"... I think Amber's death will be able to help thousands of other people out here who have lost, are losing, or soon will lose their children."* — Angela Pattison

I didn't know *how* I was going to do it, but the reason *why* was clear. For Amber and the millions of others who were living with this terrible disease... who were suffering and dying from it, I had to tell her story... to beg the world to work *together* to first and foremost *prevent* cancer. And, if they were too late, to treat it humanely and cure cancer. Amber's journey and her incredible insights into life and death, would be needed by so many. For those who were afraid, she would bring comfort and reassurance. For the hopeless, she would give hope. For those who doubted God, His power, or life after death, she would restore their faith and trust. From a child, these answers would spring. I had no doubt at all about my Life Task. My path was laid before me. All I needed to do was take the first step in faith.

Waiting to see Bernie

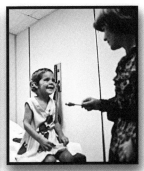

Off Burton's serum now, the tumor was growing rapidly / With the hope that I would buy her a pearl necklace / Picking out "wedding rings" so that Gary, Todd, Amber, and I could get "married" / In Bernie's Examining Room, she's "playing doctor" / Despite the growing tumor, Amber was still smiling / Our last visit with Bambi and her dog, Snipples

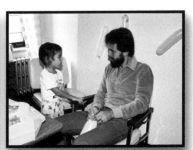
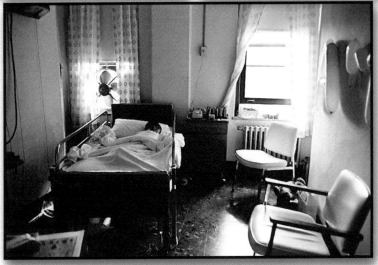

St. Raphael's Hospital in New Haven, CT

*Clockwise:* Knowing she would not be cured, we took her to see Father D'Orio, a man of God. / At the Boston Aquarium having "the time of our life" / Butterflies! / By now, the tumor had paralyzed the right side of her face.

# Chapter 14

## Crossing the Threshold

*"The call of death is the call of love. Death can be sweet if we answer in the affirmative, if we accept it as one of the great eternal forms of life and transformation."* —Hermann Hesse

Being human was still difficult for me, but Amber inspired me to try... to allow myself this luxury. She continued to teach me about life, love, and happiness. With a full heart, I followed her example and did my best to learn and integrate the lessons she was teaching me through her life and now her death.

· **Life:** No matter *how* much time we have on this earth, we should do all we can to set aside the bad, glorify the good, and express our appreciation to our fellow human beings as often as we can. We have the power to change another life... to lift someone up, with only a few words, a smile, or a touch.

· **Love:** It is not limited to what we can see, feel, and hear. The temporal world and everything in it will be replaced. The only true love comes from one soul to another. Once it is shared, it will never be broken, not even by death.

· **Happiness:** It does not come without knowing the depths of despair, suffering, and trauma. For it is only *after* we know these things, that we can fully open to the joy and contentment that is given to us by God... by the higher power.

From the time she was conceived, I knew Amber. It was a knowing that could not be explained with words or that anyone could understand or accept or believe. They really didn't need to for it to be so. We were... we ARE intertwined, connected, indivisible. It was remarkable to realize this. I knew I needed to be steadfast in my role as "scribe." I focused on recording the rest of our life together. The closer I came to seeing the end, the more fanatical I was about documenting. Every waking moment was captured on film or tape. Hundreds of hours of voice... of photos... of movie footage... of her drawings. I wasn't sure what I would do with them, but I knew I would need them someday. I filled one cassette case with 50 tapes and asked Gary to pick up another at the store. I was on a mission and I needed supplies.

Her physical decline was heartbreaking to watch... to stand by helplessly... to accept her fate. She was wasting away, but like a concentration camp survivor, she clung to the finest shreds of life. The instinct to survive, though it was waning, could not be taken from her. Her eyes had lost their sparkle; they were simply sunken orbs. Her legs could no longer hold her body; we carried her everywhere. Her body was shrinking before my eyes as quickly as the tumor was growing. *"How can she still be alive???"* Her spirit was the only force sustaining her; it *definitely wasn't* her body.

I spent my time tending to her, talking with her, reading to her, stroking her. The rest of the time I stayed busy doing chores around the house and preparing for her death. We talked about it freely now. "Amber, what do you think Heaven's like?" "Oh... I think it's a BIG white house, *real pretty,* with lots of rooms and you can have anything you want—cookies, candy, ice cream. And DO anything you want." "When you get there, will you save me a place?" "Sure, Mom, I'll save Gary and Todd a place, too."

### *October 17, 10:15 pm*

*Amber got "zapped" today at St. Raphael's Hospital. Radiation is now used to ease her pain, not cure her. Dr. Knowlton, her radiologist, is more than willing to work with us as a team and not an adversary. He is a good man FIRST and a good doctor SECOND. That's the way it should be.*

*As I left Amber and the Treatment Room behind, I stepped into a gathering of people: Nurses, doctors, technicians, hospital workers, and a priest. I don't know how they knew she was in the hospital, but regardless, they came to pay tribute. Our eyes met. Without words, they told me they shared my pain. I felt that human acknowledgment of crossing paths down the road of life, if only for a few moments. We stood in silence, bound together by the little girl we watched on closed circuit TV. "Amber is bringing us together," I thought.*

*Earlier this evening, she woke up from her nap crying and sobbing out of control. "Mom, I had a dream about two swans. They said, 'We will devour the Good Guys!!!' There were butterflies all lined up, and they had faces. The ducks were eating at them!!!" I don't know how to interpret her dreams, but I'm sure they express how she's feeling deep inside. I wish I could reach inside and fill her with joy once again. One more time, just a little spark of joy.*

*She told me that her head and eyes were hurting. "Mom, it feels like there's water sloshing around in my head... like there's a wheel in my ear." I took a flashlight and looked inside her ear. The hole was gone; the tumor had taken over; it was solid and white like cottage cheese. I wondered at this THING... this inanimate OBJECT. "How can it be killing my little girl??? It looks so harmless... so benign." My hatred for cancer had to be hidden… had to be buried for now.*

*I am looking over to the lump of blankets that is Amber, asleep on the couch. "Is she..." I hold my breath, waiting to see if the lump will rise and fall. "Yes... she's alive." Then I let my breath go.*

As I watched her, day after day, laying on the sofa, watching TV, playing with her dolls, drawing, or playing "doctor," I'd think, "Any day now... I wonder if today will be the day." I just couldn't believe it was humanly possible to live in a body like that. The tumor was nearly the size of her head *outside!* There was just as much growing *inside her skull!* No longer eating, her strength and fortitude and fierce determination to live replaced all sustenance. She was on her way to Heaven and food was not needed to get there.

To the outside world, what was happening inside the walls of our home was surreal. We would have occasional visitors: Gary's parents—Gramma and Grampa Stiewing, the Murray's, Jan, Nancy and Sarah, Linda Bouvier, Harry and Diane, our neighbors when we lived aboard Sea Wing. My family was nonexistent. They "couldn't handle it," as my mother told me over the phone months before. Many people couldn't handle it. If I believed I had a choice, *I couldn't handle it either.* But I was Amber's mother. Caring for her was something I needed to do... I *wanted* to do to show her my love... my undying devotion then and now.

It took a tremendous amount of courage and selflessness to come into this "house of death." People seemed to be paying their last respects, to do what they could to encourage and support her, and to honor Amber while she was still alive to see them. She lived for these visits; she longed to be loved and embraced. Although she was leaving people; she needed to know that people were not leaving her. It was a lesson in dying that Bernie pointed out so poignantly. "We are losing *her,* but she is leaving *all of us.*"

Michael lived a block and a half away, but we saw him only once since we had returned from the Bahamas. For her sake, I would quietly, secretly call him. "Amber needs you *now.*" I didn't want her to overhear; I didn't want her to face his rejection ever again. He came by on his way to work to drop off some books for her. He didn't stay long. She was sleeping upstairs and missed his visit. When she woke up, I made some sort of excuse for him—I lied through my teeth—to save her from suffering his indifference and insensitivity anymore. But I couldn't spend time immersed in the past. My focus had to be in the future, however little remained on this earth. My anger for him was replaced by compassion and empathy for Amber. *She needed me to be happy and whole.* And I was—at all costs, even the cost of being honest with myself.

Amber's death was hers to orchestrate, not mine. I listened to my heart and relinquished control. "Where would you like to die, Amber, at home or in the hospital?" "HOME, for sure. I don't wanna go to the hospital, Mom, okay?" "What do you want to wear to Heaven?" "Ummm... I'll pick it out, Mom. Will you take me upstairs so I can pick it out?" I carried her upstairs and sat her on her bed while she pointed, commanded, and listed her outfit. "I wanna wear my school clothes. *Those* brown pants and... oh, yeah... *that* shirt! And my school shoes. I want to wear my school shoes," she said as though she was REALLY picking out an outfit to wear to school, not Heaven. I set everything aside, along with her black, patent leather shoes, and tenderly placed it on her dresser. No doubt she'd be wearing them soon.

We buried ourselves in the house; rarely went outside anymore. Gary made occasional trips to the grocery store, the post office, or the pharmacy. He was our link... our ambassador. It was too difficult to travel with Amber and too painful to deal with the public. They'd stare, sometimes with their mouth wide open; other times a look of shock would spread across their face and they'd quickly turn away. Children would point and be frightened and cling to their parents as if to say, "Mommy, can that happen to *me?*" I'd look at people hurrying here and there—normal, happy mothers and fathers with their normal, happy, *healthy* children. All of those *other* children. I could feel the simmering rage bubbling under my skin, though I didn't recognize it at the time. I felt uncomfortable, that's all... just a little uncomfortable.

I could keep her out of pain, try to entertain and distract her during her waking hours, and ease her through the transition from life to death. The one thing I could *not* do was stop the tumor from growing, rotting, and smelling. Like a sickening, toxic cloud that surrounded her, the *smell* could not be ignored; could not be washed away. I could close my eyes and make the sight of it disappear, but I couldn't stop breathing the odor that emanated from it. It would stay with me long after her body was gone.

One day after Amber's bath, I wrapped her in a towel and held her in my arms; her head rested on my shoulder. I gave myself up to my mothering instincts and wallowed in my feelings of love for her. I hoped that this moment would linger. "God, it feels *so* wonderful to hold her... it reminds me of when she was a baby and I'd feel her little naked body, wrapped in a towel... her body so warm... she smelled so sweet..." The tumor was nearly touching my face. "My God, it *stinks!* From a sweet-smelling babe, to *this! How did this happen? And WHY???*" I would ask this question again and again, each time expecting an answer from God. My thoughts were interrupted.

"Hey, Mom, what's that smell? Did you fart or somethin'?" Knowing the truth, I lied. "Yup, I farted." "Mommy... *pee-yew!*" I glared at the tumor, now next to my face. My mind was screaming, "*I hate you... Oh God, how I hate you!!!*" My urge was to hit it and smash it and beat it to death. I held myself back. I buried my primal urge to protect my daughter from harm... to kill anyone or anything that threatened to kill her. "I know I'll kill Amber, not the *cancer*." Clinging to her cancer-ridden body, I still didn't want to let her go. I didn't want to let her die but knew I had no choice now. Though she was in my arms, she was now in God's hands. Soon, I would let her go completely.

People were hungry for more news about Amber; they were naturally curious and concerned; they truly cared. The stories that were published in the newspapers throughout her journey, though poignant and touching, were only one dimensional. When Channel 3 called to ask for an interview, I didn't hesitate to say yes. My journey with Amber was so unbelievable and she was so incredibly brave and wise, I wanted to share it, not hide away in the house like so many millions of people with cancer were doing. To shed light on the issue—even camera lights—was to keep Amber's *spirit* alive, open the eyes of the world to cancer, and give them a reason to find a cure. That was my hope. That was my motivation.

She was the perfect example of what cancer is and what it can do. Only months before, a budding child model, beautiful inside and out. Now, a beautiful child, dying from cancer, a cancer you could SEE. God spoke to me again. "Amber is My messenger. You are My scribe. When the time to bring her message to the world is right, you will know." I had no doubt her life and death had purpose and meaning. It was pointless for anyone else to go through this Hell; Amber was sent from Heaven to make sure they didn't. *This* was the reason she was put here on earth—to literally show the world how much we need to stop cancer from killing so many. The only way this can happen is to stop the fighting, the politics, and the competition... to come together... to prevent, treat, and cure cancer. Who was I to stand in her way... in God's way? I swallowed my pride, shame, anger, and embarrassment. I let the reporters come in.

*Channel 3, "Eyewitness News"*

- *Announcer: A sad report, really. A heartbreaking story tonight out of Milford, where a mother and child are struggling against cancer. A struggle that no longer has any chance of being won. Doctors say the little girl is dying. Channel 3's Pam Cross, reports the four year old child understands that.*

- *Pam: This is not a story for everyone. It's a strong report about death... about cancer and dying. It's about a four year old girl's dying, and her mother's indignation with the medical community. (Camera scans Amber's modeling portfolio.) This is Amber Calistro a year ago. Her mother began a portfolio, hoping she would be a successful child model. That summer, Patti Calistro found a small lump behind Amber's right ear. Right away she thought, "Cancer." But the doctors disagreed.*

- *Me: Generally they would say to me, "Lots of kids get lots of lumps and bumps... don't worry about it." I wanted to believe them and sometimes, I did; for periods of days, I would. But a nagging doubt led me to want to see what was inside.*

- *Pam: It was over six months before doctors diagnosed rhabdomyosarcoma—a very rare form of cancer. Patti Calistro says if they'd known sooner, they might've had a better chance of arresting the disease. Amber was operated on once in Connecticut. Later, she received Lawrence Burton's controversial blood therapy in the Bahamas.*

- *Me: She started experiencing pain at the beginning of September; but until that time, she had no side effects; no pain. We were snorkeling... playing. Amber was going to school and dance lessons in the Bahamas. We admitted her to St. Raphael's and under the direction of Bernie Siegel, who was willing to work WITH us, we had a lot of tests run. At that time, the surgeons brought me their opinions, and I decided it would do her more harm than good to have surgery.*

- *Pam: Patti Calistro, who is a single mother and an artist, has been busy collecting Amber's last words. She wants to spearhead an independent movement to investigate the state of cancer research and she responds sharply to those who criticize her for allowing Amber's death to become public.*

- **Me:** *I'm not trying to force this on anybody. But at the same time, I do believe in freedom of choice. I feel if people DO want to know about it, they should have the choice to learn about it. It's something that each one of us has to come to grips with while we're living, or we spend our whole life dying.*

- **Pam:** *I'm Pam Cross, Eyewitness News, Milford.*

I was doing my best to cope, but I was tense, tired, and anxious. I *had* to keep these feelings away from Amber. She needed a strong, steadfast, unwavering mother, not the weak and vulnerable woman I was inside. Gary was there to listen to me, but I couldn't even *feel* my pain, much less *talk* about it. Forming my feelings into thoughts and then words was impossible; it was a luxury I couldn't afford.

Throughout my childhood, I learned how to cope with disaster. To get through this hell, I had to stay numb, nearly dead. I refused to live it, feel it, or admit to myself that MY DAUGHTER WAS DYING. To the world, I was strong, stoic, competent—"Patti, Side A," the shell. My body was controlled. My demeanor was stiff and hard. I simply could not allow my "cracks" to be visible. The truth was only for me and God to know, no one else. They never saw "Patti, the person" because I kept her invisible, buried deep within the walls of my body. She had to be imprisoned or all hell would break loose.

It was survival, plain and simple. I refused to see the ugly reality. Instead, I forced it to become something good. I learned my lesson well. My childhood was my school... my time to cultivate the positive attitude I needed to cling to now. "Mom and Dad aren't 'bad,' they're just sick. They're doing the best that they can. They don't really *hate* me, they just don't *know* me. I'm not neglected, I'm just learning how to be independent." Feel? That was something I just couldn't do. I didn't know how, and besides, I didn't even know what "feelings" were. Perhaps at the time, it was better that I didn't.

<u>*October 18, 3 pm*</u>

*This morning Amber told me about another dream she had.  It was revealing.  I thank God for her "dream gifts."  Unwittingly, she answered a question that has plagued me since I was a little girl: What's at the end of the rainbow?  "Mom, I had a dream."  "What about, Amber?"  "I dreamed that God came and took my hand and walked me to the other side of the rainbow."  "What was on the other side?"  "His house."*

*So THAT'S where the rainbow ends: At God's doorstep!  No wonder she wanted... she NEEDED her "Rainbow Room" to get to the other side and cross over God's threshold to Heaven.  "Mom, can I have a 'Rainbow Room' with rainbows all over?" she'd ask me over and over after we returned from the Bahamas.  Thanks to Gary and the people who loved her, her fervent wish was granted.  She finally got her very own room, the first since leaving Connecticut and Michael.  It's decorated just the way she wants it—with a rainbow prism that shoots rainbows all over the walls when the sun shines through it.*

*Amber is starting to "slumber."  It's quite unlike sleep; it's more like she's hovering between life and death.  Her breathing is hard and labored with long pauses between each breath.  Rather than see her awake and in excruciating pain, I want to see her this way.  Instead of hearing, "YIKES! MOMMY! I want to go to God NOW! RIGHT NOOOWW!!!  God, are You listening, God???  Her pleas have been replaced.  I now hear the sporadic sounds of her temporary peace.*

Human dignity is something that no one can take from us. The ability to be proud and capable and human; we are all born with it and we all HOPE to die with it.  I was reminded of this while I watched Amber struggle to hold a cup of soda in her hand. As the Morphine made her groggy, her hand would start to fall. I'd reach out to take it from her... to stop it from falling and spilling all over her.  "Amber, do you want me to take that for you?" Indignant at my request, she'd firmly, slowly say, "No, Mom, I can hold it... *really I can!*"  This was repeated again and again.  I was afraid she would spill it, she was refusing to let her independence go. "I can take care of it *myself!*"  It wasn't the *cup* she held onto so tightly, it was her *dignity*—the last character trait of "being human" to go.

Hospice was coming three times a week to check on us... on Amber. Various nurses would examine her, they'd talk to Gary and me about the dying process, and make sure we had everything we needed. Some days, the nurses would spend a good deal of time with us. It was comforting and the company from the "outside" was appreciated. Besides the TV, I had no idea what was happening in the world, not that anything else mattered.

### October 25, 6 pm

*I am sitting on the floor in the kitchen. Amber is on the couch in her "slumber." Gary's cooking. Ruth, a nurse from Hospice is talking with us. To keep the increasing pain that Amber is having under control, I have increased her dose of morphine to 2cc every three to four hours and 2cc of Sparine every twelve hours. Although she is drugged and drowsy, she is out of pain and her mind is as sharp as ever.*

*As the tumor continues to grow and bleed, she is getting weaker and weaker. She can't walk anymore. Gary and I carry her to the bathroom, upstairs to her bedroom, or from the floor to the couch. Her voice is barely audible. Her urine is turning darker. As the Morphine wears off, she complains of aches and pains in her left armpit and her belly. For the past two weeks, she's had a constant fever.*

*I cannot believe that this child is my daughter! She is so incredibly strong and optimistic and encouraging! Each time I ask, "Amber, how're you doin'?" Without exception, she says, "Good." Good? She's GOOD? How can she say she's GOOD??? But I realize that she IS good... she is very good... perfect, in fact. Amber is the perfect angel sent to earth from God.*

The press continued to satisfy the public's need to know; they cared; they couldn't help it. But the line between caring and intruding was fuzzy. At one time, I had been one of them—a regular person untouched by the tragedy of cancer—so I understood this need. Without having to live through it

246

themselves, they could read about someone who was, and secretly say to themselves, "I'm glad it's not me or my child." People were concerned, compassionate, and giving. I admired their courage to question. Cancer was so frightening that we couldn't even say the word until recently. It was converted to code; it was called "The Big C."

"Cancerphobia" was beginning to grip the nation and people were scared to death. With Amber's tumor on the outside of her head, people could *see* cancer itself. It wasn't hidden inside. It wasn't easy to dismiss. The press and some of the people who read Amber's story, were not used to a mother being so open and forthright about her daughter's cancer... about the details... about death itself. I put myself in their shoes to see this from their eyes; I tried to be honest, but gentle. This was new territory for all of us, and the line—the tightrope we walked—was loose and wobbly. Clinging to each other to keep from falling was all we could do.

Bob Childs, a photographer from *The Associated Press,* came by to take photographs for an upcoming article. I held Amber in my arms. I didn't think about *which* side of her head was facing the camera. He shifted uneasily between looking through the viewfinder and then at us. "Uh... can you hold her on the *other* side? I mean, with her *left* side facing the camera?" I had no idea what he was talking about. I'd actually become *accustomed* to the sight of the bulbous tumor that protruded on the right side of Amber's head. "Why?" "Well, I'm not sure... I mean, I don't think..." He grimaced and made a slight moaning sound, unable to find the right words. I realized what he was saying and shifted her to the other side. I thought to myself, "I know it's hard to look at, but it IS cancer. Just because you don't see it, doesn't mean it doesn't exist."

Although I wrote the date in my journal, I was unaware of the concept of time. I knew it was autumn; I could see the leaves change color and begin to fall from the trees. It was crisp and cold outside. Occasionally, Gary would light a fire in the fireplace and make Amber a bed in front of it. She loved watching the flames and feeling the warmth. Her enthusiasm was tempered by the drugs, but her spirit was healthy and frisky. Her words of wisdom never stopped and neither did the tape recorder.

She was laying on her bed in front of the fireplace, watching the flames dance. As I passed through the living room on my way to put her clean clothes away, she stopped me. "Mom?" "Yes, Amber." I went over to her side. "Mom, I *know* I'm here to help a lot of people." I couldn't believe my ears. I knelt down to hear her. She was lying in front of the fireplace; her face was glowing from the reflection of the flames. *"What* did you say, Amber?" Irritated that I asked her to repeat it, she said it again. "I *said...* I know I'm here to help a lot of people."

I froze in place. I was speechless... amazed... I shook my head in wonder. In my heart, I knew, but in my mind, I didn't. Hearing *her* tell me why she was here on this earth, as she was about to leave it, was too profound to be human. Finally, I was convinced. "She *is* an angel... she *IS."* I tenderly kissed her and stroked her head, then got up and went on my way. Like a robot, I climbed the stairs, walked into her room, opened her drawer, and placed her clean panties on top of the pile that was already there. I wouldn't know for some time, *exactly* what those words meant or how they would shape my life.

### *October 26, 2:22 pm*

*A Channel 30 reporter and her cameraman left a short while ago. They barely held themselves together for the interview. I wish I could've comforted them... told them it'll be okay, but I know it won't. Instead, I made a feeble attempt to let them know I understood their sympathy. I knew they couldn't possibly understand mine.*

### *Channel 30 News*

- **Darlene:** *The days are down to a few at most for four-year-old Amber Calistro of Milford, Connecticut. She knows she is dying of cancer, and her mother, Patti Calistro, says Amber is less frightened than she used to be and wants to die and be with God.*

- **Me:** *She was afraid at first, and the more we talked about it, the more enlightened I got, and the more she enlightened me. So it was a... we* *just taught each other type of process. But now she's desiring to die and be with God... and to be out of pain.*

- **Darlene:** *Patti Calistro says that she discovered the tumor growing behind Amber's right ear about a year ago. Mrs. Calistro says she's been tape recording her daughter's conversations in the past ten days, and plans to write a book on the experience. Mrs. Calistro says that she hopes the book will help others facing cancer deaths.*

- **Me:** *...to educate people that there ARE alternative therapies out there. There are more therapies than chemotherapy, surgery, and radiation. There are actually HUNDREDS of therapies out there. There are men and women—dedicated doctors and scientists, not "quacks," but dedicated humanitarians—working to alleviate the pain of cancer. Many of these alternative therapies work... and the proof is out there for the asking.*

- **Darlene:** *Patti Calistro also stated that she feels that cancer should be one of the prime issues in the presidential campaign. At the Calistro home in Milford, Connecticut, I'm Darlene Stuart-Powell, Channel 30 News.*

Though no one would say it to me directly, I knew that they couldn't understand how I could put my daughter, *who had a huge tumor on her head and was dying from cancer,* on TV. It may have seemed like that to them, but to me, she was Amber, my daughter, beautiful in every way EXCEPT for that tumor. I didn't want to hide her, or quietly slip away into history, or exploit her, either. I wanted to tell Amber's tale—all of it. And pictures helped to tell it. Pictures were the truth—the unfiltered, undeniable truth.

### October 27, 9 pm

*The tumor was oozing all over. Blood and pus continually drip out, then harden. Her speech is slurred, but her mind isn't. How can she still think? She continues to plead with me, "Mom, please help me... Mom, please... I'm begging you." I wish I had the guts to overdose her. It would be so easy; just load up the syringe with morphine and inject her.*

*THE END. But how can I do it??? I would be killing her. After all, I created this child. I gave her life. How can I take it away???*

*Nobody knows how I really feel and I don't expect them to. Unless you've been here, it's impossible to know... to conjure up these feelings. I'll try to explain:*

*Part of me — Amber — is dying. I cannot see the future, or even glimpse it. It is out of my reach. I am watching in horror as my healthy, plump, little girl, with an incredible personality, wastes away. The more days that pass by, the more tiring and complex this becomes. Amber is barely enjoying life. Even though her body is wilting, her mind is not, and she becomes frustrated at attempts to convey her messages. I am connected to her... to reality, by a thread. That thread is love. It is stretched and strained and tight. "Will it break when she dies?" I want to get on with my life; she wants to get on with her death.*

*At times, I find myself hovering between wishing she would live and wishing she would die. I look over at her, lying on the couch. I can see that for her, this is no life; it is simply existing. It is pain, broken up with very brief moments of a little bit of pain, no pleasure. I want her to die. It is too painful to watch this. Then I see her living... at least she's LIVING. Selfishly, I don't care HOW she's living; she just IS, that's all. I want her to live — exist, if she has to — for me. I don't want to live my life without her.*

*I give so much credit to those parents whose kids have serious physical or mental problems. I know I don't have the strength to go through this day in and day out. How do they do it?*

*Why do I HAVE to let Amber suffer? Isn't there a more humane way to die? Why does society place more value on the life and death of an animal? When they are suffering and dying, why do we have the choice to move the process along... perform euthanasia... kill them painlessly and with mercy... allow them to DIE WITH DIGNITY?*

*And yet human beings are allowed to suffer... needlessly suffer in excruciating pain. We prolong their inevitable death and for who?*

*Certainly not for the dying person who is not afraid to die and simply wants to get on with it and not for their loved ones who are watching their beloved EXIST in agony, not LIVE.  How can we assume to "play God..." to make the choice for someone else's life AND death?  The people who are making the laws against the practice of euthanasia have never suffered the way Amber is suffering now.*

I was tortured by not only the experience of watching my daughter die, but seeing beyond her, to the mass of humanity, to the millions of people who had gone, or were going, through the same thing.  Amber was my window.  I looked through her to see the world filled with suffering and dying people just beyond the glass.  Just as I couldn't forget her, I couldn't forget them either.  I remembered her words: "Mom, I know I'm here to help a lot of people."  Now that I knew WHY, I was beginning to understand HOW.

### *October 28, 2:02 pm*

*I took a nap earlier, with Amber laying on top of me.  It brought me back to the Bahamas... to our carefree days on our Naked Beach.  She felt so good; so much a part of me; almost as close as when I was pregnant with her.  I wanted to tuck her back inside me, protect her from the world, return her to that time of peace and utter contentment, so opposite from her life now.  It's so hard to let go... to embrace the emptiness instead of my angel.*

*Right now, she's sleeping on the sofa with her arms around Big Bird and her baby Teddy.  This morning, as I lifted her off her bed to bring her downstairs to the sofa, a large chunk of tumor stayed on her pillow.  I could FEEL a piece of me ripping off... sucking the breath right out of my lungs.  I imagine, when she slept on the tumor, pus softened the outer layer of skin and it attached itself to the pillowcase.  My God, how is she living through this?  I am only watching and yet, the sight of her living this is nearly killing me.*

*She sleeps peacefully most of the time now.  I am relieved to watch her sleeping without moaning in pain.  She has surrendered to her fate.  No longer does she cry to God, "Please don't make me suffer! God, why do you make me suffer?"   Instead, she APOLOGIZES.   I can't believe it! SHE APOLOGIZES!!!!   "Mom, I'm sorry my bump hurts... I'm sorry."*

*I am trying to capture each moment with her and never let it go.   The tape recorder has been on for the past month; I have too many tapes to count.   I took pictures of her body: Her hands with the pink nail polish, her toes that are stubby like mine, her belly button once connected to me, her cute little buns now riddled with needle holes.   Since I plan to cremate her body, I will never see them again.   "God, I can't let her go."*

*Hospice is no longer helping us.   Phyllis and Joanie came by last night to inform me that Dr. Lack, the attending physician with Hospice, had called Bernie.   She told him that she didn't agree with me in the matter of Amber's medication.   She wanted me to drop the Sparine to .1cc every twelve hours.   After several days of trying various doses, I decided to give her .2cc of Sparine every three hours.   Since I've put Amber on that schedule, she has not complained of pain, has had no medication-related side effects, and she can still be called to awareness.*

*I took offense at her accusations and the observations that she made.   How can she know what is best for Amber from only the feedback she gets from the nurses?   Why doesn't she visit or speak with me directly?   Instead, she called Bernie and told him that I was over-sedating her and that I spoke about dying in front of her.   Amber is aware of her approaching death.   I have not tried to hide this from her.   I will not deceive her.   I never have and I will not begin now.*

*Because of our differences, Phyllis and Joanie told me that Dr. Lack will not come to the house to pronounce Amber "dead."   Despite our previous arrangement, she told Bernie to do it or make other arrangements.   I called Bernie.   "Patti, they're afraid of your attitude... the fact that you are documenting Amber's death and have let reporters into your home. You're not 'wringing your hands' the way most people do. You want to be in control of Amber's pain... to have a say in how she lives AND how she dies. Hospice isn't used to this."   "What am I going to do? Who is going to come to the house to pronounce her 'dead'? Will you?"   "Patti, I will if I'm not in surgery at the time, but I can't guarantee it."*

So... here I was with my daughter standing at "death's door," wanting to fulfill her last wish and let her die peacefully at home, and with no one to pronounce her "dead" when she died. Since Bernie had suggested I call the fire department, I called them first. They referred me to the police department, who referred me back to the fire department. They told me to call the undertaker at the funeral home, who suggested I find a doctor who will come to the house to pronounce her "dead" and then they will pick up the body. INCREDIBLE!!! Amber was in the next room dying while I was in the kitchen on the phone, knee deep in bullshit, reaching out my hand for someone to help pull me out of the mire. I was desperate, no longer looking for help to save her life, but for help to let her die with peace and dignity.

I called Bernie again. "I'll do it, Patti... I *will*... but I may be in surgery when she dies. I'll tell you what, let her die at home and then bring her body to St. Raphael's Emergency Room. The funeral home will pick up her body there and take it to be cremated. I'll make all the arrangements." Again, Bernie came to our rescue. We were grateful that he saved us from the bickering and fighting and politics that surrounds cancer. He understood Amber's needs and satisfied them without question. I could now return to my dying daughter.

Amber was asking for Michael. Afraid he would create another confrontation, I didn't want to call him, but for her sake, I did. It was late at night. He hadn't been by to see her, so he didn't know if she was alive or dead. I wanted Amber to have a chance to say goodbye. She was barely awake, but she was aware. When he walked in the door, she was lying on the couch; her head was in my lap. He was there no longer than five minutes when he tried to start an argument with me, bringing up our past, unresolved marital issues, the same ones that drove us apart. I was appalled.

I brought him into the kitchen—out of earshot of Amber—and whispered in disbelief. "*Now?* You want to talk about this *now???* Your daughter is dying over there and you want to argue with *me* about our past?" He still harbored rage and resentment. It blinded him from loving Amber... from telling her what was in his heart... from helping her over the threshold. "Why can't you let it go... why can't you look past *me* and see *Amber?*" I reasoned. It was hopeless.  He began to raise his voice.  Afraid that Amber would hear, Gary and I asked him to leave.  It was no use.  He would not let it go, calm down, and focus his attention on his dying daughter.  After several failed attempts, Gary *forced* him to leave while I carried Amber upstairs to her room, to her peaceful "Rainbow Room."

### *October 30, 9:25 am*

*Today is my 27th birthday.  It would've passed unnoticed, if it wasn't for Gary.  Last night, shortly before midnight, we all sat on Amber's bed and opened the presents he bought for me.  Ever so slowly, they sang "Happy Birthday" to me.  Soon after, she closed her eyes as if to go to sleep, and slipped quietly into a coma.*

*We all slept together in Amber's double bed—Gary on the outside, me in the middle, and Amber against the wall.  Gary held me, as I held Amber.  I wanted to cry—I really did—but the tears would not come.*

*I began my conversation with God.  "Please, God, get me through this.  I have so many preconceived notions about death... about dead bodies.  Will I break down... lose control... sob and wail?"  "Maybe."  "Will I be able to touch her when she's dead?"  "Why not?  She is a part of you."  "Will I have the courage to pack up her belongings?"  "Sure you will."  "Will I have the strength to live without her?"  "You will never be without her."  I remembered her last words to me: "Mom, when I die, I'll still be Amber, I'll just be DIFFERENT."*

*Feeling drowsy now, I recalled our past and all we'd been through together.  She was my family, my world, my life, and now she was slipping away.  "I am here with Amber.  I am holding her hand.  I will take her home to the other side of the rainbow."  I drifted into a half-sleep.*

*Throughout the night, I was aware of her presence.  I'd reach over and feel her body.  "It's cold... is she dead?"  I was wide awake now.  A long moment would go by.  Then she would breathe.  Somehow, I fell into a deep sleep.*

*I woke to the sound of her heavy breathing. As I opened my eyes, I saw the sun streaming into the room and through the prism, lighting up the wall over Amber with a glorious rainbow. The bed was wet beneath her. She couldn't control herself anymore. Her body was lifeless, except for her slow, raspy breathing. I picked her up. Another clump of hair, pus, skin, and blood tore off her head and stayed on the pillow. "OH, GOD!!!" I cleaned her up and dressed her in her school clothes while Gary made a bed for her on the couch.*

### Noon

*Gary is preparing the back of my station wagon so we can transport her body to St. Raphael's. He laid Todd's Mickey Mouse sleeping bag across the back and put her favorite blanket on top to cover her up. All this seems so natural... so normal... so completely outrageous!*

### 1:45 pm

*Her breathing is quite labored; almost as though something is pulling her chest up from the outside. As she breathes, the air comes into her belly first, then travels through her lungs on the way out. Breath in... she struggles to hold on to life. Pause. Breath out... surrender.*

*And we wait...*

Knowing that a miracle was transpiring before my eyes, I could not stop documenting. Why? I simply did not have an answer or a choice. Like instinct, a natural intuitive power was driving me on. To anyone else but me and Gary, it would have seemed bazaar, but to us, it was normal. We didn't even question it. The tape recording stayed on and my camera was in my hand. I held her hand with the other.

As I looked through the lens of my camera, I saw my angel resting. Her face was so beautiful... so peaceful. She lay there without moving. Her tranquility was occasionally interrupted by her chest and belly rising to take her last breaths, then sinking to let them go. There were long moments of stillness between them. Her hand was holding the Key to Heaven, more for me than her.

She didn't need it. The Gates of Heaven were wide open, ready for her to join the host of angels and God, who were waiting on the other side. I knew she was ready to cross over, but was afraid to leave *me*. I needed to release her from the pain and suffering, her earthly ties, and above all, from me, her mother.

### *Tape Recording—2:25 pm*

- **Me:** *I love you. I love you, Amber. Oh... thanks so much for coming to me. Thank you for coming to me, Amber. You come to me again, okay?*
- *Or I'll see you in Heaven.*
- *Don't forget to save us a place, Amber. Don't forget to save us a seat and DON'T HOG UP THE BED, you hear? No hoggin.'*
- *You have the best buns in town, Baby.*
- *I love you.*
- *Rest now, Baby. Just rest, Amber. Rest.*
- *Don't cry... don't cry.*
- *I love you, Amber. I love YOU.*
- *Gary, she's crying.*
- **Gary:** *No, that's just because you were messin' with her eyes.*
- **Me:** *No... she's crying. Look! There's tears coming down and they're not stopping.*

The intervals between breaths were long, sometimes minutes. I lifted her eyelids a few times, to see if her pupils were dilated... to see if she was dead. I wanted to be present—*really present*—the moment she crossed over. I wanted to keep my promise: "Amber, I will never leave you." And I knew she would never leave me. I remembered her words: "Mom, when I die, I'll still be *Amber,* I'll just be *different."*

Leaving this earth, I wanted her to know how much she was loved... how much she taught me about love, about living. Though I'd told her countless times during her life, I wanted these words to be the last she heard before she crossed over.

- *Don't cry... don't cry... please, Amber. Don't cry, Baby. I'll be okay. I promise.*
- *Oh, I love you, Amber.*
- *I never knew love before you. Thank you for teaching me.*
- *She's dying. Her eyes are dilating.*
- *Oh!!! What a tremendous feeling of peace has come over me!!!*
- *Oh... I FEEL GOD!!!*
- *Thank You, God.*
- *Thank You, God.*
- *We praise Your name... praise Your name.*
- *2:30 pm—exactly.*
- *Thank You, God.*
- *Thank You, God.*
- *Thank You, God.*
- *She's dead.*
- *Oh... oh...*
- *God, my whole body's tingling!!! Gary, is yours??*
- *MY WHOLE BODY IS TINGLING!!! I feel as though I have ants running through my body!!!*

Gary was weeping. I was consumed by an overpowering sense of peace and warmth and joy that ran through my body and down to my soul. Like "ants" running through me, I tingled all over. It was an actual PHYSICAL FEELING!!! The miracle I had prayed for was taking place as Amber died. Now I knew. I had no doubt: God *was* real. Though I didn't SEE Him, I surely FELT Him. "Amber's death will give you life." It was October 30th—Amber's death day and my birthday. She had given me a most precious gift: A new... a *real* spiritual life.

The last moments were captured forever through the lens of my camera and the tape recorder; it was always on. Doing this was so natural and felt so good. It was as though I was gently and quietly consuming the last morsels of her life through these tools and I wanted to savor *each one* forever. If her death was simply her changing, as she reminded me, knowing the physical Amber would allow me to truly believe and live the rest of my life with the spiritual Amber.

Time stood still. There was no need to hurry... no need to rush. I held her limp body. It was empty. With my new spiritual eyes, I could see Amber flowing out into eternity. Like the rays of the sun, I could feel her warmth. Searing this into my memory, I looked—really looked—at her body. She was so incredibly still... so lifeless... almost like a porcelain doll laid to rest after a long day of play. The edges of her mouth were slightly turned up, as if she was smiling, happy to be on the other side and away from her tortured body. The massive tumor hung from her head. It was dead, too.

Her body was just that: A container. The spirit of Amber had left it behind. Now she was transformed. She was with me. I could feel her essence... her spirit... more intensely than ever before. Like a mantra, I could hear her words in my head. "Mom, when I die, I'll still be *Amber,* I'll just be *different.*" I smiled as I returned to the memory of her telling me this truth... of her giving me this gift. I heard her voice and saw the impish twinkle in her eye. No need to worry or grieve, I could feel her "difference" now.

I gently lifted her battered body and carried her to the waiting car. I placed her on the bed that Gary had made, as he tenderly lifted her head and put her rainbow pillow under it. I stood back. "She looks like she's sleeping, not *dead.*" I turned to Gary. In that moment, we were joined forever. Knowing Amber was our bond, a bond that would never be broken. I closed the door and put myself in the pilot's seat.

Off we went down the road heading for the highway, New Haven, and St. Raphael's Hospital. Once the beacon of hope; now a crossroads where her body would be picked up by the mortician to be cremated. I glanced around at the different cars, filled with people, casually driving around me. They could see her body, lying in the back of my Volkswagen station wagon. "I wonder how many of these people know she's dead. How many *other* dead people are on the road right now? God how ironic. Life *does* go on, doesn't it?"

My eyes drifted to the rear view mirror. Amber just lay there. Not a sound. Not a movement. I looked past her to the car behind me... to the man at the wheel. "He's completely unaware of this miracle before him." I began to wonder, "How many times are the miracles *right in front of us* and we don't even know it because we are so caught up... so absorbed in what we are doing or have done in the past or *will* do in the future? We box ourselves in, cut ourselves off, close our hearts so that we cannot see the miracle of our loved ones after they die?" Just as I believed that I would "see" Amber, I knew that others could, too. They just had to stay open and look.

We left the highway and again were on the side streets. A few blocks from St. Raphael's, I realized that my time with her on earth was coming to an end. THE END. I spotted a vacant parking lot behind an abandoned "7 Eleven." In one movement, I pulled in, stopped my car, grabbed my camera, got out, opened the back door, saw her in the viewfinder, and pressed the shutter. In the blink of an eye, this moment was captured. Simultaneously, God said, "Take a picture. People need to see 'dead,'" and Gary said, "What are you *doing???*" "Taking a picture." As I'm going through the motions, I say to myself, "What *are* you doing??? They'll say, 'How cold... how callous... *how could she???'* " Then I heard the voice of God, gently reassuring me. "Don't worry. I'll be with you. I'll protect you from the world." Amber's words exactly.

I got back in my car and drove to the Emergency Room. I stopped near the entrance, got out, walked to the back of the car, and opened the door. Since Bernie had called to make the arrangements, they'd been expecting us. Two orderlies greeted us with a stretcher. They offered to put her body on it. "No... thanks... I'd like to carry her in." One last time, I took her into my arms and held her body, now empty. My last physical connection to my daughter would soon be taken away. I cradled her to my heart and gently pulled her into me.

I walked towards the automatic doors, her lifeless body swaying to my step. Beyond the parting doors, I could see a crowd. Nurses, doctors, secretaries, visitors, priests, and nuns had gathered there to pay their last respects to this little girl—*their* little girl—who had fought so bravely to the very end. At once, I could see I wasn't alone, that they had suffered, too. They had hoped for her recovery, prayed for her life, and watched along with me as she slowly and painfully died. Many were crying. Their grief forced them to turn to each other for comfort. I felt no pangs of sadness or sorrow; I still felt the glory of God. I was at peace, and so was my baby.

Dr. Raine, a young intern, directed us to a small room that was separated from the Emergency Room by a curtain. I placed her body on the stretcher and studied it... absorbing every inch... filling my mind with the memory of Amber. "Perfect feet... hands... lips... eyes..." I stopped at the tumor. I moved closer to inspect it. Since she wasn't there and could feel no pain, I shook it. It felt like gelatin: Soft, powerless, sickening. It was enormous; nearly the same size as her head. "How can something so pathetic... so ugly... kill my beautiful little girl?!?!" Just under my skin, seething rage was coursing through my veins. In my mind, I could see a battlefield strewn with the bodies of all the *other* children who had died before Amber and the bodies of children yet to come.

Instantly, I felt as though I'd been injected with a tranquilizer. My hatred gave way to a new understanding. "Don't waste your life hating. Your time on this earth is too short. Take her message...take *MY* message to the world. WRITE THE BOOK. Save the others." I took a vow: "I will."

I went with Dr. Raine to fill out the death certificate. He was nervous and a little scared. Our eyes connected with a "knowing" look, and we took our comfort from that. He was new to this, I could tell. I felt pity that he would see so many more people die from cancer before his career would be over. He pitied me for my loss. We focused on the matter at hand.

It was a standard form... standard procedure. "Immediate cause: Cardiorespiratory arrest. Due to, or as a consequence of: Rhabdomyosarcoma-metastatic." In the end, Amber didn't die from cancer. Her heart and lungs stopped as a result of it.

I returned to the room where Amber's body lay on the stretcher. Gary stood beside it gazing down at the little girl he had grown to love, then father. We waited for word that the mortician had arrived. It came.

"One last walk." I wanted to take this one last walk with her. Following a nurse, I took hold of the stretcher and wheeled her body around the corner and down the corridor that led to a maze of hallways under the hospital. It was dark, chilly, and still. The corridor seemed to go on forever; winding down to places unknown. The floors were shiny, clean linoleum and the rubber wheels of the stretcher made no sound. The walls were white, with a handrail that led the way to the waiting mortician.

As we turned the corner, I saw him. He just stood there waiting for us. His hands were clasped in front. The dark suit stood in stark contrast to the white walls and floors. The light from the open door, which led to the hearse, illuminated his face; it had no expression. "Black suit... black stretcher... black body bag." We arrived.

In time with his greeting, I removed myself from my body and hovered above the scene. I studied it from a distance, just as I had many times before during my life with Amber. "The mortician respectfully standing off to the side... hands behind his back... patiently waiting his turn. Gary next to me. Me at Amber's side." All eyes were on her. I picked her up and held her once more. Her body was like a rag doll—empty and drained. Her skin had turned light blue. Her face glowed and betrayed her destiny: She was an angel now.

I placed her on top of the open, waiting bag. "A kiss... one last kiss goodbye." I bent down and touched my lips to hers. They were cold and hard. She wasn't there anymore; she was free from her mortal burden; she was now inside of me. Gary kissed her.

I slipped back into my body... back to the scene before me.

We turned and walked away. Nearing the end of the corridor, I stopped to look back. I remembered. I'd promised Amber that I would never leave her, so I stood there transfixed, just watching. I could see her porcelain face disappear as he zipped up the body bag, turned the stretcher, and without hesitation vanished, heading for the waiting hearse.

Gary found a home for us... a
place where we could be a
family... a place where she could
finally have her "Rainbow
Room..." a place where she could
die in peace.

262

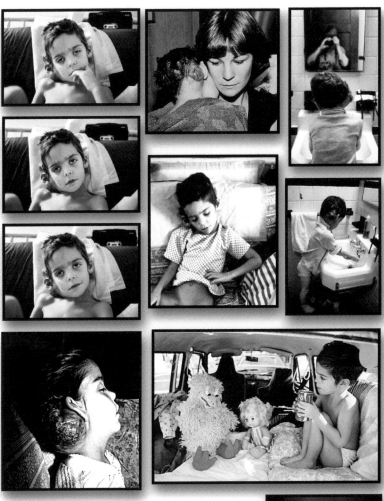

Realizing there was as much *inside* her head as outside, I stood in awe of how she lived with such grace and dignity. Amber always looked at the bright side. Each time I asked her, "Amber, how do you feel?" her answer was the same: "Good." She even managed a smile. Her dignity was something she clinged to, even when she could barely hold her cup. Hand on hip, she insisted she could do anything, even when I knew she couldn't. I set my instinct to "baby her" aside and allowed her to continue to live her life *her* way, not mine.

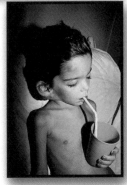

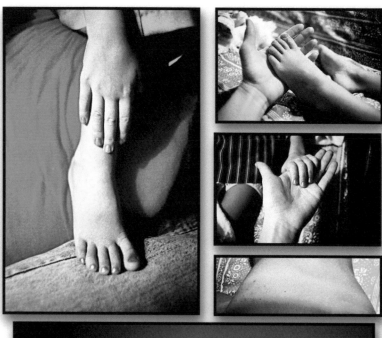

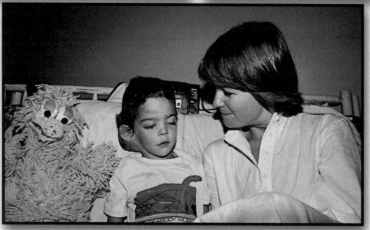

Knowing in my heart that I would cremate her body, I captured every detail I could while she was still with me—her hands, feet, and belly button that once connected her to me. Even her buns that were riddled with holes from the over 1,500 injections of Burton's serum and now more with Morphine, were beautiful to me. The tape recorder stayed on every waking moment so that each wise and wondrous thing she said would never be forgotten. "Mom, wanna play 'Beauty Parlor' and paint my nails pink?" I gladly obliged and wallowed in each moment.

Just after midnight on October 30, 1980, my 27th birthday,
Amber slipped into a coma. A few days earlier, I let her pick out
the clothes she wanted to wear to Heaven. "I wanna wear my school
clothes, Mom." I did as I was told and gladly. Setting the cancer and
circumstances aside, she was still my beautiful little girl and I loved her with
all of my heart and soul. To ease my pain after she died, she gave me the
most precious gift I've ever received: Insight into life after death. "Mom,
when I die, I'll still be Amber, I'll just be *different.*" I gave her
The Key to Heaven to hold onto when she felt she was dying. It would
help her open the Golden Gates, but I knew she wouldn't need it.
She was in God's Hands now just as The Key was in hers.

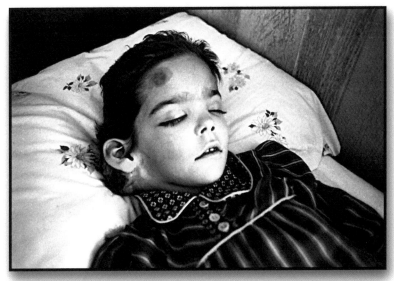

Deep in a coma, she could still hear me. As I told her how much I loved her and thanked her for showing me the meaning of love, tears began to flow down her cheeks. After wiping them away, more followed. "It's okay, Amber. I'll be okay." I reassured her. "Go now. Be with God. Be with God, Amber." The moment I finished that sentence, at 2:30 pm, she stopped breathing and began to glow. Immediately I felt an incredible, warm, outpouring of energy that I knew was God and Amber's spirit going to meet Him. "Thank you, God, thank you," was all I could say. "Thank you." I would spend the rest of my life being grateful.

# Chapter 15

# *Life Lesson / Life Task*

*"The block of granite which was an obstacle in the pathway
of the weak, became a steppingstone in the pathway
of the strong."* —Thomas Carlyle

Gary and I left the hospital. I felt light, calm, unfettered, and grateful. Amber was out of pain and with God. Her body, which held her captive and tortured her to the end, was just a shell. She felt no more pain, only glory. She was now on the other end of the rainbow. She was finally with God.

I felt His glory, too. I had come through the experience of Amber with a purpose to my life, a new set of values, and a better understanding of the meaning of life and death. Most of all, I saw myself as human: strong and vulnerable, good and bad, joyful and desperately sad. I knew I would always have these feelings and would always need God to see me through them. But now I had Amber, too. Not the baby I grew or the little girl who never grew up, but the angel I always knew she would be.

I began the slow process of learning how to live again. The hopeful part of me—my future—died that day with Amber. Just as a baby learns to breathe, eat, talk, crawl, walk, and function in society, I had to learn again, too. God became my teacher, parent, and friend. Throughout Amber's journey, I wanted to give up countless times. He had the strength to carry me through the unbearable times—the loneliness, depression, anger, rage, and exhaustion.

Returning home without her, I knew I'd need a plan. I started at the beginning. I returned to her Rainbow Room to pack up her belongings, but couldn't. I wanted to freeze time... to go back to the time before it happened. So, for three days, I avoided touching or moving anything out of place. I just wanted to live in her world as she left it. I didn't want to make "it" come true.

"You're ready," God said, with a calm and confident reassurance. I was finally ready to say it. "Amber is dead." I took my first step on my way to reliving, I opened the door to her room.

## November 1, 10 pm

*I am sitting on my bed in my room. I haven't gotten used to Amber's room being "my room" yet. I can still feel her presence here, though I know she is dead. My mothering instincts have not died and I wait to hear her voice calling me... needing me. "Mom... Mommy?" Like an echo in my mind, I can still hear her voice.*

*As I opened her closet door, I felt the first shock wave of her absence. Her clothes were hanging as usual. Her toys lay neatly on the floor, just as she left them, waiting for her return. A small pile of dirty clothes lay in the corner ready to be cleaned. This was part of the life Amber left behind. I sank to the floor — the burden was so great — and closed the door behind me. I shut out the world that took my baby from me.*

*It was pitch black. My eyes were useless, so my nose took over. I reached over to her pile of dirty clothes. Breathing deeply, I took in the odor of Amber. It was my only physical link to her now. Her dresses, pants, underwear, mittens, and dirty socks, replaced her warm touch, her smile, her giggles, that impish look in her eyes, and the sound of her calling my name.*

*I cried, but my eyes were not wet. My heart ached and so did my body. I wanted to linger in this sensory world. I wanted there to be more. "What did she leave me to find?" I opened the door and went down to the Laundry Room to search through the dirty clothes for something... for anything that would reconnect me. I found her little red change purse in the pocket of her jacket. Inside was a partially eaten Peppermint Pattie, a white marble, a bubble gum comic, and $9. I laughed. "Oh, how she loved to collect things." My memories... I still had my memories. "No one can ever take them away."*

A few days after she died, we heard a knock at the door. We could see the shadow of a man through the curtain. Gary answered it. As he turned to me, I could read his mind. A man in a black suit stood in the opening. He spoke. "Good evening. Is Mrs. Calistro here?" Gary invited him in. "I'm from the Evergreen Cemetery Association..." His words drifted off as I looked at the box in his hands. It was small, shiny, and brass-colored. A large white label covered the front. "I'm here to give you..." I finished his sentence for him. "Amber's ashes."

I asked Gary to get a plate from the kitchen and took the box from his hands. "Thank you... thank you *very* much." The number "12788" was stamped on the lid. I pried it open and looked inside. A small envelope read "Cremation Certificate." The words "Amber Marie Calistro" and "Cremation No. 12,788" were typed on the front. Inside was the certificate dated "November 3, 1980." I read it, carefully folded it, and returned it to the envelope.

As I peered inside the container, I could see a clear plastic bag filled with cream-colored ashes and bone fragments. I poured them onto the plate. The man stood there silently, almost reverently, as I carefully sifted through Amber's ashes. I was looking for her—*any part of her*—that would confirm she was alive at one time, if not now. Nearly lost in this act, I looked up to thank the man as Gary was walking him to the door. I returned to my world.

Touching her again filled me with the love that only a mother... a woman who grew this child could know. I savored the feel of her powdered bones on the tips of my fingers as I gently set aside pieces that I would keep. "A few multicolored brown pieces... almost like small pebbles. A white one... must be her tooth. A coral-colored one... not sure what that is. A black one with a white shell. Her... her buckle from her shoe!" I was surprised to see it had survived the fire. I picked it up and placed it in the palm of my hand. A subdued and saddened joy washed over me as I thought of her picking out her outfit to die in. *"Mom... I want my school shoes,"* she insisted. My thoughts drifted. "Her life will never fill them but at least I can hold this memory in the palm of my hand *now,* and *forever in my heart."*

Like I was performing a religious ritual, I returned the ashes to the bag and placed it inside the container. Keeping those few pieces out, I poured them into the small envelope with the cremation certificate. I wanted to keep them for myself, not return them to the sea. I put the envelope on top of the ashes, secured the lid, and put the container in my room for safekeeping. I thought, "How ironic. *This* container holds what's left of Amber's body while Amber's body was the container for her soul... for her spirit." It gave me comfort to know she was with me. From now on, she would always be my "Guardian Angel" and an angel to all the others who knew her as well.

Winter was fast approaching and soon the ice would trap Sea Wing at the dock. "I need to spread Amber's ashes in the Sound," I told Gary. "Why don't we ask Jim Motavalli if he'd like to come with us?" Jim had written an article titled *Amber Has Cancer* for the *New Haven Advocate*. It was subtitled *... and the 'War' on the Disease is Making Slow Progress. Why?* He'd done his homework, reported on the state of cancer and the doctors who were open to various cancer treatments, not just the "big three": Surgery, radiation, chemotherapy. He explored the world of cancer and the "Cancer Industry" itself. His heart was touched by Amber; his mind reached out to save her.

We planned to sail to the middle of the Long Island Sound with just a few close friends and scatter most of her ashes there. It was a cold, blustery day as Harry and Diane motored their sailboat out of the Housatonic River and raised the sails, just as we entered the sound. Jim Motavalli, Bob and Joyce, Gary and I, silently sailed past the breakwater, all of us lost in our own thoughts. Mine returned to the past. This river held so many of our memories: The day Amber and I met Gary and Todd at Brown's Boatyard, moving aboard and watching Gary collect oysters from the warmth of the companionway of Sea Wing, many evenings spent sitting in the cockpit as a family while we watched the sun set.

When the time felt right, Harry turned the boat into, then downwind. I walked up to the bow and opened the plastic bag, allowing her ashes to blow with the wind and settle on the surface of the water. The wind was pushing the boat forward, forcing me to say my good-byes to her body now resting at sea and heading towards my future.

A week later, Gary and I returned to the Bahamas to pack up the apartment. It felt odd to be there without Amber. Although my spiritual life had been uplifted, my physical life was devastated. My senses were floundering... groping for her. I wanted to *see* her... *touch* her... *smell* her... *hear* her. Emotionally, I was a pendulum swinging back and forth: First feeling my loss, then all I had gained from knowing her. I held on to the fact that at least I was *moving,* if not fully living.

We packed up two huge duffel bags with the things we didn't need, but someone else would: Amber's clothes and toys, household goods, and food. We took a cab to the village of Williamstown, on the outskirts of Freeport, and distributed them among the local Bahamians. Afterword, we walked down the road to the Traveler's Rest, a local roadside cafe across from the ocean, and reflected on the day. Both Gary and I felt so fortunate to *have* the things so we could give them away. We knew Amber wanted that, too.

I was reminded of Amber's Angel, Mrs. N., who had so generously paid for our stay at the clinic. When I thanked her for all she had done for Amber and for us, she modestly told us why. "Patti, it's not *MY* money it's *GOD'S* money. I'm just here to distribute it for Him." That sentence changed my life. From then on, I would redistribute God's money, too.

I returned to the 'States ready to do battle… ready to redeem Amber's death. I was going to fight for all the people who were suffering from cancer. I plunged into that world, without so much as a thought, and certainly not a plan. I lived at the library; searching for *all the* information that existed about cancer. I contacted *all the* organizations that existed *because cancer existed:* The American Cancer Society, The National Cancer Institute, hundreds of citizen action groups and others. I read *every* book I could get my hands on, watched television shows that interviewed knowledgeable guests, and attended seminars and lectures.

I did nothing halfway; there was no middle, no compromise, no balance. The energy of my grief, my burning desire to save the world, and my sense of injustice, all mixed into the pot. It was simmering with the rage I'd buried for so many years. I learned to "keep the lid on." It would take many years before I was safe enough to boil over. But the pressure needed to be released and I wanted to scream to the world, "My daughter suffered and died in vain!" I got a call from the *National Enquirer.*

"Hello, Mrs. Calistro," the reporter said, "We've been following your daughter's battle with cancer and we'd like to do a story." We made an appointment for them to come interview me. I kept the tape recording running during our interview to resolve any possible questions that might arise. On January 20, 1981, Amber's story was told: *The Love that Death Couldn't Steal.* It didn't soothe me; it made me more determined than ever to "save the others."

I discovered the dark side of cancer; the one most people don't know (or don't *want* to know). Those that do, either want to forget or have been forgotten. It was a world fueled by money, greed, and power. People who were suffering with cancer and were desperate to live were willing to try anything. They were turned into guinea pigs and used in "clinical trials"—experiments —to further a particular research facilities' "hope for a cure." They stopped being people and were turned into statistics and those statistics were manipulated to make the public think that great strides were being made toward eradicating this dreaded disease. Once the drug companies' press releases were fed to the media and the public "bought it," more money was released to those research facilities to continue the cycle.

"But *are* there 'great strides'?" I continued to dig deeper. I wanted to know. The optimistic side of me needed to know that my daughter's death was not in vain; not the result of the futile War on Cancer. The same war that claims *ONE PERSON EVERY MINUTE... OVER HALF A MILLION PEOPLE EVERY YEAR!!!*

I read Ralph Moss' *The Cancer Syndrome* (now *The Cancer Industry)* and Samuel Epstein's *The Politics of Cancer.* I was in shock, unwilling to rest until *everyone* knew what I knew. I learned that CHEMICALS caused cancer... chemicals, our immune system's inability to withstand their bombardment, with a touch of "heredity factor" thrown in for good measure. "Oh, my God, chemicals are everywhere!!! They're in our food, water, air, clothing, schools, homes, cars, workplace... in our world!"

It made sense to me: "If they know what *causes* cancer, then they know how to *prevent* it." I set out to prevent the millions of others from the agony that Amber had suffered. I continued to dig. The more I looked, the more I found. I collapsed under the weight of my newly discovered knowledge and its implications.

My feelings of anger and impotence fueled the fire that was under the "pot." Rather than lose control or boil over, I went into hiding. I stayed at home, pulled the shades down, and cried. I cried, not only for the fact that my only child had suffered and died, but that she didn't *have* to die. I cried for Amber, for me, for anyone who had ever died from cancer, for those who suffered that day, and those who would learn someday that they had cancer, too. I cried for the celebrities who died from cancer and for the homeless person that secretly died alone. I cried for the families they left behind; those who stood by and watched their loved ones suffer, unable to stop the pain, unable to stop them from dying. I wanted to cry myself to death. I wanted to join my little angel who now lived in God's house on the other side of the rainbow.

It was December. The leaves were gone. The world looked dead and I *felt* dead. Any life that I had, was buried deep inside... too deep to feel. I didn't want to celebrate the holidays and I was mad at the world because everyone else *was,* despite the fact that Amber was dead. "Let's just erase Christmas this year," I told Gary. He wanted to help me heal. He needed to focus on something positive and could not understand that I didn't. He even put up a *tree!!!* So I was mad at him, too.

One morning as I awakened from a deep sleep, I heard Amber's voice. "It's okay, Mom. I love you. Love means wiping away someone's tears." She was helping me to heal... teaching me how to live, the same way I taught her. "No need to hurry. This will take a very long time."

Putting my anger aside, I returned to the studio to find my way back to the world. Working long hours, Gary and I remodeled the space that we had abandoned to move to the Bahamas and care for Amber. We decided to divide it into three separate businesses: Studio 3, where I worked doing graphic design, The Artist's Gallery, a gallery that featured one sculptor or other 3D artist and one painting or print artist per month, and The Kid's Studio, a place where children ages 3-12 could come and explore their artistic talents.

Picasso came to mind: "Every child is an artist. The problem is how to remain an artist once he grows up." I was ready to rediscover my own inner child. I was ready to play again. It was just what I needed to create and contribute... to get lost in... to do what I could to elevate others.

Having grown up in California and now living in Milford, a quiet, conservative New England town with my studio on the "Green," I found myself bumping up against history, tradition, and culture. Like a salmon swimming upstream, I was pushing against the flow of what "was," hoping to initiate change for the better, or so I thought. I was dubbed a "Renaissance Woman," a title that caught me off guard and left me exhausted. In June, we closed the studio and moved aboard Sea Wing. We poured all of our time, effort, and money into our plan of sailing to Paradise... of escaping reality and living our dream.

My relationship with Gary was my "safe haven" and he was my rock. He stood by me throughout my ordeal with Amber and remains even now. We decided to begin again... to renew our joy for life that had died with Amber. We tried to create a baby... another life to grow... a soul who would join us forever.

On April 13, 1982, our son, Tobias Matthew Stiewing, was born. Once again, I returned to my "mothering," but this time, with a man who loved us both. It was wonderful to live with the living again and pour my love into this child. Sent down from above, he would teach me the things that Amber could not. His future was bright and I looked forward to seeing it... to sharing it with Gary. Toby was the link we created between our two children, Amber and Todd. Shortly after his birth, I realized this.

Since we were rebuilding Sea Wing in the middle of the boatyard, we moved into a friend's beekeeper's cottage overlooking the Housatonic River. As we lay in our loft, Toby asleep underneath us in his crib, I woke up with a start. I shook Gary awake. "Gary, guess what? Toby is Amber and Todd put together! Tobias… get it? TO… BI… AS; *TWO… BY… US! He's a combination of BOTH of our kids!"* We were both astounded at the miracles that continued to appear in our lives and Toby was certainly the best and the biggest.

Throughout the summer of '82, I enjoyed Toby and my family. My focus was uplifting, positive, and lively. I wanted to ride this crest for a while and needed help to do it. I had to struggle to keep my grief from overpowering me. I contacted The Compassionate Friends, a group of parents whose children have died.

The meetings were held once a month and I looked forward to them *every* month. Nobody else could understand or imagine the emptiness that filled my life. As much as they tried, people just could not feel what I felt. Some simply gave up. "Oh, Patti. It's been over a year now." What they *really* meant was: "Patti, it makes me feel uncomfortable to be around you when you talk about Amber. Just forget her, will you? She's *dead,* for God's sake. I don't want to be reminded of the sadness and the pain, even if there is some joy and happiness, too." It felt so good to be with people who *knew.* My "compassionate friends" let me talk, cry, laugh, get angry, be silent. Whatever I felt was okay; just as long as I *felt* something.

I discovered that there were two distinct groups of parents: Those whose children had died by accident and those whose children died as a result of an illness. The first group, had no chance to say goodbye, but their children died quickly and didn't suffer. The second group, could say goodbye and resolve some of their feelings, but they had to watch their children suffer and die. I was one of these.

Once I began to understand and accept my grief, I resumed my journey down the path to write the book… to "save the others." I spoke with Bernie. As usual, he directed me to the resource I needed. "Elisabeth Kubler-Ross. Have you heard of her? She's an expert on death and dying and holds workshops in different places around the world." I went to the library, read her books, then wrote her a letter. I explained my intention to write Amber's book to help others and asked her advice. She wrote back: "… Once you have the book out, and people trust who you are, the path will open to you all by itself." She asked me to call her and invited me to her *Life, Death, and Transition* workshop in New York in August of '83. "Can you have something for me by then?" "Oh... yes." I had a lot of work to do.

With this goal in mind, I bought a three-ring binder, some paper, and a box of pens. I went to the library and checked out all the books on the subject of "how to write a book." The volumes of notes, my journal, photos, movies, newspaper articles, and audio tapes I'd collected helped me to sort through my experience and make sense of the bits and pieces. With Gary's support, I worked full time on the book.

I sent letters and brochures and photographs and manuscripts to *hundreds* of literary agents and publishers. I was certain that Amber's story was *so* amazing that I would open my front door one day and find them duking it out for the book rights. WRONG. Instead of the deluge of offers, I received a mountain of rejection slips. People cared—they really did—but my "incubation period" was not over. I needed to balance my emotional state and hone my writing skills. Besides, the world was not yet ready to receive the book that would change the way we see cancer forever. "Patience. That is your Life Lesson." It would be a long lesson indeed.

I became active in politics. The local citizen action group was looking for "people with a mission." I nominated myself and with the zeal of a woman who was caught up in the "Women's Liberation" movement "burning her bra," I took on whatever cause was on the agenda. Indirectly, I believed that all "causes" had something to do with cancer... or should I say, Amber. I didn't want to forget her and I didn't want anyone else to either.

The newspapers gladly followed my crusade. I spoke on radio talk shows, television talk shows, and before our state congress. I didn't care what I had to do to get *my* message across. I was indignant at the response. "Gary, people are suffering and dying. What am I supposed to do, wait *fifteen years* to publish the book?" Gary did his best to comfort me and bolster my confidence, but his voice was only background for the words that were booming in my head: "PATIENCE is your lesson. AMBER'S BOOK is your task. You can't have one without the other." "But I just *can't* wait that long and neither can the world." I forged ahead. Like a modern day Joan of Arc, I continued my futile crusade.

The questions began to plague me. I needed to know that Amber's life, her *death*, and the reason she was put on this earth, were not in vain. "If they know what *causes* cancer, why aren't they doing something to *prevent* it? And even if it *is* too late for some people and they *do* get cancer, why, after over twenty-five years since Nixon declared the 'War on Cancer,' haven't we found a *cure?* Cancer costs the American people nearly *$80 BILLION DOLLARS A YEAR! Is money* the reason we continue to let people die? If we *did* find a cure, what would all the people who make a living from cancer—pharmaceutical companies, oncologists, cancer centers, organizations, etc.—*do for work? IF* the United States government is sincerely fighting 'The War on Cancer' and promising to find a cure, is there a plan to retrain and reemploy these people? And *if* not, *why* not?" I had no answers, only searing questions and nagging doubts.

I decided to go to the source for answers: Washington, DC. "Surely *they* will know." I called ahead to make appointments with those people who I deemed most influential... most *responsible* for the state of cancer today: The people at the top.

We packed up Toby and left Shelton, Connecticut. We drove all night, arriving in Bethesda, Maryland, at 3 in the morning. My appointment with Vincent DeVita, head of The National Cancer Institute, wasn't until 8:30, so we looked for a place to get some sleep. We were broke. My crusade had cost us. So we agreed to find a park, spread some blankets on the ground, and sleep until the sun came up. At the crack of dawn, we went to a restaurant for breakfast. I slipped into the restroom, changed into my "meeting-an-important-person" outfit, freshened up, and emerged as "Joan of Arc," ready to do battle.

My meeting with Dr. DeVita lasted about two hours. I asked his permission to record it. He agreed. "Document... I have to document everything." We approached each other with caution and began our conversation. We were far apart on the issue of cancer, but for the first time, I discounted my own "conspiracy theory." DeVita explained his point of view. "This is about individuals—each person acting alone or maybe in concert with a few others. This 'War on Cancer' is not *one big war*, it's thousands, maybe *millions*, of individual... of personal wars. We are divided and fighting on our own."

I began to see that he was a man... simply a man who believed in *his* cause as much as I believed in mine. He was *one person*, not the *whole cancer world*. He strongly supported continued funding for traditional therapies and dismissed anything else as "quackery." I pressed him to open his mind to the complimentary therapies that were working worldwide. "There is a conference on 'Alternative Cancer Therapies' in Los Angeles next weekend. Are you planning to send someone from the National Cancer Institute?" "No, we don't believe they have any value." He was courteous but completely indoctrinated to one way of thinking and unwilling to budge.

I kept my other appointments at the EPA and Congress. They entertained me but gave me no real answers to the convoluted questions I was asking. What I *really* wanted to know was: "Why did Amber die and did she die in vain?"

My last "performance" was at The White House. I created a "sandwich sign" to wear. On the front was a life-sized, beautiful modeling photo of Amber, while on the back were two photos: One of her ghastly tumor with "CANCER" written under it; the other of her dead in the back of my car with "KILLS" under it. "Cancer kills." That was my message and I wanted the world to stop and take notice.

Setting fear and trepidation aside, I strapped the sign on and began my arduous trek around the perimeter of The White House. With each lap I took, I'd look across the street at Gary and Toby playing in the park and cheering me on. "Hi, Mommy!" I heard as I watched my innocent son excited to see me. He waved excitedly. I pleaded with God. I wanted to give up. "I want to stop this battle. I want to ignore cancer, just like every body else does. I want to be normal... typical... invisible. I'm tired of fighting."

My pleas were ignored and my legs kept moving. I fought the wind as it tried to rip the sign off my body. I fought God as He nudged me along the sidewalk. *"Please*, God. Let me stop. I've had enough. Besides, no one is listening... can't You see that?" People were avoiding me... hurrying away from my path. "People *will* listen to Amber. In the meantime, you can't stop until you're done... until Amber's book is done. It *will* happen all in good time... *MY* time, not yours. You can't force people to look at something they can't even see." My family faded into the distance as I took another lap. "Oh, God, I just want to be with my family. I want to raise my son and live in peace. *This is too damn hard!!!"*

Their eyes were filled with fear. People were looking at me like I was a nut... too radical... nearly insane... a lunatic for sure. And they were right. Some refused to take the brochure I'd created to explain the ravages of cancer and the devastation it caused for me and my little girl. "No... no... no thanks." They hurried on, trying to escape the reality of cancer that I forced upon them. "Well, God, if Amber can suffer and die for the masses, I can feel tired, rejected, humiliated, and foolish."

Dan Beegan, a reporter from *The Associated Press,* met me in front of The White House. I did my best to project confidence, strength, and optimism, but I was discouraged and feeling rejected. I wanted to quit. I wanted God to leave me alone. "Go pick on someone else, dammit!" That afternoon, I checked into a hotel on the outskirts of town to ignore cancer, enjoy my family, and lick my wounds.

I shifted the focus of my life to my family, but in brief spurts, I reached out to the world for help. I wrote Richard Stolley, managing editor for *Life* magazine, asking him for one page to tell Amber's story to the world. He kindly replied; he tried to let me down gently. I wasn't satisfied. I called. "I want one page... just *one...* to tell Amber's story with pictures." He painfully told me the truth. "Patti, people don't need to be slugged in the face with cancer. They pick up a magazine to feel good. They don't want to see this." I knew he was right, but I had to convince him. "Yes, but people also have a natural curiosity for blood, guts, and gore. Look at how many 'rubber-neckers' pass an accident scene straining to see body parts." "Patti, that's an *accident.* This is something we all have a part in creating." I thanked him for his time and hung up to digest what he said. He *was* right, but I couldn't admit it. I was too stubborn, too consumed by my own rage and grief, to see the truth.

Gary did his best to distract me. We poured our hearts, our souls, and all of our money into Sea Wing, the sloop we had lived aboard then dry-docked while we cared for Amber. It was our "dream boat," a sort of "escape hatch" from society. We planned to sail away to Paradise and the Virgin Islands... away from the chemicals, pollution, cold weather, and reality. We devoted ourselves for a year on this project. And then it turned to two, then three. Shortly after we launched her, we fell in love with Stormalong, a 45' Hans Christian, and repeated the long restoration process again. It would be awhile before I could break free.

As long as I was "connected," I was compelled to continue my crusade. A producer from *The Good Day Show* in Massachusetts called. He wanted me to appear on a show titled *A Parent's Right to Choose.* Since the Chad Green fiasco, it became an issue whether parents had the *right* to choose the therapy for their children. I eagerly accepted the opportunity to speak out in agreement with "freedom of choice." Chad's legacy would not be forgotten and neither would Amber's.

While speaking to the public, I had hope that I was *doing* something to stop the madness... to make sense out of the chaotic world of cancer. I found it impossible to sit back, watch, and do nothing while millions of people were "dying like flies." I appeared on the *Good Morning* show in New York with Regis Philbin and Kathy Lee Gifford. They were gracious, but at a loss at how to treat someone like me: A parent who had a child die. It seemed I was every parent's worst nightmare. People were curious, but worried it would happen to them; as if knowing me might somehow "curse" them.

As the cameras rolled, I tried to be concise—not too emotional, educated—not the "wild-eyed grieving mother" who was outraged that "the doctors didn't believe me." Instead, I was robotic, unfeeling, calculated, logical. I remained on the set after the show to field questions from the crew and the audience. They were hungry and grasping for answers. I did the best I could to pacify them with the knowledge and resources I had obtained. I left feeling certain, "Amber's book is not only *wanted,* but *needed* as well. People *do* want to know." But I also knew that now was not the time. I needed to heal, find my balance and know a sense of peace.

With Sea Wing sold and the restoration of Stormalong complete, the time had come for us to "cut the cord." Just as Amber was now free from her body... free from her pain, I was released from my own. "Paradise awaits!" I repeated to myself as we outfitted the boat. The promise of a new life in the Virgin Islands, held its spell over us. Throughout the years with Gary, *My* Dream had turned to *Our* Dream. Though the scenery was different—no house on a hill, no fancy car, no closets and closets of coordinated clothes, or two children—My Dream, now *Our* Dream, was becoming a reality.

It had been nearly six years since Amber had died. Finally, it was time to slip away and find some peace and solitude. On October 20, 1986, we untied our lines, pulled away from the docks at Milford Marina, and set our sails on a course to freedom and the island of St. Croix. It would be the final destination in our "journey of a lifetime," a chance to rest and recuperate. The radical revolutionary that I had become, was longing to be the calm and contented woman of my dreams. I'd spent the first half of my life fighting: To survive, to belong, and then for the chance for my daughter to live. I was weary, tired of my life of pain. I wanted to stop running, to reflect, to live a simple and uncomplicated life with my family, away from the public eye. I didn't want my past to follow me and dictate my future. I just wanted to be Patti, a person I needed to know and love. I wanted to live, *really* live, not spend the rest of my life dying.

We were sailing along at a nice clip and would be out to sea in no time. We rounded the end of the Long Island Sound—the same 'Sound that held Amber's ashes—and lazily sailed along towards New York City and the East River. It was dusk and the sun was beginning to fade. I laid out dinner on the gimbaled dining table below and invited the crew to dig in. As we enjoyed the evening meal on the deck, we were transfixed by the scene: The skyline of New York framed the people that lined its banks, looking into our world and beyond to the sea. A deep, iridescent blue was the background canvas for the grey and black buildings, filled to the brim with the twinkling office lights; people still hard at work on the job. The air was crisp and cool. As we sailed along in Stormalong, I stood on the bowsprit with the wind in my face like a figurehead of a ship leading the way to explore uncharted worlds. *This* was my moment of freedom; a moment I would burn into my being, never to forget.

The wind filled the sails as we cut through the water, heading out to sea, leaving it all behind. The people standing along the shore were wistfully watching. I answered their thoughts with my own. "I am breaking free and *you* can, too!" Then I spoke to myself. "Look at the skyline of The City over there. People stopping, staring, watching me sail into the sunset; secretly wishing they could trade places." I felt strangely connected to them, but not absorbed. I was leaving. "I'll come back to save you, I promise." I knew my journey was only a reprieve. I would need to return to complete my Life Task, my reason for being on earth. "Mom, I know I'm here to help a lot of people." "Yes, Amber, I know."

The last rays of sun peaked around the Statue of Liberty, our American symbol of freedom, just as we turned our boat and sailed into the open ocean... the twilight... the stars. The iridescent blue of the sky melted into the water within moments. Since there was no moon, it was impossible to distinguish the line between sea and sky. We were sailing through space. "At sea at last!" For the first time in my life, I felt free. Except for the ship-to-shore radio, we had no contact with the outside world. I relished the thought. "No pressure... no traffic... no people... no image to uphold... no cancer to eradicate." Again, I was dreaming.

The last photo of my beautiful little girl / Her ashes, what remained of this child I grew deep inside / Spreading her ashes in the Long Island Sound

We returned to the Bahamas
to collect our things and discovered what Amber left
behind. Her "Sheepy," tap shoes, toys and angel
wings would not be needed now.

We opened Studio 3, a commercial art studio, in January of 1981 and closed it in June. We turned our attention to our family and rebuilding Sea Wing so that we could sail away to Paradise... away from cancer once and for all.

STUDIO 3
15 river street
milford, ct. 06460
877-5208

murals · storefronts · signs
diesel trucks · commissions
patricia a. calistro

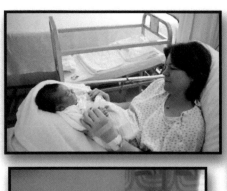

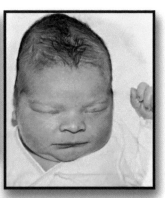

On April 13, 1982, Tobias Matthew Stiewing was born. He is both of our children—Amber and Todd—together. "Two... by... us," was a pleasant surprise to realize one day.

With Grampa and Gramma Stiewing / Toby was a happy child / The "sandwich sign" I wore when I walked around The White House during my "Cancer Crusade" / Sailing away to Paradise in our second boat, Stormalong

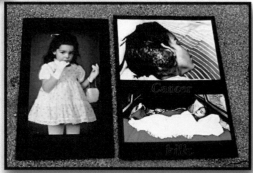

# Chapter 16

# *First Edition*

*"God gives every bird its food, but He does not
throw it into its nest."* —J.G. Holland

**This chapter was the original Epilogue, written in April 1996 in
our home in Pompano Beach, Florida, a few months before the
first edition of "Embrace the Angel" was published.**

It's been almost ten years since I "sailed away to Paradise..."
to freedom... to my needed break from the world of cancer. As it
turns out, my *attempt* to fulfill my Dream was just that—an
attempt. God had other plans for me. My journey to tell Amber's
story and save the world has taken a few twists and turns; not all
of them were followed with enthusiasm. Yet, each delay and
detour has brought me closer to my goal... closer to this book.

After leaving New York harbor, heading for our new life in
St. Croix, we sailed offshore, motored down the Inter-coastal
Waterway, and ended up docking in Beaufort, North Carolina. It
was the last stop… the launching point for our trip to Paradise and
the ideal life that awaited.

Since Toby was now three and a half, he enjoyed the
adventure of living on a boat. He would stand on the bow pulpit
and wave to other boats that went by or yell to the people on the
docks as we were pulling in, "Hi! I'm Toby!" We knew he would
have no trouble making friends or feeling comfortable and
confident in strange circumstances.

On October 30, 1986, my thirty-third birthday and the sixth
anniversary of Amber's death, we were ready to make the thirteen
day ocean crossing to the end point on our chart: St. Thomas, in
the US Virgin Islands. Stormalong was well stocked with supplies,
our sailing skills were honed, and the "weather window" was
perfect. In preparation for our journey, Gary checked the oil. I

could see that something was wrong the minute I saw his face. "There's water in the oil." I looked at the dip stick. A creamy, white goo clung to it. He wiped it off and checked it again. The same result. "We've got a problem. Water's gotten into the engine... into the oil. We can't make the crossing today."

For the next few days, we tried every trick in the book to find the source of the water and fix it, all to no avail. It was now November and our "weather window" was beginning to close. Finally, it shut. For the next three months, we stayed in Beaufort to find the source of the water infiltration and repair it. Crossing the Gulf Stream that runs south to north up the East Coast was dangerous and we needed to be prudent and safe. "Let's stay put and fix it right." We both agreed.

We worked with a local mechanic who told us to pull the engine out of the boat and place it on skids he put on the dock. Using our boom as a "come-along," we made the preparations. A "Nor'easter—" where the sea is whipped, counter clockwise, into the eastern seaboard—was fast approaching. It would be upon us in a matter of hours. We had no choice but to go for it. "Gary, are you sure we should do this?" I hesitated but knew time was of the essence as our money was running out. "Living aboard builds character," I remembered hearing or saying to myself or reading somewhere. This was just another building block.

Finding more problems with the engine, we stayed in Beaufort for three months while the mechanics repaired them. Gary, being resourceful and caring as always, found odd boat jobs nearby. When those dried up, he took a bus up to Annapolis, Maryland, to work with his friend, Peter Paglia, in his wood shop, Atlantic Woodworks. We were grateful for the money *and* the friendship. We were "down to the dregs."

Our "$25 Christmas" was upon us and we vowed to make the most of it. Gary was working in Annapolis so Toby and I borrowed the loaner car at the marina where we were docked and went shopping. We got a small, artificial tree for $8, a bit of tinsel, and decorated the tree with his toys and other objects. I secretly bought him a couple of "Hot Wheels" from Santa. Gary returned from working in Annapolis just in time to celebrate Christmas. We did not have much in money or things, but having come through our ordeal with Amber, our values had certainly adjusted. Health, family, friends, and home were the most important things in life, in that order. We were wealthy; we had an abundance of all of them.

In January, the engine was finally repaired and in place and we were ready to move on. We needed to build up our savings before we made the crossing to the Virgin Islands. "Do we continue heading south to Florida and take a chance at finding work or motor back up the Inter-coastal to Annapolis and have security?" That was the dilemma. After much debate and discussion, we went with more security. Although it was the middle of winter, we knew we could live aboard; we'd done it before in Connecticut. We set off on our journey to Annapolis. It was quite the adventure as we motored our way through the heavy fog and ice covered water, but we made it to City Dock. We'd stay for the winter. Our plan was to work, pay off our debts, and then carry on to live our dream in the Caribbean.

Winter went, spring came, then summer. We were finding our niche and beginning to settle down in this quaint harbor town on the Chesapeake Bay. We put Toby in school, Gary continued to work at the Peter's shop, and I started a business varnishing boats, a trade I'd begun while living aboard in Milford. It was possible to bury the torment and ignore the reality of cancer. Nobody knew me. I could get on a boat, keep my head down, and work on the brightwork, taking care to make it as "perfect" as humanly possible. "Ahh... peace at last," I'd sigh as I set about sanding and varnishing. I was in hiding and I knew it. I also knew that I couldn't hide forever. One day, I would *have* to complete my Life Task but only when the timing was right. And it wasn't right yet.

Too impatient to wait, I needed to take action... to stop people from dying. No matter how much I tried to ignore it, I couldn't. Every day I was reminded that cancer continued to kill. As I stood in line at the grocery store, watched the news on TV, talked with the parents at Toby's school, or picked up a paper, somebody—somewhere—was suffering with cancer. *EVERY MINUTE, SOMEONE WAS DYING:* Another movie star, politician, writer, philanthropist, TV personality, sports figure, neighbor, friend, or stranger. I simply could not set this issue aside and go on with my life, letting all those people suffer and die, and wait for someone else to speak out on their behalf. Once again, I jumped back in the fray.

I dug out the "third draft" of Amber's book, dusted it off, and assembled the voluminous notes and materials I had continued to collect through the years. In the winter of '88, I hunkered down in our boat and buried myself again in my obsession. I sat down to write what I hoped would be the *"last* draft" of the book.

In the meantime, Gary and I were growing apart. "Our Dream" together became *"My* Dream." We ended our marriage in March of '89. Though we remained close, our personal goals and priorities were worlds apart. We continued to raise Toby together with the same commitment to parenting that we shared with Amber and Todd: Love, trust, respect, caring, discipline, manners, and compassion for others. I was fortunate enough to have the opportunity to redeem my own childhood by raising Toby and watching him develop into a fine young man. He has all the qualities of Amber and Todd, yet he's clearly an individual in his own right.

Believing that our future was not in Annapolis but in Pompano Beach, Florida, Toby and I moved into a house with Aunt Anne. She needed a family as much as we did. Uncle Bill had died a few years earlier and I was now divorced from Gary. We clung to each other and the hope of creating a family... a safe haven... an oasis to cherish as we faced our day-to-day living. It was good to provide a fulfilling life for Aunt Anne and Toby, but a struggle to keep it afloat on my own.

The house was a "Money Pit," just like the movie. With no man and no resources, I was left to get it done... to put my construction skills to use... to transform this house into a home for me, Toby, and Aunt Anne. I set to work repairing and remodeling. Most of my time was spent fixing, painting, and maintaining our home. It didn't leave much time for Toby but I did my best to carve out "quality time" to be "Mom." I knew I was only one person and a very fragile one at that. Once again, I had to hide it for the sake of my son.

Along with seeing myself as human, I began to see others in the same light. "The Enemy" in the War on Cancer, was only men and women who had the same goal that I did: Eradicate cancer in our lifetime. The *way* they chose to achieve it varied drastically from mine in some cases; paralleled it in others. I came to see that pointing a finger to *blame* them for propagating cancer, only stopped me from looking further; from continuing my pledge to *work together to save the others.* Amber was the symbol under which to unite. "They *will* listen to Amber." *MY* message died as Amber's gave birth in my imagination... in my mind... and, eventually, on my computer screen.

All the bitterness, rage, and resentment that fueled my previous attempts at publishing, were replaced by realistic compassion and forgiveness. I tore down my walls of resistance and let Amber write this book. "How would *she* see this person? What would *she* say... think... feel about this situation?" I realized that *all* of us are human without exception, even the doctors who misdiagnosed Amber's cancer. We are human *first* and what we choose to do with our humanity *second. What we do for a living comes second to how we are living our lives.*

I sat down to write the *fourth* draft of Amber's book but now it had a title: *Embrace the Angel,* God's words to me when I emerged from the shower in Montreal and saw Amber sleeping on her back with her toes shoes poking through the blankets and her ballerina outfit on. Draft after draft, I grew with each one. I discovered more bits of wisdom... of insight... of direction from God. Letting go of *my* words, thoughts, and deeds and "letting God," moved me closer to the final draft.

This draft was different from the others; it had feeling and passion. Putting off the inevitable, was really at the core of why I couldn't face or relive the pain. I could see that some of the roadblocks on the path to publishing the book were placed there by me. "I'm not ready to 'take Amber's book to the world' until I...

...spend a month or so on an island 'fine tuning' the manuscript."
...have enough money to publish it myself."
...grow my nails."
...buy a computer and printer and 'do it right'."
...lose weight."

...meet a man who can support me so I can work on the book full time.

...finish working on my house."

...quit varnishing boats."

...raise my son."

...overcome my fear of being successful, having people discover who I *really* am, giving up my privacy, having money."

...get my braces off."

...meet a philanthropist who believes in my cause and supports it."

...am sure—without a doubt—that the world will not reject me."

...can guarantee that I won't be hurt."

...clean my car... my living room... my yard... my teeth."

...see Toby graduate high school and be on his own, so he won't have to suffer any teasing or ridicule from anything I wrote."

...am prepared for the onslaught of criticism."

...trim the trees, sweep the pool, paint the roof, stain the deck, and re-coat the driveway."

...am certain that *God* is directing my steps, not me."

All valid reasons why I couldn't move forward. In the end, I did what I could: I tried. I knew that God knew best, not me. His direction and me following it, was more important than my need to be right or successful or put it off any longer. I was compelled to write and let the world slip away while I did it. I put myself in "neutral" and maintained my life—Toby, Aunt Anne, house, car, job, surviving—but my writing was in "drive" and going 100 miles an hour.

I planned to debut it at the Miami Book Fair International in November of 1994. "This is the place for *Embrace the Angel* to be discovered." I was certain that a publisher would scoop it up and beg me to sign a contract on the spot. I printed thirty-five "review copies," made some signs, created a display, brochures, photos, and had the location for my booth. The day before the opening, Hurricane Gordon made a U-turn and returned to South Florida, just in time to cancel the fair. I was crushed and floundering. "What do I do *now*, God?"

This roadblock was only a temporary defeat but a defeat, nonetheless. I wondered, "Why I can't I be given a chance at completing my goal. Dammit, God, why are You making this *impossible?*" "You're not ready. Have patience. I will tell you when." I *was* ready. I was ready to give up. I was tired of being alone, frustrated by the constant struggle, and needed the support of family and friends. We moved back to Annapolis.

In September of '95, I saw an announcement in *The Capital*, our local newspaper, for Hospice volunteers. I realized that my goal was noble, but my methods were not. I needed to return... to remember *why* I was given this enormous Life Task: "Amber was one person but *each* person who suffers from cancer needs a voice." I didn't need to save the *whole world*, only each person in it. I signed up to volunteer.

The training was intense and very thorough. I'd volunteered my time to many causes quite often in my life, but this organization was different. The people at Hospice of the Chesapeake were more concerned about me and my needs than what I could do for them. I was pleasantly surprised. They not only trained me to understand grief and the dying process, but they helped me to put my life in perspective and refocus my goals.

My goal was to publish a book that not only was needed, but *wanted* as well. I knew that it wouldn't get done the "traditional" way: First, you find a publisher who believes in your book, then publishes it, and trickles it out to the public through the major bookstores and the media.

I believed *Embrace the Angel* would come into its own the other way around. I would self-publish it because *I* believed in the need to tell Amber's story, open up the door to cancer, and unite the cancer community under a common goal. I would start the flow by distributing it to people around me, and then let it spread on its own... person to person... neighbor to friend, etc. This book was too controversial for anyone but me to take the risk and publish it.

I also came to the realization that I couldn't do it alone; I needed help from the public, those who had the most to gain or lose from knowing Amber's story. I asked Kathy Edwards, the feature editor at *The Capital*, to publish a story asking the public to read and review *Embrace the Angel* and send me their comments. Mary Grace Gallagher wrote a touching story and at the end of the article printed my address and asked for feedback. February and March of '96, I sent "review copies" back and forth to many people who responded. The encouragement I received was tremendous:

- *"Once I picked it up, I couldn't put it down."*
- *"When I finished the book, I felt completely full—full of Amber, full of Patti, full of love and compassion, especially the desire to reach out and help. It's like you gave me a wonderful gift. I shall look forward to Amber's book being released."*
- *"There are so many people I wanted to share this book with. I forced myself to send it right back so you can get on with getting it published!"*
- *"To everyone I say: If you think you love your children now, wait until you've read 'Embrace the Angel.' This book will make you tuck your children in bed a little tighter and give them that extra kiss each night."*
- *"I wish you luck in everything you do and look forward to seeing the book in stores."*
- *"The story was compelling! You have the gift of bringing one right into your life—the pain, the joy, the horror, the hope is all there... those whom it reaches will never be the same after reading it. Patti has opened the door for many who dare to be different in their approach to cancer treatment. She has made enough inroads already to guarantee that those who need Amber's gift, will find her."*
- *What took you so long to write this?!? Amber's story truly touched my heart. You were blessed to have such an Angel. I doubt, seriously, if any adult could endure what Amber did with such grace and dignity. She was surely sent from Heaven above to teach us all a lesson about living and dying."*
- *"I stayed up all night reading it."*
- *"Let me applaud you for having the discipline, patience, as well as the creativity to put this book together. I found it extremely interesting. Congratulations!"*

Without the support of these people who made the time to read Amber's book and write their impressions and feedback, I would have tucked the book away and learned to live with the regret. Instead, I sat at my computer typing away for days on end. I was determined to publish this book.

The process I went through in *writing* this book *nearly* equaled the pain I shared with Amber over fifteen years ago. Each time, with each "draft," I'd relive the horrendous experience of watching her suffer, then die. But this agony is *nothing* compared to the short span of *her* life with cancer. When I look back at her journey and all that she went through, I stand in awe and admiration.

She endured it all: The ridicule from the first tumor, the traumatic surgery and barrage of tests, enduring coffee enemas and a multitude of pills daily, getting radiation and losing her hair, over *300 blood pulls and nearly 1000 injections* in the Bahamas, and her incredibly painful death. Yet, when I asked her, "Amber, how do you feel?" Her answer was always the same. "Good." Only an angel would say that, I'm sure. To have the power to rise above this earthly pain and see the good, is truly a gift from God. Her life is her gift to you. Treasure her words and learn from her pain. Embrace the angel. She is your solace... your safe place... your refuge and your hope.

Amber is a messenger. But more than that, she is our guide from God... our eyes into the beyond... our guardian angel gently nudging us to be the best we can be and leave this earth a better place for our children.

Our dream of escape was never realized. On October 30, 1986, we found water in Stormalong's oil and returned to Annapolis.

Despite our divorce, Gary and I set aside our differences and raised Toby together / The "Money Pit" I bought in Florida

I have the BEST life: The "Man of My Dreams," a mom-in-law who I adore, a family who cares, friends who sustain me, and my health.

Annie, our beloved
Jack Russell, came
into our lives
in November
of 2005.

302

Before Toby left for deployment to the Persian Gulf in October of 2007, we decided to go on a "Cheating Death" vacation. White water rafting and zip-lining, we would tempt fate. I nearly lost my life when I got caught under a rock in the rapids.

*Clockwise:* Toby meets the love of his life: Kimberly, a sweet, talented, kind-hearted young woman who loves my son / Going zip-lining together on our "Cheating Death" vacation / Their doggies: Soco and Mali

2010 was our "Up in the Air" year: Glider rides (John was the pilot for his since he flew helicopters for the Navy), skydiving with Toby and Kimberly, and a hot air balloon ride over Napa Valley!

*Clockwise:* Ireland 2005 / Dingle Peninsula / With my good friend, Susan / At Bunratty Castle / One of many pubs / Irish graveyard / Richard, Susan, and us

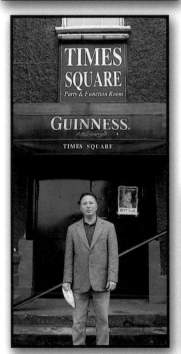

*Clockwise:* Italy 2008 / At Mamma Agata's / Positano / Amalfi Coast / At the Coliseum with Mom

*Clockwise:* A HUGE and warm welcome from our family in Corleone, Sicily / Our family / Mom and Rosa walking the narrow streets

2009 Southern Caribbean
cruise on Celebrity's
*Millennium* to celebrate both
of our birthdays / Dennis and
Joanie, our new neighbors

Cozumel 2010 to celebrate our 10th wedding anniversary

Our 2010 Garlic & Grapes
trip to California

311

Our home... our oasis / THE Outdoor Kitchen w/Pizza Oven, John's great masterpiece / My Studio (with Annie perched in the window), where I breathed life into this book once again / Gary installing a skylight over our bed in the Master Bedroom

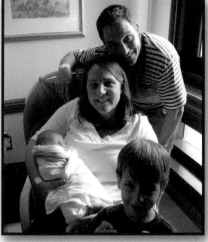

My life is good. Filled with good neighbors, good friends, good times, and good health. Yes, there *is* life after death. While we are left on this earth without hearing, seeing, touching, or embracing our loved ones, we can know their spirit lives in our hearts forever. And *that* is where we will find them, but *different*, as Amber reminds us. Stay open and they will pour in.

## I *love...*

...my family.
...my friends.
...my future.
...living with passion and joy.
...sharing my life with loved ones.
...growing things.
...traveling to see the world.
...elevating others.
...spending my time wisely.
...embracing life to the fullest.
...walking in the Metaphorest
with Annie and listening
to God for instructions.

# Epilogue

Today is the thirty year anniversary of Amber's death and my fifty-seven birthday. It is the perfect time to remember... to reflect... to gather the parts of my past that I need to let go. Completing this rewrite, republishing it, and then seeing it on the bookshelf, is my way of "closing the book" on this journey and opening up my future for what lies ahead.

As I sit here in my Studio, watching the crystal which hangs in the skylight spread its multitude of rainbows across my periwinkle walls, I'm reminded of Amber's "Rainbow Room." I am feeling contented, excited, even exhilarated. Having spent the last several months writing and rewriting the first edition of *Embrace the Angel,* I am finally at a place of peace. I am ready to launch it, let go, and move in another direction.

The past thirty years have been filled with every emotion, thought, and feeling that you can imagine... that you have probably experienced in your own life as well. For me, this time has been one of discovery, transition, challenge, and learning. I am forever grateful to Amber and to God for teaching me to keep my heart open to love, not closed from pain. Doing so, has allowed me to "see the change" that Amber knew her death would bring. A prophecy from a soon-to-be angel, her words continue to transform my life: "Mom, when I die, I'll still be *Amber,* I'll just be *different."* She continues to teach me "the difference" as I travel along my path to teach others.

My journey with Amber transformed me from a young woman with no purpose in life to a woman with a mission to elevate others... from drifting without a destination to staying focused on the mark on my internal compass... from wondering why God chose me to knowing exactly why He put me on this earth. My childhood prepared me to be the mother to my own children that I wanted from my own. The trials and tribulations in my life gave me the tools, confidence, and persistence to keep going until I found a solution. Recalling what Amber endured with grace and dignity, taught me about what is *really* important in life: Sharing my life with loved ones, maintaining my health, spending my limited time on earth wisely, and using my "Power Within" for good.

As with any life story, mine is filled with people who touched me deeply—whether our time together was for a moment or for years. I crossed paths with thousands of people during my time here on earth. We were deliberately meant to meet and exchange our "life lessons." Each one added a thread to my tapestry of life. All made me who I am today.

After our divorce in 1986, Gary and I set our differences aside and continued to parent Toby together. I concentrated on raising my son and earning a living working on the brightwork—the teak wood trim—of boats. It was difficult and physically exhausting but it paid the bills and allowed me to enjoy my obscurity and solitude.

With my portion of the proceeds from the sale of Stormalong, our 43' Hans Christian that we lived aboard, I produced a how-to video titled *Secrets of the Trade: Brightwork, the Art of Varnishing.* It was fun and exciting to write the script and hire a company to film me. It was my reward for all the days I worked in the snow and frigid winds of winter; the rain, sun, heat and humidity of summer, and in every other condition you can imagine.

Although very involved with my community, I knew there was something missing. Toby was a teenager who began emerging into his own life, one separate from my own. From

Amber, I learned that *people do die* and so I raised him to be a healthy, happy, man able to get along in this world without me, should I die first. He learned this lesson well.

After 10 years of being single, I was ready to move in another direction... to develop my own life, one without my children in my sight but always in my heart. It was during a trip to Europe with my good friend Susan and her family, that my path became clear.

We celebrated a lovely Christmas week in England at her parents, Dori and Ken's home, then I went on to France on my own. I landed in Paris with no plan, only a desire to see the country, know the people, and find myself. I bought a "Eurail Train Pass" and launched my expedition, heading south to Toulouse to spend the New Year. I found myself alone in my hotel room at midnight with a bottle of wine, a loaf of bread, and a chunk of cheese. I called Gary and spoke with Toby. "Hi Mom!" My heart melted. "Are you having fun in France?" I was, but still, something or *someone* was missing.

Taking the train from Marseilles to Geneva, Switzerland, was magical. I sat alone in the passenger cabin "ooohing and aaahing" at the incredible beauty of the pristine mountains, streams, and villages around me. It was a memory in the making and I looked around, hoping to share this incredible scene with someone—anyone who was near enough to hear me—stranger or not. The cabin was empty. I was alone. This realization drowned out the deafening silence.

It was then that I realized I'd come full circle... that I'd arrived at the other end of the "Soul Mate Spectrum." From "I don't need a man" to "I don't want a man" to "I'd be *nice* to have a man in my life" to "I NEED a man to share my life with." This took me by surprise, but I knew it was right. "When I get back to the 'States, I'm going to find a man, someone who is caring, loving, and will share the 'Four Corner Foundation' that anchors my life: Morals, values, interests, and goals." The oh, so true Swedish proverb, came to mind: "Shared joy is double joy. Shared sorrow is half sorrow."

Knowing that the Man of My Dreams had not... *would* not come knocking at my door, I joined an online matchmaking site.

Dating was different this time; it was more about what *I* could do for him than what *he* could do for me. "Mine" would become "ours," we would give without expectation, be willing to compromise, and not measure words, deeds, or love. We would see our relationship as an empty glass into which we both poured ourselves. Once we "emptied our glasses" into our relationship, it would be impossible to see who gave what and where the dividing line was. I'd learned a lot from my two previous failed marriages, and I was determined not to make it three. "I only have so much time on this earth and I have to use it wisely," was a thought I repeated often.

After several months of searching, I met John on July 4, 1998, a day filled with firecrackers and celebration of our country's independence, of our dependence on one another. It was an irony that was recognized. We met at a bookstore, a neutral, public place, recommended for online meetings. I suspected he might "be the one" but restrained myself and enjoyed his company without expectations. "Want to head into DC and watch the fireworks on The Mall?" "Sure, let's do it!" I was ready to take the plunge.

Taking a train into Washington, DC, we landed on the National Mall and merged into the crowd's current. I could only see him; the rest were strangers, merely moving objects in the background. As the evening progressed, I shared my life—all of it, both good and bad. He didn't flinch. "It will take a *really* strong man to be in my life... to love me with all of his heart," I thought. By the end of the night, I knew. "He *is* the one."

We've been together for nearly thirteen years now. John has truly transformed me from a restless crusader to a contented woman (still with an exuberant joy for living), very much in love with my husband, truly grateful for the blessings I've been given. Sharing my life with him, his family and mine, our friends, and Annie, our Jack Russell, has been the fulfillment of my early dreams and satisfied my deepest desire to belong, to be cared for, to be accepted without hesitation for exactly who I am.

Living my life in the light, away from the shadows of CancerWorld, gave me the chance to grow and flourish. I was able to take some of the lessons learned in my childhood—"Be prepared for anything" and "Make sense out of chaos"—and transform them into ways which would help others.

I got involved in my community as Outreach Coordinator for the City of Annapolis Office of Emergency Management, delivering workshops and presentations on "Preparedness" throughout the region. It was my passion! I was able to empower others to feel more secure in our uncertain world. Rather than live in fear of the unknown, they could relax, knowing that they and their loved ones would be comfortable with enough food, water, and supplies to last through whatever crisis came—whether it was a snowstorm, job loss, terrorist attack, or hurricane.

Learning how to transform chaos into calm as a little girl, I began to study the art and science of Professional Organizing. It was a great career choice, as I was able to use all the skills and tools I'd collected from the various jobs throughout my life: Design, carpentry, business, helping others overcome challenges and reach their potential. It was a productive outlet and a powerful way to change people's lives by changing the *things* that were in it.

My life has been powerful and peaceful; full to the brim with memories, challenges, opportunities, experiences, and people. Most of all, it's the *people* in my life who add color, dimension, and meaning. People, and the precious time we spend with them, are what matter in the end.

Here is an update on the people who were (and some still are) a part of Amber's story and my life:

## Toby...

...is in the Navy keeping us safe and protected. It's been over eight years now and he plans to stay the full twenty and retire at forty-one. I admire and respect the man he has become and the life he has created: A woman he loves at his side, a full circle of good friends, and family he knows he can count on and trust. He and his girlfriend, Kimberly, along with their two dogs, Soco and Mali, live just a few hours away in Virginia Beach.

It's been wonderful to have a second child in this life! I've been given another chance to "mother" and enjoy watching my child grow up, not be snatched away so suddenly. The privilege of being a parent with all the struggles and challenges that are part of the package, has made me feel both redeemed and blessed beyond words.

## Gary...

...is still in my life... is still in *our* lives. He is a good man and a great friend to both John and me. We invite him to our parties and gatherings and he does the same. He lives just a short drive away on the banks of the Chesapeake Bay in the home of his dreams. Building it over a period of several years *and with his own two hands,* is a testament to—not only his skills as a carpenter and builder—but his fortitude and commitment to realizing his dreams and enduring the discomfort, with a smile on his face, until they come true.

Though now divorced, he has two beautiful children, Benah and Eli, who he adores. Sad that his marriage ended, but having stood at my side through Amber's ordeal, he is no stranger to tragedy. His uplifting, positive, hardworking lifestyle suits him. My hope and prayer is that he, too, will be blessed with a "Soul Mate" who will give without measure, support the best in him, and is longing to share her life with him.

## Todd...

Todd has grown into manhood. He is now a 3rd and 4th grade teacher at an Expeditionary Learning school in Santa Fe, New Mexico, where he lives with his wife Chrissy and their daughter Sadie Bay. He enjoys working with children, playing music, camping, bike riding, and soccer. His reaction to Amber's death is almost a surrealistic distant memory of an extraordinary time, a painful love, then loss.

## Patti...

...my sister-in-law and Amber's aunt, is doing very well. With her big heart and open arms, she welcomed Amber and I into her and my brother, Joey's, home after our short stay with my parents when we left Michael. Her life with him was hell and thankfully, she escaped and found true and lasting love. She married John, the wonderful man who rescued her from a life of misery, and together they have built a life of happiness and joy. They have two grown sons, retired early, and are now enjoying fixing up their cabin in the mountains, taking long trips in their RV, and spending time with family and friends. It's been so good to keep in touch throughout the years.

## My Immediate Family...

...has faded into a distant, painful collection of dire circumstances and unspeakable events. Choosing to surround myself with people who care for and truly love me, I let them go. It was a decision that I've never regretted; it is one that I fully understand. "I do not have the power to change anyone else but me," was a lesson that was hard to learn and even harder to live. I stopped living in a fantasy world of "I wish I had a family who..." and started taking the steps to help people who wanted—who needed—my help and Amber's inspiration. I focused on completing the manuscript and publishing the first edition of this book.

## Kathy...

...died in 2004 from heart disease which, in my opinion, was brought on by overwhelming heartbreak and sadness. She left behind four children: Raymond and Courtney from her first marriage; Michael and Buddy from her second. Michael was the one who found her dead. He described his life with Kathy and this memory in an email to me. It was heartbreaking to read.

*"...It was just my mother and I in the same house. My brother had left for college. She worked taking care of elderly people in their homes. Years after she stopped working, she went on Social Security. She would close herself off to the world, staying in her bedroom watching nothing but television. Prescription drugs would slowly transform her... would take her out of touch with reality. Pain killers, muscle relaxers, and*

antidepressants would be the mix she took. I would try to stay out of the house as much as possible. I couldn't bear to see my mother like this. It's hard to see someone give up on life. When I did interact with her, it was like talking to a child. Her mind was overtaken by pills. I would get frustrated and try to push her away.

I was attending the community college and I had a part-time job, so I was always out of the house. I was very busy. I would tell my mother, "You're living like you're already dead. You're still young! Live life." Her life became nothing. Full of anger at the people who she thought had screwed her over throughout her life, she decided to become completely antisocial. She gave up on the human race. I could not stand the way she felt about life. I was young and wanted to experience life. I didn't want her toxic ways to affect me.

The year was 2004. I would go to work, college, then hang out with my friends. Always away from the house. I would come home late at night and check my mother to make sure she was still breathing. One night she caught me checking on her and the next day she asked about it. I told her about my fear of finding her dead. She told me not to worry. She's in great health with her heart. I would still continue to check on her every night when I came home.

On September the 23rd, I had a full day. I went to school, then work, then back to school again. After school, I hung out with my friends at Denny's. I came home a little after 11pm. It was dark in the house. I walked up to my mother's door. I noticed the light of television coming from underneath it. I also noticed that our dog Oliver was in there. This was very odd because my mother ALWAYS had Oliver in her room in the mornings and kept him in the living room at night.

I turned the door knob and slowly entered. Oliver was very frantic. My mother was laying on her back with her arms at her side. I started to shout at her, yelling "Mom!" louder and louder, as Oliver kept barking. I tried to wake her up. I was shouting and shaking her. Her skin was cold to the touch. Her lips were sealed shut, and her color was abnormal. I was in the state of shock. I sat by her for a few minutes. I knew she was gone. I talked to her but knew I was talking to an empty vessel. Just words like, "Why did you do this to yourself mom? Oh mom..."

I then got up and decided to call the paramedics. They wanted me to perform CPR on her. They wanted me to drag her to the floor and *do it there. I couldn't, she was dead weight. The paramedics finally came. I stayed out of the room. One of them came out and said, "Sorry for your loss." That's when it hit me. I went down to my knees and started crying. Time slowed down at that point. Now it was my responsibility to let everybody know. Letting each person know was harder and harder. My mother passed away that night. It was the hardest thing I've ever had to deal with. I wish she didn't give up so easily on life. Later the autopsy came out and we discovered her cause of death was a heart attack.*

*My mother was an amazing person. When she was at her best, she would bring joy to so many lives. She was full of love. I will always remember how great my mother was before the dark part of her life. I wish that mother was alive today."*

Incredibly, both Buddy and Michael are doing very well. They've taken their painful past and used it as a powerful "spring board" to excel in their own lives. Michael is an impersonator for the Los Angeles Lakers' center, Pau Gasol, and enjoying the spotlight in Hollywood. Buddy works as an Event Coordinator at a college in northern California and wrote to update me on his life with Kathy, the lessons he learned, and the events surrounding her death.

*"...I was at school, close to graduation, when I got the call that mom passed away. Long story short, I flew down and took care of all the life decisions that needed to be made, funeral arrangements, what we were going to do with the house and so on.*

*Mom and I we're really close until the end. One thing that I remember her saying frequently was you need an education to get out of this lifestyle. I don't think without her saying that I would've have gotten as far as I did in school. She was the type of person who was kind and loving when she was in a good place, but once she went to the bad place, you knew.*

*Growing up I remember all the moments that alcohol was present in our lives. Our dad's alcoholism—until we had to leave him in 1992—grandma, Harry's and mom's. I always felt safe when one person in the family was sober, but once we left our father and mom was the only one around drinking, I felt so helpless. I think her drinking was a place of remorse and regret for the unfortunate events that happened in her life. Leaving Raymond and Courtney on the East Coast, her father beating*

*her, our father beating her, one bad experience after another. I think if she*
*was more confident, things would have been very different.*

*Her dreams... I remember she would have these ideas every now*
*and then. An idea to help cancer patients with wigs or helping others who*
*were less fortunate. She would get so passionate, but they would fall to*
*the side. I feel she was always in survival mode, which I learned growing*
*up and still fight against today. This isn't a way to live. It just keeps you*
*always wondering and thinking about what's next, instead of living in*
*the moment.*

Reading through their emails, I got a sense of *them* living through the same tragic life that *I* did, all those years ago. It was a life that I never believed in or followed or wished upon my own children. My parents were examples what *not* to do, say, or think. Thank God I could see through the victim-centered role they played and decided to take control of my own life, realize my Power Within, and raise my own children as I had always wanted to be raised.

Courtney and Raymond are still living in New Jersey. Courtney has married a wonderful man, BJ, and has three wonderful boys. She is the mother that Kathy wanted to be—loving, fun, caring, devoted, interested, and involved—but couldn't. Deprived of the skills and tools, my sister never realized that *she had the power* to build her own life... to shape it any way she wanted... to live the life of *her* dreams, just as her daughter is today.

## Michael...

...moved to Loveland, Colorado, remarried, and had two more children. The last time I spoke with him was the winter of 1986. Gary and I had parted. Toby and I went to live aboard a client's yacht for the winter. He had just had a son who was 6 months old. That was the last time I spoke with him. We made our peace. He died from Amyotrophic Lateral Sclerosis (ALS or Lou Gehrig's Disease)—believe it not—on Amber's birthday, February 28th. It appears that he finally found contentment and happiness with his family and had another chance at fatherhood before he "crossed over" and is now with Amber. Here is his obituary:

*Publish date: 3/1/2007*

*Michael James CALISTRO, 56, of Loveland, passed away Feb. 28, 2007, after a two-year battle with ALS. Michael was born Sept. 5, 1950, in New Britain, Connecticut, to Michael John and Marie (Spielman) Calistro. He married Debbie on Sept. 21, 1986, in Denver. Michael loved his Lord and Savior Jesus Christ, was a member of Resurrection Fellowship and an active member of the men's 6:33 group there. He was an avid outdoorsman. Michael was also a master at restoring classic muscle cars. His witty sense of humor carried him through life, especially in the difficult challenges of his illness. He was a lover of music, played guitar, sang and wrote songs. Photography was also a favorite hobby of his. He finished his career at Hewlett-Packard as an 11-year veteran. Michael is survived by his wife, Debbie of Loveland; sons, Nathan Calistro and Stephen Calistro of Loveland; daughter, Krissy Bacheller and husband Greg of Centennial; brothers, Mark Calistro and wife Carley of Longmont, and R.J. Huck and wife Sheryl of New Britain, Connecticut; sisters, Terri Fabrizio and Marie Calistro, both of Bristol, Connecticut; grandchildren, Katelyn and Rachael Bacheller; nephews, Mark Calistro and Cameron Carter, both of Longmont; and nieces, Sandi Calistro of Arvada, and Jennifer Fabrizio of Bristol, Conn. He was preceded in death by his parents and by one daughter, Amber Calistro.*

I couldn't republish this book without doing all I could to seek closure and perhaps bring a sense of peace to my life with Michael... to my memory of our time together. Bringing his life to light, after Amber and I left him in Connecticut, was important to me... to this story itself. I hoped that he found true love with his new family and children, but I needed to know for myself and for you, my reader. I also prayed that the father that Amber had missed, became the deep, loving, caring father for his other children.

Knowing I could not rewrite history, I reached out to his widow, Debbie, to see if there was something she wanted to contribute... to balance the behavior of a young man who couldn't find a way to father all those years ago... to bring some sense of fulfillment to Michael's life with Amber... to help me understand and accept my past. I found her on FaceBook.

### *Patti DiMiceli / November 6, 2010 at 1:23 pm*

Hi Deborah. I am Michael's daughter, Amber's, mother, Patti. First, let me say that I am sorry for your loss and for Michael's suffering. Despite our differences at the time of Amber's death, I am glad that I was able to talk with him in 1986 and make our peace before his passing. He died on Amber's birthday, just as she died on mine.

Second, I'm finishing up the rewrite of Amber's book and currently working on the Epilogue. Though I can't rewrite history, I wanted to reach out to you and give you the opportunity to update the reader on Michael's life after Amber. It appears that he found happiness and contentment with you and your sons, as well as peace with God. I am very grateful for that.

Please let me know if you'd like to communicate. Or, if you prefer not to, that's okay. I just wanted to reach out as a courtesy to you and your family.

### *Deborah Calistro / November 16, 2010 at 11:00 pm*

Re: Amber's Book

Hey Patti,

Sorry about the delay in responding. Real life is sometimes more pressing than social networking. I appreciate your consideration but there is not much to tell that would benefit your readers. Michael and I had a great marriage and, along with our two boys, we have enjoyed Krissy's extended family, too. Mike has two beautiful granddaughters. We now know there was a really great birthday party surprise for Amber on the day of his death. Although all of his children have an aspect of who he was, Amber is the most to look like him. Nathan, as you can see, has talent, but Stephen has his great heart and love of life. Krissy has his mental ability. I pray for his seed. If you have any specific questions, feel free to ask.

God bless you

Debbie

### *Patti DiMiceli / November 17, 2010 at 7:38 am*

*Debbie...*

*Thanks for responding... for updating me. It is a comfort to know he had you and his family at his side and that he and Amber are in Heaven looking out for us. The one "gift" that changed my life forever, she gave to me on my birthday. Just before she died, she told me, "Mom, when I die, I'll still be Amber, I'll just be DIFFERENT." So, I know she did not "pass away..." I did not "lose a child." She simple changed and has been "with" me ever since.*

*I guess the one question I have would be, "How was he as a father?" Sadly, he did not "father" Amber at that time and it was painful for all of us. No doubt it was not just Michael, but the combination of Michael and me. And so my hope and prayer is that he was able to "redeem" this part of his life and excel with Krissy, Nathan, and Stephen.*

*This is not a judgement at all. Again, we made our peace and time has turned any negative thoughts or feelings I may have had into love and compassion. It means a great deal to me that I can write the Epilogue with a loving, open heart. Though I cannot change history... my history with Michael, I can move forward in a positive, uplifting way which is directed by God.*

*Thanks, Debbie, for opening up your heart to me.*
*Patti*

### <u>Deborah Calistro / November 17 at 8:57 am</u>

*Patti,*

*Very valid question, based on the way he was raised. When I met Mike he said he did not want to have any more children and if he had remained in that idea we would have not gotten married. What really changed him was when he experienced the love and acceptance of his Heavenly father through Jesus. It improved him as a loving and forgiving man. Just as he received he gave out. Krissy actually came to live with us after high school and the healing began. I think my kids would say he was tuff, but just... We, in combination, raised two very well adjusted boys.*

*On the medical side, he had no cancer, but struggled with heart disease. We were shocked when the diagnosis of ALS came and 2 years later his death.*

*God Bless you*
*Debbie*

<u>*Deborah Calistro / November 17, 2010 at 9:05 am*</u>

Hey Patti..... just a PS: Our granddaughter's birthday is also 2/28. She will be 10 this Feb and looks at this to be a positive thing that her granddad's heavenly birthday is the same as hers.

<u>*Patti DiMiceli / November 17, 2010 at 9:43 am*</u>

Oh my God—literally! I am still shaking my head that your granddaughter's birthday is the SAME as Amber's and Michael's "spiritual birth." There are SO many "signs" that God has given me in my life, both then and now. He was the one who guided me through Amber's time with cancer, keeping the journal, and writing the book. The moment that she died, I actually FELT God!!! If I hadn't recorded the moment, I would've probably let it slip into my "memory bank" to collect dust or justified it as... um... whatever.

Do you think your boys and perhaps Krissy would want to write something about their dad for the Epilogue. It may give some balance to him as a father... as a man.

Know that I am very sensitive to all of you. I also want to do all I can to ensure that Michael's life AFTER Amber—especially his fathering—is brought to light in a loving, caring way; that his "tale is told." I did write Nathan a note on FB awhile back but have not heard from him. Whatever the answer, it is meant to be.

Best...
Patti

<u>*Patti DiMiceli / November 20, 2010 at 4:04 pm*</u>

Hi Debbie. Working on the Epilogue today. Would you mind if I published your FaceBook entries / notes to me? Very well said and it'd be a good balance.
Patti

<u>*Deborah Calistro / November 23, 2010 at 8:13 am*</u>

Good morning Patti,

Sure go ahead and quote me. I forgot to ask what the name of the book is...?

<u>*Patti DiMiceli / November 23, 2010 at 9:53 am*</u>

*Hi Debbie. It's called "Embrace the Angel." I'm attaching a YouTube video that WBAL-TV put together for me when they did a news segment on me in 1996. It'll give you some idea of who Amber was. You will definitely see Michael!*

*Thanks for agreeing to "balance out" the old version with the new. No doubt it will bring a sense of peace to many. If Stephen, Nathan, or Krissy would like to contribute, I would be honored. Do you think I should ask them?*

*Here's the link to the YouTube video: http://www.youtube.com/ watch?v=UrrbTOb6k6I*

*Best...*

*Patti*

*I Walk Through Your Dreams*

*www.youtube.com*

*WBAL TV's gift to me: Amber's Short Life*

## The Bristol's...

...sold their farm, Hickory Ledges, in Canton, Connecticut and bought another farm in Vermont in the early '80's. Bob continued doing what he loved: Farming. He grew berries, veggies, and always loaded up whoever stopped by with the fruits of his labor. He died in 2003 from melanoma. Always a giver, he ignored his cancer until it was too late.

Jane now lives on the Vermont farm alone and is as feisty and optimistic as ever. After over twenty-five years, I visited with Jane while she spent some time with her daughter, Lin, and son-in-law, Paul, at their home on the eastern shore of Maryland. It was a fine autumn day. The sun highlighted the red, orange, and yellow leaves as we sat in the kitchen looking out over the water. Seeing Jane again was like a dream... a sweet and enduring memory of our time together way back when. Sharing the memories of Amber with someone who knew her in her short time on earth was blissful. Like a warm blanket in a cold winter storm, Jane has always comforted me in ways that are heartfelt and true.

## Dr. Burton's Immunotherapy Clinic...

...is now called the Immune Augmentation Therapy Centre. It is still located in Freeport, opposite the Rand Memorial Hospital. In an email to Dr. Clement in November of 2010, I asked him about the clinic, the people who worked there, and Dr. Burton. His reply:

*"Dr. Burton died at home in Freeport in 1993. He divorced Esther Burton about 2 years before he died and married a patient, Betty Abernathy. She died the same year and then he married Jamie Baker, about 30 years younger than him. Jamie Burton is still alive and well. The clinic is still alive and well, but very quiet, mostly due to the recession. People are still coming back for tune ups as usual.*

*June Austin died this year, but Lynn Austin, Lee Malone, Gary, Edney, and Louis are still working. Carl and Eda Murino retired back to New York and we have a younger MD, Kevin Bethel, training to take over from me. Eddie (Put Put) Houghtaling, who was Burton's "go-fer" is very very old and unwell but still pops in the clinic.*

*The main I.A.T treatment remains in an improved state and we now also have a tumor-specific vaccine treatment which has proven very useful. Check immunemedicine.com to see our new pictures..."*

## Bernie...

...was then, and is now, a "guiding light" in my life. He has continued to change the world, one person... one word... one book at a time. He and his wife, Bobbie, have collaborated on many works and workshops, letting their love spill out and embrace millions of people. In a recent email I sent him on the progress of the rewrite and asking him for a list of his books, I attached the photo I took of the prism that shined in my eyes as I wrote this Epilogue. He updated me on what he is doing today.

*"quite an image*
*attaching bio which lists books*
*can get things through wisdom of the ages*
*i am still teaching and running support groups*

*and connecting with the world via internet*

*peace*
*bernie"*

## My "Wake Up Call"

*(PLEASE NOTE: This section describes my close encounter with declining health and what I did to reverse it, including techniques and products. Please consult your own doctor and "team of teacher/healers" before attempting any of the therapies or using the products below. What worked for me, may or may not work for you.)*

"That which is to give Light must endure burning." Victor Frankl's words never seemed more true. I was beginning to feel the heat. Knowing that returning to the book... to the time of trauma and pain, to relive my journey with Amber would be stressful, I braced myself. I continued my daily walks through the woods with Annie where I listened to God, found my peace, and balanced my soul. I took care of myself—body, mind, and spirit—so that I could withstand the impact of reaching back... of digging deep to find the answers that the first edition asked. It was my Life Task to share Amber's message with the world, I knew, and I was driven to complete it. What I didn't know was the toll it would take.

I tried my best to manage, but inevitably, my body absorbed what my mind could not. Unexplained pain began to manifest itself in my abdomen. I knew something was wrong. "I have cancer. I'm filled with cancer." Fearing that my premonition of long ago would come true, I refused to listen and stayed on my path to publishing, my self-imposed deadline. But the words kept creeping in. "I will die when I finish the book." That was my thought for years; it was the reason I would not return to and complete my Life Task. I didn't want to die. I didn't want to go through what Amber did. I didn't want to go through cancer ever again. Fear held me in its grip and I couldn't... I wouldn't let it go. I knew I needed help to get through this.

I made an appointment with Dr. Scott Smith, a psychologist who I'd worked with before, to help me sort through the myriad of emotions, feelings, sadness, and grief. As I progressed with the rewrite of the second edition, Scott opened my eyes to the fear that stopped me and the potential that was hidden inside me unused. He became my guide as I tried to navigate through the turmoil that threatened to derail me. "Mind over matter" was never more true.

He helped me to understand my own "magical thinking." My inner brain believed this irrational fear was true, just as we do when we watch a movie and cry or laugh. Though we know it's only a movie, it's real to us at the time, and so we react *as if* it were true... as if it were real. I needed to change my perspective, to look at my fear differently.

"If a friend were to say these negative things to you all the time, you wouldn't take it, would you? You'd fight back and stand up for yourself," he told me. "Keep doing what you're doing to stay healthy and don't let your 'negative friend' get you off course." And so, for the next week I did just that. Each time a negative thought came into my mind, I repeated a new mantra: "I am healthy. I am strong. I am capable." I continued to live this belief. I also went to my doctor for a physical, just to rule out the cancer I feared.

Jaime Taylor, the Physician's Assistant at my doctor's office, was caring and empathetic, just as I knew she would be. She ordered a series of blood tests. A couple of weeks later, I sat in her Examining Room and examined her face as she read the results on her computer screen. Her eyes stopped and she looked at me. "Your liver enzymes are slightly elevated." My heart stopped. "It's also known as elevated transaminases." My blood ran cold. "I'd like you to have another blood test in four to six weeks as well as an ultrasound of your abdomen." I left her office in a trance, got in my car, and pointed myself towards home.

On one hand, I wanted to pretend. "Everything's okay... I'm worrying about nothing... She didn't seem too concerned... I'll just wait, do nothing, and get the follow up tests in a month or so." On the other hand, I wanted to take control, not be a victim, learn what "transaminases" was, how I got it, and what I could do to heal myself. I was still debating as I walked in my front door. "Should I or shouldn't I???"

I grabbed my laptop and nervously looked it up. "Elevated Transaminases: In general, any damage to the liver will cause medium elevations in these transaminases (usually called liver enzymes, though of course they are not the only enzymes in the liver). Diagnosis requires synthesis of many pieces of information, including the patient's history, physical examination, and possibly imaging or other laboratory examinations. However, very high elevations of the transaminases suggests severe liver damage, such as viral hepatitis, liver injury from lack of blood flow, or injury from drugs or toxins." My mind started racing to catch up with my fast-beating heart.

Like it or not, I needed to get a grip... to gain control over this possible life-threatening diagnosis. I spent the next several hours digging for more. The more research I read, the better I began to feel. "I *can* do something about this. I don't *have* to be a victim." I landed on the "Gallbladder/Liver Flush." It was nontoxic, cost only a few dollars, and made sense to me. My common sense had always served me well. Detoxifying my body —ridding it (as much as possible) of the years and years of accumulated poisons—and supporting my filter, my liver, was the path I would take. I decided to buy Andreas Moritz' book and assemble the ingredients: "Epsom salts, organic olive oil, grapefruit, and apple juice." I would follow it to the letter.

I knew that I was responsible for healing myself, but I didn't know how to begin and I couldn't do it alone. I would need to enlist the help of people who were trained to heal the *whole person*, not just one body part. My mind, body, and spirit all played a part in getting me to this state and each had to play a role in returning me to good health. I assembled my team of teacher/healers:

- *Irit Weir*, LSc (Licensed Acupuncturist), MS (Masters of Science), of the Acupuncture Clinic of Napa, introduced me to the practical concept of "Total Biology: Learning the true nature of disease and becoming empowered to heal oneself." She pointed the way for me to restore my own health: Heal my mind and my body will follow. She also gave me the confidence to do it.

- *Scott Smith*, PhD, from Spectrum Behavioral Health, guided me through the accumulated emotions and feelings that stopped me from fully embracing life, living my potential, and fulfilling my Life Task. Teaching me how to diffuse my stress by explaining its causes and sources, he gave me the information I needed to take positive action... to change my perspective and see my world differently. He refocused me to stay "on course" and use my time on earth wisely.
- *Tamara Trujillo*, LMT (Licensed Massage Therapist), of Hands on Health, massaged my body and soothed my spirit and soul with her healing hands. She allowed me time to "melt," relax, succumb, and let go of my stress.
- *Argo Duenas*, Certified with I-ACT (International Association for Colon Hydrotherapy), from Back to Nature, cleaned my colon of years of accumulated toxins and touched my spirit with her gentle, caring, way of healing souls.
- *Michael Wells*, DPT (Doctor of Physical Therapy) and *Holly Hatton*, PTA (Physical Therapy Assistant) of Annapolis Physical Therapy, used techniques and tools to help me work out the aches, pains, and kinks in my body.
- *Frederick Sutter*, MD (Medical Doctor), from Center for Wellness Medicine, evaluated me as a whole person, not simply a patient, and gave me recommendations which empowered me to take control of my own state of health.
- *Margaret Wright*, MS (Master of Science), BSN (Bachelor of Science, Nursing), CNHP (Certified Natural Health Professional), of An Ounce of Prevention, changed the way I look at food forever. Her knowledge, coupled with a true sense of caring for me and passion for her work, opened my eyes to "actually eating," being completely aware of what I am eating and the path it will take.

I left Margaret's office with new knowledge and one purpose in mind: Find out exactly what happens to the food I eat after I take the first bite. What organs, enzymes, and gastric juices play a role in digesting my food? How *does* it get from one end to the other... from "Point A" to "Point B"? How does my body absorb the nutrients? What role does fat play? What can I do to make this better? Being a "visual learner," I needed to see.

When I got home, I headed upstairs to my studio, sat down at my computer, and typed "digestion... gall bladder... liver" into Google. Many illustrations popped up, including videos on YouTube. I was astounded. For the first time in my life, I could actually *see* food being digested! I also understood the vital role each organ plays in maintaining our health and how toxins can destroy it. From that moment on, I would think twice about what went past my lips. Seeing and understanding the process of digestion was exactly what I needed to affirm my commitment, change my life, and create a lifestyle that would support my healing.

I couldn't believe that I hadn't done this sooner but was so grateful that my "wake up call" happened when it did. I still had a chance to restore my health, but it would take a very long time, just as long as it had to get me to this place: a lifetime. I was prepared to stay the course and determined to do what was in my power to improve the results of my upcoming blood test and ultrasound. I had only six weeks to do it.

Realizing that there were hundreds, perhaps *thousands* of choices I made every day, I began to choose more wisely and realize that each choice had consequences which affected my health. Although I *thought* I'd been careful about the choices I made, my body was telling me something different. The aches and pains I felt were real. The accumulated toxins were overloading my body, mind, and spirit.

The stress of rewriting this book... of resurrecting the pain, was also playing havoc with my body. Research on stress revealed some of the effects that I was seeing in myself—elevated cholesterol levels, excess abdominal fat, and high blood sugar levels—amongst a long list of others I hadn't seen. Watching the PBS special, *Stress: Portrait of a Killer*, featuring Dr. Robert Sapolsky's thirty year study of the relationship between stress in animals and humans, was an awakening. Riveting and profound, it made me question, "What damage have stress hormones done to my body and how can I reverse the damage?"

"De-stress," I decided, "I need to make a concerted effort to lower my level of stress whenever I can and stop it completely on a regular basis." From getting regular massages to scheduling time in the sauna, I began to carve out time to let go... to relinquish my control... to surrender to the moment... to allow myself the luxury of being taken care of by someone who cared. It was a life-changing decision, not temporary and not "spur of the moment."

## My New Life

With a renewed sense of hope, I launched my new life. Everything I did... I ate... I chose, took on new meaning. My morning walks in the woods at Quiet Waters Park with Annie became my private time with God; a time to listen, observe, understand, and see into my future. There was magic in the woods. Life was on display and the metaphors were astounding. The trees were like people. Each one had a story to tell and I was listening to the wisdom God imparted. I needed to share that wisdom. *Walking in the Metaphorest with Annie,* my next book, was born.

I did the "Gallbladder/Liver Flush" and felt better within days. Getting regular massages, plenty of exercise, keeping my colon cleaned, and improving my eating habits were clearly making a difference. The idea of "Actually Eating" took shape and I was fully present and real as I ate my food. The dull ache in my abdomen stopped, I felt cleaner and more energetic than I had in years, and my spirits lifted. Hope replaced doom. I felt like my body was not betraying me, but instead, was supporting me. "Detoxifying my body was the right choice," I confirmed to myself.

As I moved through my days and nights, I began to take notes... to write down the choices, products, and actions that helped me... that might helps others. Realizing that perfection can only be applied to God and the angels, I tried to find a balance between needs and wants, good and bad, pure and toxic.

Buying organic food, rather than processed, whenever possible worked best for me. More expensive at times, I figured I would eat less food but better quality. The folks at Vital Farms (pastured eggs) got it right: "More people are becoming aware of the benefits of eating meat and poultry from grass-fed animals. From cows to pigs to chickens, they were all meant to graze. Since we are what we eat, we are what these animals eat." They proudly call the hens that lay these delicious eggs, their "Girls." I liked the practical philosophy that they lived and the business model they believed in. I bought their eggs.

So many choices were before me. I needed to keep track. Here is *my* list of products, along with some of the sources I found in my area or the internet. Just a reminder: I am constantly learning, changing, adding and altering, but as of this writing, this is what works for me. Your list will be different, I'm sure.

## Food:

- Organic food (Whole Foods, Trader Joe's, some grocery stores).
- "Pastured," *not pasteurized,* eggs (Vital Farms)
- Green tea, white tea, green tea extract
- "Ezekiel 4:9" sprouted breads (Food for Life Co., found in most grocery stores).
- "Great Harvest Bread Co." (I make the special trip across town.)
- Wheatgrass juice (I grow my own from supplies I get online: www.wheatgrasskits.com or buy it from Robek's)
- Purified water: "Watts Premier RO-Pure 4-Stage Reverse Osmosis System" (Costco, Amazon)
- Wash all fruits and veggies with either a store-bought natural product or vinegar
- Cook and store food with stainless steel, glass, and ceramic (no plastic)
- Carry a set of stainless steel utensils with me: Fork, knife, spoon (Camping sections)

## Body Work:

- Deep breathing ("Google" the many techniques & benefits)
- Plenty of fresh air, especially in the woods or near plants/trees
- Use a "skin brush" to stimulate circulation

- Check eyes 1x a year
- Get a "skin survey" 1x a year for skin cancer
- Soak my sore muscles in Epsom Salts
- Keep olive oil, non-refrigerated organic coconut oil, jojoba oil in my shower for hair/skin
- Buy only wireless bras or remove wires if needed (Research "push-up bras and cancer.")
- Get a massage often (Lots of benefits, including immunity boost, increased circulation, etc.)
- Lymphatic massage (Removes harmful substances from the tissues, immunity boost, etc.)
- Get my teeth cleaned 2x a year (Dr. Vernon Sheen)
- See psychologist once a week (Dr. Scott Smith)
- Lift weights, exercise 3x a week in addition to daily hour-long walks in the woods with Annie
- Far infrared sauna 2x a week (Evolutions Body Clinic)
- Removed acrylic nails and now cut my natural nails short
- Get a colonic at least 4x a year (change of seasons), more if I'm detoxing. (Argo Duenas)
- Sleep at least 8 hours a night. More or less as necessary.

**Body Products:**

- Take plant-based vitamins & minerals when possible (Whole Foods, online)
- Use "Dr. Hauschka" cosmetics (Whole Foods)
- "Aveda" hair coloring and cosmetics (Aveda Salons)
- Wear natural fiber clothing (silk, wool, cotton, bamboo, etc.) as much as possible
- Use "Aloe Life" natural lubricant (one of the side effects of menopause)
- Electric toothbrush (Oral B)
- Brush with"Tom's" or "Burt's Bees" toothpaste
- Dip my toothbrush in a 50/50 mixture of myrrh & goldenseal powder (Penn Herb Co.)
- Gargle with salt water
- Water Pik with "IPSAB" herbal gum treatment (Whole Foods)
- Least toxic "night guard" (I grind my teeth.)

- Shoes: Merrel, Clark's "Unstructured," Crocs (for wide feet) are widely available
- Rose water + glycerin to clean my face
- "Dust Bee Gone" dust mask (Amazon) is effective down to three microns

**Home:**

- Air out my sheets (Gulp! Don't make your bed!) often
- Use a water filter on my shower head
- Cotton sheets (The BEST: "Pinzon 400-thread count 100% Egyptian cotton on Amazon)
- All natural air freshener (you can make your own without toxic chemicals or buy it)
- Clean home w/vinegar, baking soda, salt (Great internet resources for specifics)
- Use "Method" line of nontoxic cleaning products (Target, Whole Foods, most stores)
- Compost kitchen scraps to use in my organic garden
- Recycle (Make it easy by putting a garbage can w/lid and liners in your kitchen. Sam's Club)
- Only NO VOC paints (Maryland Paint Co. is my source but there are companies in your area)
- Cotton or wool rugs w/no VOC pads (Overstock.com, Home Depot)
- Wood, not particleboard, furniture
- Reduce plastic in the home, toys, etc.
- Wash clothes w/all-natural detergents and softeners
- No fluorescent or halogen light bulbs (Google "fluorescent or halogen lights cancer")
- Install a low-flow toilet (Toto)
- Air out dry cleaning *at least* 24 hours

**Garden:**

- Keep an organic yard and garden (Gardens Alive! + many other sources) w/out poisons
- Use beneficial insects to control pests

- Set up a rain barrel and a rain garden
- Use plenty of organic mulch

**Must Read, Hear, or See:**

- *The Food Revolution,* by John Robbins, author of the Pulitzer Prize winning *Diet for a New America,* which transformed the way we eat... the way we live.
- *Food, Inc.,* a visually stunning movie, examines the costs of putting value and convenience over nutrition and environmental impact.
- *YOU: The Owner's Manual: An Insider's Guide to the Body that Will Make You Healthier and Younger,* the first "How to" manual for our bodies, similar to a manual for your car, computer program, appliances, home maintenance, etc.

All of these choices were made one at a time. There are others on my "To Do" list: Take a yoga class, finish reading Andreas Moritz' *Timeless Secrets of Health & Rejuvenation,* lend out my DVD of the film *Food, Inc.* to more friends, get a salt water hot tub, learn more about my body and make more informed choices. The road to good health is a journey, not a destination.

Six weeks after my initial blood test, I went in for another, as well as an ultrasound. My blood tests came back with my liver enzymes within the "normal" range. The ultrasound showed "fat deposits" in my liver. I was relieved by the results of the blood test and curious about how the fat deposits in my liver got there and what I could do to change it. It appears that 50% of people have a "fatty liver," even children, but have no symptoms. Being overweight (belly fat) is one cause, along with a few others. Losing the twenty pounds I'd gained since menopause, eating less unhealthy fats, exercising more, and reducing stress would help to restore my liver to its healthy state, but it would take time and a lifelong commitment.

In the meantime, I am truly living my life to the fullest, working to realize my dreams, and reveling in the love of my husband, family, and friends. John and I just completed our Up in the Air Year: Soaring in a glider, riding in a hot air balloon, and diving from an airplane! I am healthy, strong, and happy. My life has meaning and purpose. My sense of wonder and joy has been restored. I am truly embracing life and have learned, through this journey, that embracing life is the key to embracing death, our path to the beyond.

## My Horizon

Filled to the brim with childlike wonder and anticipation of what lies ahead, I am in a place of peace and contentment. My future is bright and calls me. "It is possible. *Anything is possible,*" I say to myself. Those words opened up my horizon and made me see. I now look forward to creating the memories that will lift me up, carry me through my future pain, and sustain me in my times of doubt and anguish.

I want to...

...spread Amber's message of hope, power, and possibility.

...continue to enjoy good health and the love of family and friends.

...redistribute God's money.

...share my story with the world.

...lift up others as I have been lifted.

...get on the water with John and Annie.

...travel the world to see the difference of culture and the similarity of people.

...wallow in the tranquility of this peaceful place I have found.

I am excited about the projects, people, and places in my future:

· **Current books "simmering on the back burner:"**
  1) *Walking Through the Metaphorest with Annie,* a collection of photographs and insights from my walks through the woods at Quiet Waters Park with our Jack Russell, Annie, and listening to God.
  2) *Embrace the Angel, Amber's Words of Wisdom,* an in-depth look at the insights she gave me, especially the last month of her life, captured by the tape recorder that stayed on during her every waking moment.

- **Conducting workshops and giving presentations** which include transforming grief into greatness, realizing your "Power Within," changing your perspective, and discovering your "Life Task."
- **Traveling** has always been my passion, along with sharing these adventures through writing.
- **Partnering with people** and organizations who are focused on preventing, then treating if they have to, and ultimately curing cancer, as well as those who help others crossover the threshold.

## Looking Forward

So much of my journey with Amber, both then and now, has been about recognizing, harnessing, and using the power that exists in each of us to elevate others. We can do this in so many ways; some which are secret, known only to us and God; others more visible and shared; all profound and life changing.

Each day, we make hundreds, perhaps thousands, of choices; some may seem insignificant. Where to go, what to do, how to behave, which food to eat, whether to pay attention to this or that, and on and on. Choosing the one, big or small, which will do the most good for ourselves and others, will make our world a better place to live now and our death more meaningful when it comes. Choosing, then taking action, can be done one step at a time and be as simple as choosing one word over another. A small step, really, but the impact can be far-reaching.

Several years ago, during the Christmas season, I was standing in line waiting to pay for my gifts. Caught up in the holiday rush, I was swept along, not really paying attention to anyone else. I was alone in my own world. Until I stopped. I was in line. I had to stop.

In the abrupt void, I began to relax, ponder, observe. As I did, voices began rushing in. People all around me were talking. They were upset at having to wait in line, tired of all the running around to buy gifts, burdened by the stress that the holiday season brings. I wondered, "What if we backed up our holiday season to Thanksgiving and, instead of getting ready to buy, we began a season of 'giving thanks?' We'd thank everyone who ever did a nice thing for us or show appreciation to the people who populate our world or turn our attention to those we love and spend time building memories. I'd call it the 'Gratitude Season.' It would begin right after Halloween and last throughout Christmas. Maybe it would last *all year long!*" My imagination was brought back to reality.

"Oh, God, I can't wait for Christmas to be over," one said. "I can't even *afford* Christmas," lamented another, "Guess I'll max out my credit cards again." "I'm *so busy* I don't have time to even *think,* much less spend time with my family," said the woman who unknowingly changed my life.

The volume was suddenly turned down. I could only hear me say "busy... busy... busy," over and over again. I began to contemplate the word and its meaning in my life. It was only one teensy, weensy four letter word, but its impact was huge. I thought about how much I used that word to excuse my poor manners or behavior or to ignore someone or to be inconsiderate or... well... to be *rude.*

"Do I use 'busy' as an excuse to not return a phone call or an email or send a letter to a loved one or get involved in my community... my neighborhood... my life? How many times have I said I was 'busy' and failed to fulfill an obligation or responsibility or commitment? Is 'busy' a choice or does it happen *to* me?" I questioned.

Without hesitation, the answers came pouring in. "'Busy' is *not* something that happens *to* you. You are not a victim. Things don't happen *to* you. You are in control. *'Busy' is a choice.* You are *choosing* to be involved with something or someone else. Replace the word 'busy' with 'involved' and see the difference in your life."

And I have. At first it was hard. I would catch myself often. "Oh, I've been so b... b... *involved.*" Then I would take the proper action—whether it was to apologize, fulfill my obligation, take responsibility, or make amends. That one word changed the way I live my life and the decisions I make about how I use my precious time on this earth. I was in control. I had the power. I began to look around for other ways to make a difference.

Like Mrs. N, Amber's benefactor, I wanted to "spread God's money around." Unlike Mrs. N, I didn't have a lot of it. So, I gave a little extra where it made an instant impact: To parking garage attendants, waiters/waitresses, the sanitation workers who picked up my trash—anyone who I thought needed to know how much I appreciated them, their efforts, and their hard work. Sometimes it would be left behind with a note of appreciation, other times handed to them with a smile, always a way to use my power... to use God's power to make this a better world one small gesture... one person at a time.

Our world is filled with the light of millions of people who use their Power Within to make a difference, for the better, in this world. One of these shining stars is my good friend, Alison's son, Sam Versey, a student at Penn State University. He's involved in the largest student-run philanthropic organization in the world, THON, which aims to conquer childhood cancer.

From their website welcome: *"The Penn State IFC/Panhellenic Dance Marathon, affectionately referred to as THON, is excited to have you join us in our fight to conquer childhood cancer.*

*In 1973, a small group of dedicated Penn State students held our first Dance Marathon. That year, 39 dance couples participated and raised $2,000. Since then, THON's presence in the Penn State community has grown exponentially. THON now has 15,000 student volunteers, 700 dancers, and has raised more than $69 million, benefiting The Four Diamonds Fund at Penn State Children's Hospital.*
*THON is now a yearlong effort that raises funds and awareness for the fight against pediatric cancer. With the support of students from all across the commonwealth of Pennsylvania, and THON Alumni all around the world, we continue to make great strides towards finding a cure for all childhood cancers!"*

Our children are our hope. And if Sam's big heart, good works, and commitment to easing the suffering of our children are any indication of the future, I am confident that we are in good hands and comforted enough to take one final look back.

I am honored to be chosen as Amber's mother ... to know her, the lessons she taught me... the lessons she taught *us*. I have the love and support of so many who have known me from the beginning and stood by me no matter what. Despite the time and distance, we are connected by Amber and all that she symbolizes.

Knowing the meaning of life, the reason I am here, and what happens when my body dies, allows me to let go of my past and move forward towards my future. Free from my tether at last, I am ready to focus on my own happiness, live my life with passion and excitement, wallow in the sweet simplicity of my home life with John and Annie, and rest in the comfort of my family and friends.

Nearing the end of my journey, I look forward to my future that awaits. I will finally fulfill the longing in my heart to *truly* embrace my angel again. This time it will be forever.

見 一 玄 卜 示 力

To understand the meaning of these characters and the purpose of this book, please visit:

**www.embracetheangel.com**

On our website: You can see Amber's life in movies, hear her voice in numerous recordings, delight in her drawings, and read the newspaper articles which chronicled our journey. Other documents will be posted as they are uncovered. All editions of *Embrace the Angel* are available on our website, including a limited quantity of newly discovered "first editions." Signed copies are available on request.

Please help spread Amber's message of hope, Heaven, and the miracle of life and death. Tell your family, friends, colleagues, and neighbors about this book and our website.

Your voice is vital.

# Biographies

## BERNARD S. SIEGEL, MD...

...who prefers to be called Bernie, not Dr. Siegel, was born in Brooklyn, NY. He attended Colgate University and Cornell University Medical College. He holds membership in two scholastic honor societies, Phi Beta Kappa and Alpha Omega Alpha and graduated with honors. His surgical training took place at Yale New Haven Hospital, West Haven Veteran's Hospital and the Children's Hospital of Pittsburgh. He retired from practice as an assistant clinical professor of surgery at Yale of general and pediatric surgery in 1989 to speak to patients and their caregivers.

In 1978 he originated Exceptional Cancer Patients, a specific form of individual and group therapy using patients' drawings, dreams, images and feelings. ECaP is based on "carefrontation," a safe, loving therapeutic confrontation, which facilitates personal lifestyle changes, personal empowerment and healing of the individual's life. The physical, spiritual and psychological benefits which followed led to his desire to make everyone aware of his or her healing potential. He realized exceptional behavior is what we are all capable of.

Bernie, and his wife and coworker Bobbie, live in a suburb of New Haven, Connecticut. They have five children and eight grandchildren. Bernie and Bobbie have co-authored their children, books and articles. Their home with its many children, pets and interests resembled a cross between a family art gallery, museum, zoo and automobile repair shop. It still resembles these things, although the children are trying to improve its appearance to avoid embarrassment.

In 1986 his first book, *Love. Medicine & Miracles,* was published. This event redirected his life. Many books followed.
- **1989:** *Peace, Love & Healing*
- **1993:** *How To Live Between Office Visits*
- **1998:** *Prescriptions for Living* was born from Bernie's realization that we all need help dealing with the difficulties of life, not just

the physical ones. It helps people to become aware of the eternal truths and wisdom of the sages through Bernie's stories and insights rather than wait for a personal disaster. He wants to help people fix their lives before they are broken, and thus not have to become strong at the broken places.

- **2003:** *Help Me to Heal* empowers patients and their caregivers and *365 Prescriptions for the Soul* provides daily inspiration and practical wisdom.
- **2004:** *Smudge Bunny,* a children's book about how difficulties can become blessings.
- **2005:** *101 Exercises For The Soul* teaches us how to incorporate changes into our daily lives.
- **2006:** *Love, Magic & Mud Pies,* a prescriptions for parenting book.
- **2008:** *Buddy's Candle,* for children of all ages, relates to dealing with the loss of a loved one—be it a pet or parent.
- **2009:** *Faith, Hope & Healing* contains inspiring survivor stories and Bernie's reflections about what they teach us.
- **2010:** *Words Swords,* Bernie provides meaningful poetry about life, nature, faith, and relationships, and a chance to write and react with your own.
- **2011:** A book on daily miracles revealing our human potential.

He is currently working on other books with the goal of humanizing medical education and medical care, as well as, empowering patients and teaching survival behavior to enhance immune system competency.

Woody Allen once said, "If I had one wish it would be to be somebody else." Bernie's wish was to be a few inches taller. His work has been such a growth experience that he is now a few inches taller. His prediction is that in the next decade the role of consciousness, spirituality, non-local healing, body memory and heart energy will all be explored as scientific subjects.

For many, Bernie needs no introduction. He has touched many lives all over our planet. In 1978 he began talking about patient empowerment and the choice to live fully and die in peace. As a physician, who has cared for and counseled innumerable people whose mortality has been threatened by an illness, Bernie embraces a philosophy of living and dying that stands at the forefront of the medical ethics and spiritual issues our society grapples with today. He continues to assist in the groundbreaking fields of healing, personally struggling to live the message of kindness and love. His web site: www.BernieSiegelMD.com

## BARBARA H. SIEGEL...

...graduated from Oswego State Teachers College with a BS in Early Childhood Education. As she says, "It prepared me to educate and train Bernie." Even he admits that her guidance has helped him become the person he is today. Bobbie and Bernie married in 1954.

After raising five children and teaching kindergarten she began to help Bernie with his ECaP (Exceptional Cancer Patients) groups and workshops. She has worked with many participants to help with their drawing interpretations and make the workshop groups aware of the importance of humor in healing. She often contributes one-liners to presentations to allow people to experience humor and see how laughter affects them physically. This leads to her getting more grateful comments than Bernie. She and Bernie both enjoy a home still filled with their children's things, pets and love.

## SCOTT E. SMITH...

...is a licensed clinical psychologist who lives in Annapolis, Maryland with his wife and three children. He grew up in Severna Park where he was active in sports, sailing and studies. After attending Washington and Lee University he entered graduate school at McGill University in Montreal, Canada. While at McGill, Scott worked on research which measured the effects of substance abuse on the brain and behavior as well as performing pioneering work on the relationship between brain biochemical precursors such as tryptophan and depression. His research was published in several notable journals and textbooks. He was selected as the "Outstanding Psychology Student" his senior year and was presented with the prestigious NCAA Scholar-Athlete award to help continue his study of psychology in graduate school. He graduated Magna Cum Laude and as a member of Phi Beta Kappa.

Scott was the first of his class to complete his Ph.D. before beginning his clinical internship at Walter Reed Army Medical Center where he studied child and adolescent evaluation and treatment, adult evaluation and treatment, hypnotherapy and liaison with medical services. During his tours as an Army Psychologist, he served as the Chief of Adult Outpatient Psychology at Madigan Army Medical Center in Tacoma, Washington and as Chief of the Psychology Section at Kimbrough Army Community Hospital located on Ft. Meade, MD. While in the Army he earned the Desert Storm service ribbon and the Expert Field Medical Badge.

After leaving the military, Scott entered private practice with Spectrum Behavioral Health, where he has been serving his patients since 1988 and writes a biweekly psychology column for *The Capital*, one of the nation's oldest newspapers. His writing has been referenced in the *Washington Post*, the *Indianapolis Star*, the *Chicago Sun Times* and *Rosie* magazine.

Scott has a general practice where he works with individuals of all ages in conducting evaluations and providing treatment for children, adolescents and adults. His areas of expertise include working with anxiety, depression, mood disorders, trauma, abuse, behavioral disorders, adjustment issues, habit disorders, chronic pain and illness, stress management, family problems, divorce, school related difficulties, learning disabilities, ADHD, couples and family therapy. He also testifies as an expert in psychology in forensic matters and conducts evaluations related to security clearance issues.

Following the death of his father from cancer and with the impending death of his mother from the same illness, he and his family settled nearby in Annapolis to raise their children. An avid sportsman, Scott has enjoyed coaching children in sports as well as practicing sports psychology as a hobby and sidelight to his clinical practice. As a sidelight, he enjoys applying psychological principles to performance enhancement and he has worked with athletes at the recreational, high school, college and professional levels. He was the psychological consultant for the Baltimore-based "Whitbread Around the World" racing team.

# ALISON KELLY...

...is a motivational speaker, trainer and facilitator. She delivers inspiring presentations to thousands of individuals each year at meetings, conferences and customized workshops. A firm believer in the power of each individual to affect change and influence others, she strives to motivate people to leave their mark in this world through their everyday actions, positive attitude and personal awareness.

A Graduate from the National College of Ireland, she has more than 20 years of experience in human resource management, consulting, quality management and training with Fortune 500 companies, colleges and federal, state and local government services. She has received numerous awards and recognition for her excellence in design and delivery of training. Her extensive management and consulting skills, coupled with her energetic and empathetic approach, energizes participants of her workshops to take charge of their life.

Combining her passion for inspiring people with her love of both her home country, Ireland, and her adopted homeland America, Alison injects humor, compassion and real life examples into each topic she teaches.

Her book *Through My Irish Eyes* is a collection of her experiences of the people who have used their influence to motivate others and change the world for the better. Alison's website is www.akellyassociates.com.

**Amber's Drawing**

"What Matters Most"

# The Cover

Over thirty years ago, this book was formed in my mind. I could *see* the cover and know the contents. Each element, each image would have special relevance and invite the reader to indulge... to feel empowered... to understand the meaning of life and death. So clear was this picture, that it became *real*. I could see this book on the bookshelf, feel it in my hands, and know that my angel would live in these pages.

Since the first edition was published in 1996, my last name has changed from Stiewing to DiMiceli. After ten years of being single, I was willing to take the plunge... to love and to *be in love* again but only after meeting my husband, John. Before him, I imagined I would remain single for the rest of my life. His love changed me. He is the foundation for my life and the Man of My Dreams.

The background color is indigo blue or what I call "blurple," a combination of blue and purple. Combined with the orange glow behind Amber, it reminds me of the heavens during that magical "between time." It is the sunrise—the beginning of a new day... a new life. It is the sunset —the end of a day... the completion of a life well-lived. It is the passageway from life to death, that transformational time before we crossover.

The stone arch is from a photograph I took while on vacation with my mom-in-law, Maria, and John in 2008. We were returning to Corleone, Sicily, the beautiful town where their family stills lives today. On our way, we stopped in Taormina, the closest place to Heaven I've visited while traveling this earth. It was enchanting, mystical, and spiritually gratifying. I long to return... to linger.

Amber is standing on the threshold between life and death, ready to move through the doorway, on to eternity, and into the dimension where we will meet; a place where I will finally embrace my angel forever.

One of many portfolio shots meant to launch her modeling career, Amber's spirit was captured in this photograph—literally. As with most of the photos in this series, her body seems to radiate an aura or glowing effect. As if she knew the future, her hand is poised to hold the Key to Heaven, the same key that she held in her hand as she died to help her open the Gates of Heaven.

The design was envisioned and executed by me but could not have been realized without the help of Marghi Barnes, a good woman, artist, caring soul, and amazing Photoshop wiz. You can reach her at divineplanet2000@yahoo.com.

CPSIA information can be obtained
at www.ICGtesting.com
Printed in the USA
235432LV00003B

9 780983 180388